Shaping
Canton

Peter Cookson Smith

Shaping Canton

The Mountains are High
and the Emperor Far Away

ORO Editions — Novato, California

OU MER D

PROVINCE DE QUANG-TONG.

Contents

Jean-Baptiste D'Anville,1735: Province de
Quang-Tong (Courtesy of Wattis Fine Art).

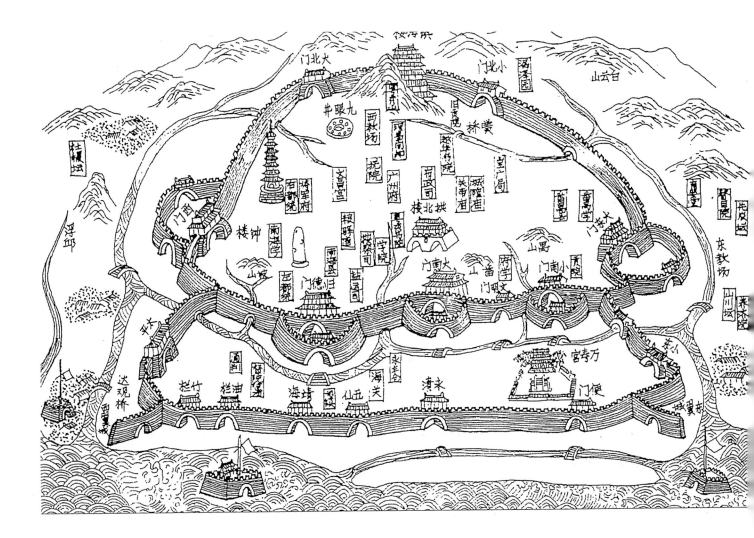

Preface

Canton sits on the east bank of the Pearl River, around 80 miles from its entry into the South China Sea. Its name by which the city is popularly known, is said to be derived from the Portuguese Cantäo, which applied to the old walled city. "Guangzhou," following its designation as the prefecture's seat of Government in 1918, takes its name from the ancient Guang Province.

The mountains are high and the emperor is far away (shān gāo, huángdi yuan) comes from an ancient Chinese proverb dating back to the 13[th]thirteenth-century Yuan dynasty. It alludes to a past age where those who operated at a suitably convenient distance from Peking were apt to disregard the proclamations of central authorities or even Imperial edicts that they deemed less than relevant to local circumstances or personal interests. In the context of past events, this perfectly encapsulates the position of Canton, at least up to the fall of the Qing dynasty, situated 1,316 miles from the capital and sheltered by the Baiyun Mountains whose thirty peaks were often shrouded in white clouds.

The day of my first arrival in Hong Kong on the September 9, 1976, marked an unanticipated watershed in modern Chinese history, as it coincided with the death of Mao Tse-tung. My first impressive view of the city was therefore further distinguished by long lines of people, patiently queuing outside various branches of the Bank of China to sign the books of condolence. At the time it seemed to do little in terms of resolving the marked insularity on both sides of what was then an almost insurmountable land border, guarded by military representatives with mutual interests to protect.

In December 1978, the metaphorical bamboo curtain, that had until then been only slightly ajar, was made somewhat more permeable by the planned reforms, set out at the 3rd Plenum of the 11th Central Committee by Deng Xiaoping. These did not unfold as a "grand design" but as a tentative approach that would set China on a new economic and social trajectory, and heralded a rapid transformation toward economic growth accompanied by tight political control. The vehicle for this was the Four Modernizations in agriculture, industry, defense, and technology.

As a result of this my first visit to Canton was in late 1979, coinciding with new accords that were opening up Guangdong Province to both business and professional interests. Within two years my firm and I, who by that time were engaged with Hong Kong's new town and rehousing programs, became increasingly involved in some of the early urban planning and design projects in southern China. These were being hastily assembled as part of modernization initiatives that were to open up overseas investment, and unleashed forces that have propelled China to the forefront of global economic importance in the twenty-first century.

The route into China's many southern cities at the turn of the 1980s was less than straightforward or convenient. Canton was a five-hour journey on the Kowloon-Canton Railway, or a seemingly endless road journey that involved various river crossings via car ferry. A visit further afield normally demanded a combination of rail, road, and air travel to a destination that we can now reach by air from Hong Kong within an hour. It generally involved an overnight stay in Canton's Dongfang Hotel, well within walking distance of the station, with an early flight the next morning, and finally a pick-up and an overland journey to the point of arrival. But it was the "getting there" that often provoked the learning experience.

Canton remained the largest city within the dependent territory of Hong Kong's immediate ambit, but with a population of only three million people, contained within a compressed topography where the Beiyun Mountains define its northern edges, and the alluvial plain to the south around the Pearl River tributaries was largely given over to agriculture.

Working visits to Canton required periods of stay in a government guest house, set in a quiet compound where meetings were usually held. Bedrooms were surprisingly large and comfortable, with stuffed armchairs and beds protected by giant mosquito nets. Mealtimes were rigidly enforced, and if one arrived late for the 6 a.m. bowl of congee it quickly disappeared back to the kitchen. Lunch followed a not dissimilar pattern at 12 noon, followed by a compulsory siesta, during which I took to exploring the adjoining streets, the Temple of the Six Banyan Trees with the remarkable Hua Pagoda, and the even older Guangxiao Temple, with the nineteenth-century spires of the Sacred Heart Cathedral puncturing the horizon.

The collection of craft of all types and sizes along the Pearl River was so great it almost obscured the water's surface. This included passenger ferries that crossed to the riverside wharfs of the Liwan district, seemingly unhindered by the competition of countless small crafts that followed their own personalisedpersonalized itineraries along the Zhujiang.

The city was in the process of building China's first international hotel—the White Swan—and we would occasionally drive from Macau on weekends to monitor progress. It was financed and conceived as one of several public initiatives by the Hong Kong businessman and philanthropist Henry Fok Ying-tung, who was later appointed as vice chairman of the 10th National Committee of the Chinese People's Political Consultative Conference—the country's top political advisory body. As a member of the FIFA executive committee he also brought football teams to Canton to play in front of 50,000 wildly cheering and denim-suited supporters, which gave me, as an occasional visitor, something to do in the evening—even participating in pre-game kickabouts.

The hotel opening that I attended in February 1983 was followed two days later by an invitation to all local residents who came in their thousands to experience the grand central atrium with its imposing waterfall feature. Soon afterwards it hosted more impressive visitors including Hu Yao-bang, Zhao Zi-yang, Deng Xiao-ping, and later Queen Elizabeth II. The privileged location of what was to become the first international hotel in China was situated on the southern bank of Shamian Island overlooking the Pearl River, and provided the first tall building insertion in what was a grand collection of British and French buildings that formed the Canton concession area dating from the mid-nineteenth century. Ten years later the Fok Ying Tung Foundation became the first foreign investor in Nansha, now a city district of Guangzhou, with the objective of developing a city for the twenty-first 21st century as part of the Pearl River Delta Region.

To the north and across a canal via a narrow bridge were the markets, with sights both impressive and startling, and as far as the livestock section went, not for the faint-hearted. This led to the compressed street system that was formally the center-point of the Thirteen Hongs, through the now pedestrian Shangxiajiu Street, and along Zhongshan Lu to the Temple of the City God. To the east of Shamian was the bund with its tree-lined promenade and collection of older treaty port buildings, including the Port Authority building. Further to the north, Liuhuahu Park provided boating opportunities on the lake, while Yuexiu Park to the east incorporated the Five Rams statue and Zhenhai Tower, and at its southern fringe the Sun Yat-sen Memorial Hall.

Through the closing decades of the twentieth century and into the twenty-first, our work in Mainland China extended to a number of the largest cities including Beijing, Shanghai, Xian, and Chengdu. However, Canton has remained as an always engaging destination at the head of the designated Greater Bay Area. Its active program of urban regeneration has equipped the city with the means to meet the new demands of a carbon-neutral future while embracing necessary goals of livability.

The history of Canton is a complex and multi-facetted one. Its trading relationship with the West extended back to the maritime silk route that flourished between the second century BCE and the fifteenth century CE, and connected China with Southeast Asia, the Indian subcontinent, the Arabian Peninsula and Europe. From the sixteenth century international trade with the West advanced considerably following the arrival of the Portuguese in 1552, which effectively exploited pre-existing trading conditions. By the beginning of the eighteenth century many parts of Asia were becoming active bases for expanding commercial networks, including trading links with Chinese ports, but with independent physical identities that reflected a strong Western influence in administration, planning, and city making. In this sense "modernization" was, in significant ways, essentially equated with Westernization, under which sweeping political forces of change over the next two centuries would shape emerging cultural identities. By the early nineteenth century, during the Qing dynasty, only 10 percent of China's population lived in urban situationettings. The combined total of China's top ten cities amounted to only two percent of the total population of 300 million that had doubled over the preceding 150 years, as Imperial policy favored a balanced pattern of growth between market towns and villages. However, some of the most significant urban entities in China were the major port cities, situated around the natural coastal harbors and river deltas, of which Canton was the most important as a center for trading activity.

Well before the problems that beset China from the mid-nineteenth century, both inter-provincial and external trading conditions were extremely robust, with commodities including tribute grain and silver shipments distributed through a system of waterway transport.[1] The beneficial mutuality of close Chinese bureaucratic and merchant contact through *guangxi* also acted to protect vested interests on both sides, and resisted or excluded foreign traders from traditional avenues of commerce. It can in fact be argued that China's political and market systems were, in their somewhat isolated context, both sophisticated and self-sustaining, and therefore in little need of external interjections to forcibly alter their course. However, the need for new instruments of change and accompanying institutional adjustments were virtually inevitable in re-shaping its position within rapidly evolving world events.

Canton and other port cities were established as beachheads of foreign influence during a period of massive Western expansionism and trading ambition. The Treaty Ports exerted a strong hold on urban politics, economic growth, and new patterns of urbanization, with foreign settlement opening up parts of the country to Western cultural influence just as it expanded its commercial horizons. In a more elusive way, the new "gateways" into and out of China, transformed not only attitudes to modernization but almost inadvertently fueled changing political attitudes, offering an alternative urbanism outside hidebound standards and state control.

The foreign occupants of hastily constructed "concession areas" in the mid-nineteenth century arrived with fortuitous advantages from an industrialized and militarized Western world. However, the initial capacity to coerce was fated to erode over the following century as forms of occupation gave way, first to commercial collaboration, and finally to subdued exit. This echoed and interfaced with the parallel process of change within China itself. By the beginning of the twentieth century, the Treaty Port period had begun to give way to a new era of revolution, military occupation and instability over the middle decades of the twentieth century. This led to the Socialist Planned Economy between 1949 and 1976, followed by the reforms of 1979. The reinvigorated city of Canton slowly began to re-emerge as a significant force through the continuing modernizations that heralded unprecedented urban growth, while Guangdong Province as a whole has greatly contributed to China's emergence into the global marketplace.

John Fairbank, the noted Harvard historian, identified British activity in China during the early and middle years of the nineteenth century as the turning point in the "interface" between China and the West.[2] In a number of ways this can be simplified into what, after the Treaty of Nanking, it had more or less become—an opening up of China through a commercial exploitation by foreign interests. It is, however, a more complicated and ultimately more ambiguous process than this, leading directly to the revolutionary events of the twentieth century, with an emerging social and political order that continues to reverberate through its intense transition from national disintegration and isolationism to strategic remodeling, economic regeneration, and world stature. In all, the period that extended over almost two centuries reflected a frequently unstable but inevitable transition from the old to the new China.

The sudden Western presence, crudely superimposed on a very different societal structure, might be considered, in retrospect, as a timely stimulus toward internationalism, just as much as it was an imperialist intrusion. This being said, Niall Ferguson has ventured to suggest that the British historically regarded forceful occupation and attempted jurisdiction over foreign territories as an inherent part of their "civilizing mission."[3] At the same time, China's somewhat passive response toward a militant presence of "barbarian" invaders could be explained through the potential benefits of new trading trajectories rather than a critical challenge to the very structure of its society.

From the mid-nineteenth century, the Concession Areas grafted awkwardly onto older city forms or transposed on completely separate sites along river shorelines, almost inadvertently contributed to a new urban order through a combination of new port works, imported industrialization techniques, the integration of rail routes, and the gradual formation of new business and commercial centers. New areas of land reclamation, created to facilitate new growth areas and port works, evolved into multi-story commercial and diplomatic enclaves that absorbed evolving development typologies. These not only helped to establish present-day urban identities but effectively realigned city growth processes toward the newer urban quarters and commercial districts that created a focus for business development. However, many of these measures at the time ran counter to deeply ingrained organizationaloperational patterns within the country, and only superficially brought about a genuine amalgamation of interests. At a more elusive level, it can be quite legitimately supposed that the overall intention of European powers was not imposed imperialism but trading concessions. This was facilitated by an adroit single-mindedness in terms of establishing separate compounds within or at the fringe of existing port cities, where both land use and municipal control could be exerted independently of external constraints, but where there was a common bond. Canton and other treaty ports, which included Hong Kong, formed the start of what has been termed the "Western Century" in China, whereby the country experienced a remarkable transition from the disintegrating Manchu state to foreign partnership and a new international order.

From a historical perspective, while interactions between Chinese and foreign communities shaped the growing city of Canton and its institutional development, urbanization patterns also reflected the underlying robustness and continuity of the historic trading dynamic, irrespective of Western influence. It might be said, therefore, that foreign intervention, with its imperialistic overtones, redirected but did not alter the overall course of urbanization. For a time, however, the symbolism associated with Canton and other treaty ports informed and circumscribed the relationship between Chinese and foreign residents, just as it reflected new tiers of economic organization and urban definition. Fresh planning concepts for growth and expansion were introduced into Chinese cities, establishing a different morphological basis than the narrow streets and tightly packed courtyards of the older walled conurbations. There was also a possible need, however ambiguous, to reflect cultural differences through architectural patterns—not merely the distinctions between foreign and Chinese styles, but between the national characteristics of different concession areas.

Scholars of recent Chinese history tend to have put different interpretations on events, either contending that the treaty ports were crucial in overcoming an almost feudal society and leading China into an emerging industrial and trading world that could have only been resisted for a short time, or alternatively reasoning that treaty ports had little real political significance. In fact, the foreign settlements acted as the focus for largely independent mercantile and even city-building regimes, but were relatively disengaged from both revolutionary forces that were gathering momentum during the early twentieth century, and invading forces that eventually signaled their demise. It is perhaps prudent to broadly subscribe to the former view, with the ports propelling an emerging

role as trading gateways, particularly during their later years, while acknowledging that Canton had, for the most part, a thriving merchant class well before the advent of foreign merchant traders.

The gradual disintegration of a long established imperial order can be largely attributed to the dislocation that China faced at the end of the nineteenth century, exacerbated by military struggles that it could scarcely contain. What is beyond dispute is that Western residents and Chinese formed an unofficial alliance, outside the established order of the time, to further both individual and collective commercial interests that had strong urban and political repercussions. This also contributed to the breakdown of the rigid demarcation between the traditional bureaucrat and the urbanizing merchant class.

The nineteenth century treaties were undoubtedly unequal, but the re-vamped urban management under the much maligned "extraterritoriality" for a time acted as a bridgehead toward modernization, ultimately proving to be an essential tool for the regularization of economic activities that would, sooner or later, have been inevitable. The supplanting of tribute by the treaty system, and its subsequent rationalization of administration, in effect cut loose the ancient instruments of ritual and gradually prepared the path for new institutional development, while advanced modes of planning established a workable city infrastructure that opened the door to investment in China's urbanization, and activated new urban ideologies.

Concentrations of capital in the hands of both foreign and Chinese banks facilitated the continued expansion of the Chinese merchant class, and by the turn of the twentieth century Chinese investors and management input were represented in around 60 percent of all foreign capital ventures. The tight network of commercial guild associations helped to maintain a high degree of separation from foreign financial institutions run on more formal lines, and Chinese financial bodies remained dominant in terms of domestic operations.

The path to modernization in China took a bewilderingly different course from that of many colonized Asian countries. There are several possible reasons for this, beginning with the paradoxical situation that prevailed until 1911, whereby foreign influence and ideology failed to implant a sufficiently viable new order, despite a weak and progressively ineffectual dynastic leadership, partly due to the dislocation and civil unrest initiated and prolonged by the foreign occupation itself. It led many disaffected Chinese intellectuals to question the established order and inherent resistance to change, and generated a commitment to a bourgeoning Chinese nationalism and a realm of support for Western-style modernization as an agent of economic transformation.

In socio-cultural terms, China possessed a long-established and self-sufficient identity that was intuitively resistant to external pressure—even the prevailing Manchurian Qing dynasty adapted to the indigenous Han model. It proved to be relatively accepting of Western cultural overtures, including new patterns of modernization that became insinuated within established cities, and remained relatively immune to the confrontational pressures of foreign intrusion. The overthrow of the Qing dynasty in 1911 as a result of revolutionary forces that had been gaining momentum since 1894, gave way to a civil struggle and war with Japan that culminated in the Communist victory in 1949. This came to represent a series of conflicts and reconciliations, many of which were interrelated: those between invasive forces and political imperatives; those between social struggle and ideological principles; those between the entrenched Confucianist order and the inevitable pressures of a new internationalism; and those between the modernizing impetus of urbanization and the conservative rural heartland, steeped in tradition.

The modernizing forces associated with Canton and other port cities had little or no interface with the vast rural realm that allowed the established system of self-sufficiency to continue, impervious to the central bureaucracy and the distant currents of urban change. This separation survived relatively unchanged until the post-1949 period up to the late 1970s, during which time economic upheaval was compounded by problems of mismanagement of agricultural policies, impossible industrialization targets, and mass deprivation.

Contemporary China, with its emphasis on rapid city growth, has, to a significant extent, optimized the responsive urban legacy and latent capital markets of the major port cities. Canton today is China's third largest city and its most prosperous. It still retains within its morphology a physical legacy of the early concessions and resulting urban form. The monumental but fragmented residue of foreign occupation, enshrined in Lingnan traditions of brick, stone, and architectural ornament in relation to place and situation, now infuses the present day city with a mellow and timeless sense of place.

The road to modernization has been fraught with hurdles, revolution, and reform. In the twenty-first century it has led to a type of state-controlled capitalism, with a guarded acceptance that this represents a nuanced interpretation of orthodox Marxism, but arguably one which is suited to the unified tradition of Chinese society, even as China accepts the implications of the global marketplace.

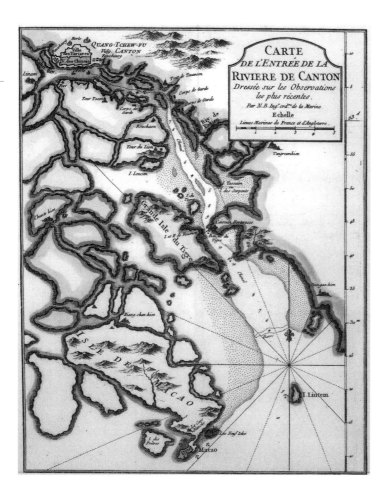

...neteenth-century plan of the ...arl River Delta.

As such, much of the twentieth century can be considered an unstable period of transition up to the present modernizations, which still hold within them many pre-modern conditions. The unequal treaties of the nineteenth century, coupled with the cataclysmic events that evolved from this, arguably fed the political undercurrents. This in turn induced a strengthened sense of purpose in restoring territorial integrity, that was later to embrace the return of Hong Kong to China in 1997 followed by the return of Macau in 1999 under Special Administrative Area status.

Globalization and the return of overseas educated Chinese increasingly impart Western values and an international outlook, but as Chinese society matures so does a sense of nationalism. This includes a forceful definition of patriotism and respectful identification with the new China as it plays a leading role on the world stage.

There is not a little irony in the fact that the Royal Mint in nineteenth-century London that received the shipment of millions of taels of silver that China was forced to hand over to Britain as reparation at the conclusion of the Opium Wars, is now owned by the Chinese government and houses its embassy.

Introduction

On December 13, 1978, at the end of a routine gathering of the Chinese Communist Party, held in the wake of the Cultural Revolution, Deng Xiaoping as the new leader of the Party following Hua Guofeng, stood up to set out a pragmatic vision for the future of China. In his speech he broke with the route adopted for the Socialist Planned Economy in 1949. He proposed that China should aspire to defeat poverty that afflicted some 90 percent of its population, and set in motion a strategy for revival that would surpass the world's most advanced economies. Several days later at a CCP conclave, Deng's visionary proposal was formally adopted. It represented in many ways the culmination of more than a century of persistent change, conflict, and confusion.

A contemporary view of one city's history, is a matter of both reference and reconstruction, helping to infuse our perspective on the past with our knowledge and evidence from the present. On top of this there lies an elusive topography of association and interpretation that must be woven into the existing record by both local and national events. Canton has for several centuries held a central position in regard to economic, social, and urban change in China, and is one of its oldest cities, extending back some 3,000 years to the Qin dynasty. The city represented a major trading center during the T'ang dynasty and became a provincial capital in the fourteenth century. Defensive fortifications around the city extended through the Ming dynasty while maintaining a symbiotic relationship with its agricultural hinterland. Three centuries later it was placed under siege for almost a year by the invading Manchurian army before its fall in 1650. Accelerating urban growth reflected new trading trajectories and the commercial undertakings of its merchant guilds together with their overlapping affiliations. The growth in population led to its gradual expansion to the southwest, outside the city wall, relatively independent of the older city, with an elaborate web of narrow streets and thoroughfares containing different quarters for its Chinese and Tartar inhabitants. Its wealthier sectors housed mansions for the leading mandarins and "Co-hong" traders, while foreign merchants from the nineteenth century constructed their trading houses or "factories" fronting onto the Pearl River, serviced from the port of Whampoa.

Canton, with its associated foreign capital and buccaneering knowhow, undoubtedly propelled new economic and social trajectories but these were largely ineffective as a politically integrating force in the face of fundamental social and political change. Technological innovation became a less than material tool of modernization with trade, finance, and industrial production in total contributing only a small amount of gross domestic product prior to the end of treaty port operations in the early 1940s when Western influence became increasingly marginalized before being extinguished entirely in the post-1949 period.

The residue from a historical interaction of cultures and events still swirls around contemporary relationships and occasionally creates unfathomable tensions, but this challenges the need for necessary forms of understanding derived from mutual interests. In the post-modern world, China's economic success reflects a resourceful exploitation of globalization's many benefits without suffering national fragmentation or disintegration. In this, government treads a narrow line between maintaining responsive economic development with measures that ensure stability and cosmopolitan values. As a technology-led development model propels China to the forefront of the global economy, the country continues to pursue an aggressive urbanization strategy that is necessary to anchor domestic consumption.

The book is set out as follows:

Chapter 1 *The Mandate of Heaven* explores the ancient rules governing city development in China that can be traced back to the Zhou dynasty and an established social protocol known as the *Zhou-li*—the mandate allotted to the Emperor. This reflected the Confucian conception of place in harmony with the natural order and a hierarchical organization of urban quarters.

Chapter 2 *Avenues of Trade* examines the early maritime connections that led to the development and growth of the trans-oceanic trade, that along with the Maritime Silk Road helped to consolidate a supporting system of port cities in Southern China.

Chapter 3 *Adventurism and Hostilities* sets out the situation that revolved around the evolving trading associations and the opium trade that formed a catalyst to hostilities.

Chapter 4 *Beachheads of Foreign Influence* sets out the Treaty Port settlement pattern, extended trading access and treaty law. Together these contributed to a new direction of development in Canton following the Treaty of Tientsin in the aftermath of the Taiping Rebellion.

Chapter 5 *An Emerging Modernism* examines the responsiveness of Canton to new ideas and interventions as a result of increased economic influence. By the early part of the twentieth century Canton, as the principal gateway into China, was becoming receptive to innovative planning and restructuring initiatives as part of a new Republican program, shaped by investment in urban infrastructure.

Chapter 6 *Forces of Transformation* discusses the compelling forces of revolution. These began to emerge in the early twentieth century in the wake of the Boxer rebellion, and gradually stoked up a wave of nationalist sentiment and opposition to the imperial system.

Chapter 7 sets out the ramifications of the *Socialist Planned Economy* between 1949 and 1976. The Sino-Japanese and civil wars had left Chinese cities in a state of degradation. At that time the country was somewhat isolated internationally with trade restricted to Communist Bloc countries, effectively constraining the inherent locational advantages of Canton.

Chapter 8 *Reforms, Challenges, and Resurgence* examines the steps taken to set China on a new path that was to transform Guangdong Province and China as a whole through a commitment to establish a new policy of reform. By 1978, the socialist transformation had stagnated and Deng Xiaoping was in a position to set China on a new economic and social trajectory.

Chapter 9 *Remaking the Canton Metropolis* focusses on the reconfiguration of the Canton conurbation, and the production of increasingly diversified urban initiatives, with a gentrification of older urban districts, and new business, residential, and cultural urban quarters reflecting a restructuring and upgrading of the city, with urbanization becoming the driver of economic growth.

Chapter 10 *The Political Paradox* charts China's alchemy of contemporary factors that have fashioned a political system responsive to the unified tradition of Chinese society. It is argued that this is closely related to the three harmonious belief systems of Chinese culture—Confucianism, Taoism, and Buddhism that are centered around philosophical teachings that appear to be suited to the unified tradition of Chinese society. It is arguably the "Chinese characteristics" associated with the current political model that accords with the goal of a more equal society and best meets community needs as a whole. As a global power, China now aspires to shape and influence an international order by driving multi-lateral agreements that meet the so-called "four-pronged" political goals of governing the country by law, deepening reform, maintaining a disciplined political approach, and building a prosperous society.

Temple of the Five Immortals or "Genii." The shrine extends back t the Song dynasty.

The present temple was erected along with the bell tower under the Ming dynasty in 1378 and wa effectively reconstructed in 1889

Chapter 1

The Mandate of Heaven

The first emperor of Qin—from 221 to 210 BCE, toward the end of the Warring States Period—sanctioned migration from the north to the Guangdong region, and to assist this the Lingqu canal was constructed leading to an integration of Han migrants and the native Yue people, the building of walled settlements and the introduction of advanced agricultural techniques. The regulation of China's maritime trade went back to the Tang dynasty between 618 CE and 907 CE with strict supervision of foreign vessels and merchandise. At the time, the majority of the population were concentrated along the river valleys where local industries included shipbuilding, porcelain, and paper manufacturing.

The rules governing city development in China can be traced back to the Eastern and Western Zhou dynasty, one of the most culturally significant Chinese dynasties, which lasted from 1046 BCE to 256 BCE. During the course of several hundred years, the Zhou rulers instituted a basis for a carefully ordered and unified way of life. Intellectual thought and philosophical precepts both articulated and anchored the workings of society, and established a strict dialogue between urban planning and an established social protocol known as the *Zhou-li*. This represented a work on organizational theory and became one of the "Three Rites" of ritual texts attributed to Confucius. The culturally specific forms of the imperial city symbolically represented both the power of the Middle Kingdom and a value system of social organization. It was expressed through clearly defined but complex correlations and rules that regulated the workings of a profoundly hierarchical society. The Zhou-li was divided into six sections: the offices of heaven dealing with general governance; the offices of earth relating to the division of land and taxation; and the offices of spring, summer, autumn, and winter, dealing respectively with education, military, justice, and territorial matters. The "winter" office sets out standards and guidelines for city design in terms of planning, architecture, and technology.[4] This comprised an ideological sense of ritual, guiding and standardizing urban design as a reflection of a socio-political order that remained largely unchanged for almost three thousand years. The rules for this were set out in the *Ying-guo Zhi-du* which regulated city layout through a system of tight controls that interfaced directly with underlying moral codes and principles.

Throughout three millennia, China's agricultural investment was almost totally directed toward the fertile and easily cultivated southern and south-western flanks, as the land beyond its northern boundary mainly comprised steppeland and pastoral uses. However, it was this area that became the main source of periodic invasion, primarily by Mongol and then by Manchurian forces. The Manchu controlled an extensive empire beyond Chinese boundaries, including Tibet, outer Mongolia, and Turkistan. Qing dynasty policy was therefore focused on securing and maintaining these northern frontiers as well as supervising the traditional economic and social order within China. Unity was also assisted through China's geographic advantages, in particular the Yellow River basin, which provided a convenient latticework of connections between centers. It also promoted political and cultural influences that had a homogenizing effect, whereby rigid social class structures inhibited any sense of nationalism. Invading powers from the north, which were equipped more for military rather than imperial domination, were essentially dependent on China's prevailing governmental and bureaucratic institutions and sought to maintain them.

Much of what the West knew about China came from the diaries of Marco Polo, the Venetian explorer, who had spent 17 years at the Mongol court of Kublai Khan, returning to Italy in 1295 with tales of China's prescience in manufacturing, science, and publishing. The emperor was assumed to rule the "Celestial Empire" under a heavenly mandate.

The mandate allotted to the emperor was reflected in an extended system of public office through which scholar-officials followed traditional unifying principles of government that accommodated certain checks and balances rather than stimulating radical change. The process was perpetuated by a formal examination and appointment system based on a philosophical understanding of Chinese classical traditions. This acted to consolidate the mandarinate by assimilating the most able and responsible candidates, but perhaps also the more conservative ones, into the established ranks of the imperial bureaucracy. Intellectual distinction, through a high level of literacy, was absorbed and sustained within a framework of long-standing political responsibility, and was reinforced by a legal code based not so much on absolute principles and protection of individual rights, but on maintenance of social harmony.[5] The examination system was lauded in Europe in the eighteenth century by philosophers such as Voltaire as a model of meritocracy, free of external influences and steeped in the morality laid down by Confucius.

A patterned conception of place was reflected not merely in relation to the cardinal points of the compass but to the center. This leaned heavily on the canonical history of Confucianism where the human being occupies a central position in the universe by emphasizing the cyclical forces of history. Built elements were arranged both in accordance with tradition, and with reference to the enigmatic influences of geomantically favorable locations. A dynamic balance was preserved that required only an intuitive harmony with the natural order. Urbanization tended to represent a formulaic blending of physical development with an intricate pattern of established relationships, which was reflected in a hierarchical physical organization of city quarters. This made urban settlements vulnerable to the exigencies of dynastic and governmental shifts, whereby the capital city might be moved in its entirety from one location to another. However, while the population of China doubled to more than 300 million between 1650 and 1900, the level of urbanization was only around seven

Foreign traders proceeding from Macau to Canton could observe several brick-built octangular pagodas up to nine stories in height, standing on hill forms that stood back from the river, includin the Whampoa Pagoda and the Lo Creek Pagoda, both dating from the Ming dynasty.

The form of the pagoda is derive from the Buddhist stupas first constructed in ancient India as tombs or temples. Buddhism was introduced into China by invited Buddhist masters who brought with them ancient scriptures, and the first pagoda to be built in China was during the Eastern Ha period. The Chinese character ta means Buddhist tower, but can also embrace earth or soil, while the character si means temple. The design became increasingly elaborate over the centuries, with the crowning steeple taking on the traditional form of the stupa itself. The olde pagodas had an underground component to enshrine holy relics and other sacred items, and above this was an elaborate base, originally constructed from wood to give structural support for the levels above. The various levels were built in wood or brick offering opportunities for simple or decorative elements based on traditional Chinese design characteristics. In Canton its later purpose was to ward off ev influences and ensure protectio that might well have included the need for divine intervention to protect the waterfront communities from the foreign "devils."

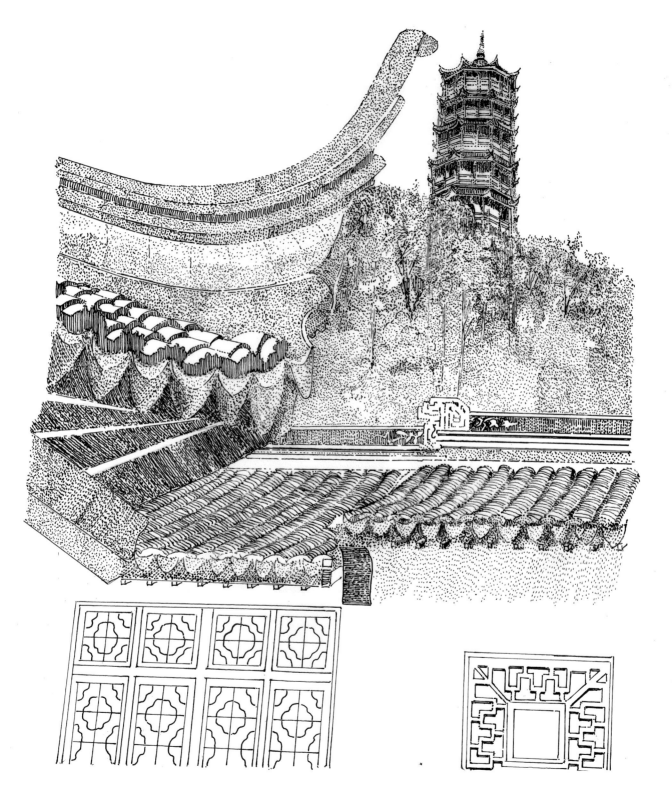

percent having markedly declined from a high of twelve percent during the Song and Ming periods, but with a higher rate of internal migration.[6]

Confucianism, which had become honed over two millennia from around 221 BCE, was reinforced by the system itself, so that the ideology governing the workings of the state was indoctrinated into its officials. The dominant Confucian tradition was not a static one, as it evolved through its close association with Buddhist and Taoist institutions but was perpetuated through the elitist culture of the examination system. China was held to be at the center of the world, and so ingrained was the Confucian code of conduct and ethical rules of behavior that those who refused to subscribe to it were therefore, by default, "barbarian." This was reinforced by ceremonial rites and intricate patterns of etiquette that acted to preserve the fundamental hierarchical order of the state with the emperor at the apex of the Middle Kingdom.

Cities were largely designed with the main offices of state located in the center, facing south. Ceremonial buildings including temples were located on the eastern and western sides, with a public market on the northern edge. The gridded primary street system divided the city into distinct quarters, while secondary grids sub-divided these further into smaller urban blocks. Thus, cities were laid out largely as geometric entities based more on *separating* rather than *integrating* elements. This inevitably downplayed their necessary reconciliation with the forces of progress and represented a significant transition from the axial orientation and symmetrically patterned arrangement of Ming dynasty buildings, with strictly regularized layouts and urban expansion confined within the city walls. The later city forms experienced significant urban expansion stimulated by economic growth, the most important being the development of an open market system. Streets became avenues of commerce and interaction, and spatial expansion extended market operations well beyond city walls, following the flow of activity along river and road alignments, and integrating smaller towns as component parts of larger urban systems.

The formation of cities and the growth of their central functions were critical elements in regional development, primarily through shifts in the imperial capital that acted to induce cycles of regional growth and development.[7] For example, the role of Canton as a port city had a significant impact on development within the Pearl River Delta and well beyond.

Each imperial and provincial capital, no matter where they were located, required a supporting apparatus of security and control over sources of food production. These aspects in themselves created the prerequisites for commercial activity and the establishment of long-distance trading routes, with chains of supply extending across the entire country, and beyond its borders. This included the Grand Canal, built in the sixth century CE, to ensure food supplies to the capital Chang'an with its vast warehouses and shopping streets.

The larger cities grew from centers of agriculture situated around the coast, governed primarily by highly regulated administrative and military regimes. Only when these roles were consolidated was commercial life established to any great extent in the cities, the small merchant class existing to serve the elite. Successive capitals were planned largely around the imperial household, their accompanying security and bureaucratic apparatus, and the divinity associated with their role in the universal order. As feudal China was administered by officials and garrisoned by troops belonging to the dominant landlord class, there was little opportunity for the growth of commercialized urban strongholds, although during the Ming dynasty peasants were officially ordered to grow cotton for officials who operated weaving workshops.

The organizational framework of the imperial city was, in no small way, related to the bureaucracy, which created countless tiers through the ranks of chief ministers, officials, officers, clerks, merchants, artisans, and traders through to a bottom rank of service providers. The largest and most important rank was the administrative enterprise that imposed its urban imprint on carefully orchestrated districts called *hsien* with populations of around 200,000 people. The capital of each *hsien* was administered by an imperial magistrate, but an underlying social order was imposed through the elders of established clans. This balance between prescribed forms of administration, the force of community representation, and the Confucian morality that permeated society combined to establish a virtually self-regulating system of authority and order, manifested in the controlled massing of physical components. On retirement, magistrates who had acted in an upright manner earned the gratitude of the community through presentation of memorials and gifts.

The "ideal" capital, exemplified by Chang'an under the Tang dynasty, Peking under the Ming and Canton, under the Qing, comprised square or rectangular walled city plans laid out on a strict north-south axis. Gates were located on each side so that the basic internal layout represented a street grid. Urban design in the traditional city made no concession to a grand architectural centerpiece, but instead comprised an inner court, reflecting the pivotal personage of the emperor, or "Son of Heaven," that could not be filled by a building.[8] In essence, the main provincial and secondary cities followed much the same model.

Cosmic symbolism attached to city spaces tended to overwhelm the particularities of geographic situation. Thus, even rural agricultural production was, for the most part, city-centric almost precisely because the city model was geared less to economic development, and more to the metaphysical geometry of order and control. Cities came into being at the behest of the state, and pre-existing townships or trading centers that enjoyed the right credentials could be incorporated within the imperial fold. In part, the rigid layout reinforced the symbolic power of the state and its administrative components, underscoring a regularized and exclusive concentration of authority, personified by city walls.

The integral concept of enclosure is an essential component of historical urbanism in China. The root word for "city" is *cheng*, which also means "wall." Walls represented order—both physical and social. Those that defined courtyards were called *qiang* implying a defensive or securing element, while walls associated with the house were called *bi*, which implied resistance to climatic extremes. The city wall symbolized authority but also security from invasion and rebellion. The Zhou dynasty established early planning principles that divided cities into wards that effectively zoned areas of specific uses, defined by walls and wide streets. The Mongols, who were predominantly pastoral, decried the notion of city walls, but after their overthrow the Ming dynasty undertook a long program

of city reinforcement through defensive fortifications of stone and brick that extended through the Qing dynasty, although with few limitations on suburban concentrations. This relates to different realms of urban scale from the protective city fortifications to the street walls, which represented a strict demarcation and an orderly division of uses, rather than responsive interfaces. Urban perception was thereby dominated by features dictated by the city-making components that stemmed from this—gates, main axial avenues, drum towers, and ceremonial spaces that acted to both segregate and embellish the functionally specific urban quarters. This rigidly zoned approach to formal layout planning, where people generally lived in the same neighborhood in which they worked, to some extent acted to predetermine the layout of Chinese cities until the nineteenth century, and was effectively reintroduced in the *danwei* collective system of the 1950s.

In late imperial China it was possible to identify two hierarchies of "central places." The first was regulated through a system of officials within a hierarchical organization of towns and cities for purposes of administration, while the second was shaped largely through realms of economic transactions. However, by the time of the Qing dynasty the vast majority of these were commercial centers, of which only around four percent served as administrative capitals.[9] Systems of cities were circumscribed by geographic constraints, economic resources, and the physiographic framework that affected transport networks and distribution channels. Economic centers became the logical places for public institutions such as temples and educational institutions, again largely based on their hinterlands and degree of economic specialization. Adam Smith described China during this period as "one of the richest, most fertile, best cultivated, most industrious and most populous countries in the world."[10] It was also widely regarded as being both self-contained and remote.

By the nineteenth century, the commercial hinterland of major cities, including the larger port conurbations, was largely contained within specific regions. The port cities had also evolved within a highly developed system of coastal trade with each other.

Urban centers themselves were part of a hierarchical order, from the imperial and provincial capitals to a network of regional centers that reproduced the same layout principles on a progressively reduced scale, only adapting their rigidity to accord with auspicious or highly constrained site configurations. This arrangement also extended to the interdependent and complementary relationship between cities and their rural catchments. The Chinese word for landscape is *saan-sui*, which literally means "hills and water," so that city space was deemed to reverberate through a metaphysical relationship with the surrounding natural topographical forms and symbolic shapes that are taken to portend good fortune. The "environmental footprint," that now marks the theoretical ability of cities and their surrounding urban regions to be self-sustainable, was very much a part of the traditional symbiotic relationship between the city and agrarian society, where each reinforced the needs of the other. Such an enlightened system was facilitated through an effective division of the country into provinces and administrative districts, each with an organizational and food production network. While city administrations ensured productivity and maximized returns from the countryside, agricultural production sustained the cities, and through these the state. The process was symbolically recognized through an annual ceremony in the imperial capital overseen by the emperor who plowed a ceremonial furrow into the grounds of the Temple of Heaven.[11]

In turn, the sophistication of urban life was perceived as complementary to the intrinsic nature of the landscape, relating to philosophical and spiritual virtues that had been historically celebrated over the centuries in art and poetry. It has to be said, however, that while classical philosophy and literature in China make much of the simplicity and tranquility of a rural lifestyle, the scholars, artists, and sages who did much to perpetuate and romanticize this view did so from comfortable urban situations.[12]

The traditional difference between China's historical urban model, and that of Western urbanization, relates primarily to the administrative system of government under imperial rule. The walled city was effectively controlled from within by an elite group of officials, administrators, and traders, but maintained through a symbiotic relationship with the agricultural hinterland. This extends to the term *chengshi*, which includes both the urban and rural areas under the same administrative jurisdiction.[13]

Until the mid-nineteenth century, China's system of food production and the scale of internal commercial trade flows were, from available evidence, much the same as in Europe. The coastal cities had inherited a long seafaring and mercantile tradition and followed the southern littoral or *Nanyang*—the Chinese term for the shoreline of the Southern Ocean.[14] From the late seventeenth century, ships from Shanghai carried tea and textiles south to Canton and Foochow, and north to Tsingtao, Tientsin, and Dalian. In return ships brought wheat, sugar, and timber. H. H. Lindsay's report of proceedings on a voyage to the northern ports of China, enumerated up to 400 sea-going junks entering the port of Shanghai in one single week during July 1832—a volume of shipping almost equal to the Port of London, at a time when Shanghai had one of the smallest port populations.[15] Other travelers were impressed by the profusion of traffic on the inland water routes and the stone-lined Grand Canal.

Merchants involved in important trade routes, both within China and with other Asian countries, sat almost outside the Confucian social model, having little correspondence with the bureaucratic hierarchy of scholar-officials. John Francis Davis, the Chief Superintendent of British Trade in China and a future governor of Hong Kong, wrote in 1836 that the largest buildings in the smaller towns he visited, were the commercial guild halls.[16] In this sense the rigid organizational and social structure of society, together with government's monopoly over many kinds of imports and the exigencies of the established tribute system, were seriously out of step with changing economic fundamentals. While the government accepted a commitment to maintain its massive agricultural production process, and invested heavily in certain state-owned mining and manufacturing industries, there existed bourgeoning business concerns and a free labor market, particularly in the southern provinces, that revolved around mining, textile manufacturing, cotton, and porcelain—controlled for the most part by powerful merchants. These centers were mainly found along the prominent waterway systems, low-lying river deltas, and coastal settlements. The busiest areas were around the lower Yangtse basin and the Xijiang basin characterised by a complicated series of maritime connections that tended to converge on Canton. Thus, by the early part of the nineteenth century, the most dynamic centers of trade and commerce were located in the southeast of the country, some considerable distance from the Manchu capital in Peking, and had been the first to embrace trade with the West.[17]

The urban growth that occurred at an accelerating rate during the Qing dynasty was, in great part, a reflection of the growing commercial undertakings of the merchant guilds that laid out new development and built extensive housing, retail, workshop, and port-related developments together with temples, academic institutions, water reservoirs, and transport facilities. Trade associations, or *gongsuo*, combined groups of privileged craftsmen or those who provided services. Other types of guilds were known as *huiguan*, which comprised affiliations of merchants from various native places. Merchant groups tended to develop their own characteristic urban quarters made up of

The ritual of the plough was performed by the Emperors of the Ming and Qing dynasties as the "Sons of Heaven" to ensure a good harvest. This took place in the grounds of the Temple of Heaven in Beijing. Earth was represented by a square and Heaven by a circle symbolizing the connection of Heaven and Earth. This took place twice a year, during the first month of spring, and again at the ceremony of the winter solstice on the Earthly Mount. The Emperor turned up three furrows, and each of the ducal ministers nine.

The Ocean Banner Temple comprises a series of large and beautifully decorated halls, along with a library and a printing press. In the evening up to 250 priests met to recite prayers in the principal hall that displayed gilt scrolls hanging from the pillars, after which they walked in a procession around the temple.

The three images show the manifestation of Buddha—past, present, and future: Kwo-keu-fu to the right; We-keu feu whose reign is to come on the left; and Heen-tsa-fuh in the center, the regulator of human destinies.

Originally drawn by Thomas Allom 1843.

purpose-built compounds, and introduced the need for hostels and hotels to accommodate travelling merchants and scholars. Certain *gongsuo* operated ocean-going ships where shares in trading voyages were apportioned according to investment. Over time the original guilds separated into more specialized groups with sophisticated levels of skills, associations, and capital investments.[18] Even in the early part of the Qing dynasty, 50,000 workers were employed in Guangdong Province, particularly in tea processing and porcelain manufacturing.

The boundary between the gentry-scholar and peasant classes was not entirely exclusive, but social mobility and membership of the former class was based on an immersion in traditional values, so that a strong sense of history and fine arts were perpetuated. These values and credentials reinforced the effective balance and bureaucratic interface between the urban and rural realms, providing this was seen to work for the common good.[19] This clearly contrasted with the uncompromising demarcation of activities found in older European city regions. Through succeeding dynasties, city-based regimes of power, patronage, and perceived excess were succeeded by new dynasties or movements with a significant rural support base.

During the late Imperial period, autonomy flourished in the cities and there was little "official" intervention in community affairs. The educated urban elite, rather than officials, had developed both the social ideology and the wherewithal to carry out city building, feed the poor, and even raise militias. By the nineteenth century this liberal but unofficial partnership between state and society had achieved a social consensus that became almost corporatized through the overlapping affiliations of the guild structure, so that many of the city services and much infrastructure production was implemented independently of institutional bodies.[20] Projects in the public realm that might begin at a neighborhood level would then, over time, become more systematically integrated at the municipal level. This created an interesting balance between autonomy and control, based on a strong tradition of self-management.

By the beginning of the nineteenth century, the predominant source of state revenue was the "land and grain" tax, which necessitated an effective organization of works associated with efficient forms of agricultural production. This required orderly management and investment in irrigation and land-formation projects that reinforced the interface between the bureaucratic and cultural realm of the city, and the productive values of its rural surrounds. While there was clearly an economic mutuality, this system also reinforced a distinct social and cultural demarcation. The nature of China's intense agricultural system and large rural population living in and around the fertile river valleys, was dependent on a long-established and disciplined means of co-operation, where the individual was subordinate to the wider group. This relates to the Confucian concept of *min-pen*, the peasantry that lived on the "trunk" of society.[21] Elite officials were largely responsible for public works, education, and social welfare, so that there was a delicate balancing act between local hegemony and maintenance of the social and economic status quo. The family itself reflected the authority inherent in a hierarchical structure that was considered vital to the forces which underpinned an ordered society.

The Trading Continuum in Canton

Canton represents one of the oldest cities in China extending back some 3,000 years. A perhaps questionable legend has it that five spirits or *genii* arrived at the court of the Zhou monarch, assisted in their improbable airborne trajectory by five rams, bestowing future prosperity on the Baiyue people. The rams then turned to stone—a sacrificial feat signified by a sculpture located at the peak of Yuexiu Park, which has come to symbolize the city.

Zhou Tuo, a general of the Qin dynasty, unified the Lingnan area and made himself ruler, with Canton as his capital. The 2,000-year-old tomb of his grandson Zhou Mei was discovered during excavation of a central site in the city in 1983, threaded within a jade suit. Additional evidence of the city's antiquity surfaced during excavations for a new metro system in 1995, when the remnants of a palace along with carved tablets were recovered with the characters *Pan* and *Yu*, which related to the names of the surrounding hill forms. It suggests a sophisticated arrangement of buildings, gardens, and pools along with evidence of ship-building workshops that reflected maritime trading routes established by the Qin emperor before the fall of the dynasty in 206 BCE.

Following a series of military campaigns by Western Han troops aimed at acquiring the resources of what is now part of Guangdong Province, the southern kingdom became part of the Han empire, in the second century CE. During the following years, attracted by new trading routes

The legend of the five immortals embraces the five rams who introduced rice farming to Canto[n] around the time of the city's founding in 214 BCE. As they left they were said to turn to stone, giving rise to the monument on Yuenxi Hill that commemorates the event.

and the relative stability in Southern China, migration occurred from northern parts of China, and Canton quickly became the empire's most important port city and commercial center at the eastern end of the emerging maritime silk route.

Canton was a major trading center in the T'ang dynasty and became a provincial capital in the fourteenth century. Arab traders exerted an important role in the development of the city, with the Wai Shing Chi Mosque as its religious focus dating from 626 CE. Other traders from the Middle East travelled along the Silk Road and were the first Western visitors, but while trade was welcomed in the markets and bazaars, the foreign community was excluded from residence in the city. An evening drum roll signaled their necessary return to separate *fan fan*—foreign quarters outside the city walls—that provided a model for the later accommodation of western merchants, including the first European visitors. Despite the ebb and flow of trading networks over the succeeding centuries, this effective segregation lasted until barriers were broken down, both

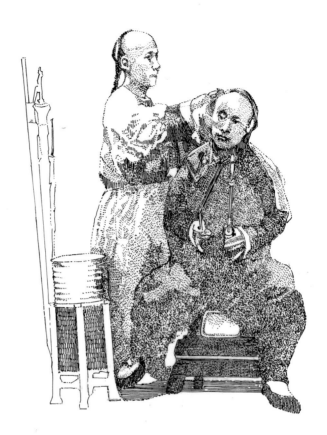

literally and figuratively, in the nineteenth century. At this time, the city was a center for manufacturing and handicrafts, and beyond its walls the urban landscape merged with the villages and
rich agricultural land around the tributaries of the Pearl River.

Growth of the city was not all plain sailing. Over the following centuries Canton suffered from rebellions against the T'ang emperor, so that by the Song dynasty in the eleventh century a brick wall was erected around the city to protect against invasion. The built-up area at the time encompassed three separate
city quarters, with fifteen outer gates. These were only combined after Canton became the seat of provincial government during the Ming dynasty, and remnants of the old wall still remain in Yuexiu Park.

In 1431 foreign trade was banned, with harsh punishments facing merchants who ignored the
imposed conditions prior to the onset of new sailing routes to the Far East. The first of these were
established by the Portuguese who were allowed trading privileges from a base in Nagasaki in return
for helping to quell the not infrequent pirate invasions, and in 1557 they were allocated the small
territory of Macau, situated at the mouth of the Pearl River. The Portuguese effectively opened
the door to the Dutch in 1601, and English merchant adventurers in 1637 under the auspices of
the English East India Company. With the Portuguese arrival, regular trading with the West began
through trade fairs. While the foreign length of stay was strictly circumscribed and residence tightly

controlled, this tended to fit well within the framework of other Portuguese trading ports in Asia that stretched from the Indonesian Spice Islands to Malacca and Goa, generating an exotic range of merchandise. The Portuguese ships also brought silver bullion from Nagasaki, encouraging the later arrival of more militant foreign powers from England and Holland. After the East India Company established a base at Amoy, the imperial court acceded to the promotion of trade with the West by opening up four ports, one of which was Canton.

In 1644 China was invaded by a Tartar army from Manchuria establishing the Qing dynasty that would last for the next 267 years. Guangdong Province was placed under siege for almost a year before the fall of Canton in 1650. After the wall was finally breached the invading army laid waste to the city, and land to the west of Sze Pai Lau (now Jiefang Road) became the new Tartar Quarter. To the east were the yamens—the domain of government officials who lived and worked in the walled enclosures. A new city extension accommodated the remainder of the urban Chinese population. The Old City was protected by a 14-meter-high wall constructed of sandstone blocks with strategically placed watchtowers, and at the time of the Manchu invasion six principal and well-fortified gates were set into the perimeter wall. The Manchus, as unpopular invaders, were concerned with a high degree of urban compartmentalism to ensure their safety through a process of controlled segregation between ethnic Chinese and the Tartars.

In Peking the inner city came to be known as the Tartar city with the native population occupying a separate area within the outer walls. This strategy was to ensure security, and to a large extent was continued in the early reform period through elements that effectively separated government and private gated developments from the wider public. This acted to fortify social boundaries, creating a cellular urban landscape around specialized development types.

Within the city wall, built originally in the eleventh century, the major avenues connecting the city gates were in place by the time of the Manchu invasion. These were named the Street of Benevolence and Love, now Zhongshan Road, and later Sze Pai Lau named after four monumental arches, now Jiefang Road.[22] Canton in the late Qing dynasty differed from many Chinese walled cities in having a less rigid layout due to its commercial trading emphasis. Successive increases in the line of the enclosing city wall, within which were housed the strictly demarcated mix of Manchurian officials and government elites, were matched by a more informal commercial expansion area or *Xiguan* to the southwest outside the confines of the wall. The layout of the *Xiguan* area evolved around a matrix of narrow streets and pathways containing a miscellaneous and largely undifferentiated mix of commercial and residential structures—the very antithesis of the walled city's ordered axiality. Trades were grouped within streets and precincts, intersected by waterways that acted as drainage canals, with security achieved through gated entrances, and their character determined by carved signboards and secure gated entranceways. The adjoining embankment was the eventual site of the foreign factories.

A 1655 plan of Canton drawn by Jan Nieuhof indicates the position of the main city features at the time. Looking north across the Pearl River it shows the position of the Governor's Palace, the various city quarters, the banqueting house, armory, and water gates, together with some fortifications on offshore islands. The major gates were used for different purposes, linking with settlements on the urban fringe and allowing in water and provisions for the inner city. On the southern wall four gates linked the old and new city areas, while the main internal routes were marked by grand *pai laus* or arches.

The result of this urban duality was that the *Xiguan* area developed virtually independently, with little official interference in its urban management. Local street and trade associations carried out construction and maintenance. As pre-modern China was largely an agrarian society, land ownership did not necessarily coincide with building implementation, so that leaseholders and business owners frequently sub-divided lots.[23] This created an elaborate web of users and increasingly complex land transfer procedures that translated physically into a largely unregulated but relatively comprehensible city building process. Gradually the increase in population concentration created unacceptable congestion and aggravated sanitation and public safety problems, with fires sometimes destroying entire neighborhoods.

The Canton trade era lasted from the beginning of the eighteenth century up to the Opium Wars that forcefully terminated the traditional "Canton System." The inherent strength of this stemmed from an ability to regulate foreign trade while at the same time being able to flexibly address the needs and requirements of the imperial court.[24] Various checks and balances allowed the customs superintendents to control trade while keeping prices competitive. Eventually, however, this type of mechanism became undermined and therefore less effective, while at the same time funds were gradually siphoned away from the central administration, which fatally weakened it.

By the time of the major nineteenth-century foreign incursions, the city had sixteen gates associated with both the old city and the newer Xiguan district. Some of the gates were ceremonial and others used for service entry and merchandise. Manchu "bannermen" troops were responsible for security and defense, and while this worked to defend the city and ensure security over two hundred years, by the mid-nineteenth century the city defenses had become vulnerable.

Eight gates were later installed around the New City including the Great Peace Gate and the Little East Gate that provided access routes between the city and adjoining settlements. Other gates included the Gate of the Five Genji, which provided access to the temple, and the Tranquil River Gate. These were well guarded by Manchu soldiers, and after darkness fell only government messengers were allowed entry.

The Eight Banner system introduced by the Manchus was used as a system of defensive units, but also acted as a practical means of social organization and land distribution. From the beginning of the Qing Dynasty the system was increased to 24 banners divided equally between Chinese, Manchu, and Tartar soldiers. Around half of the bannermen were stationed in Beijing while the remainder were sent to the most important provincial cities, including Canton. Banners were color coded according to location, with yellow at the center, blue to the north, green to the east, white to the west, and red to the south. The intention behind the division into various garrisons, was to quell any potential uprisings and act as a defensive system against invasion.

By the mid-nineteenth century 5,000 bannermen and their dependents were stationed in Canton—the descendants of a hereditary system of rank and authority—and allocated to provide security to different parts of the city. The Tartar Quarter centered around the Flower Pagoda represented a system of narrow streets with buildings constructed of adobe and painted white. The Chinese Quarter was constructed from clay bricks, but laid out in a regular way. The hierarchical division between the three ethnic groups was uneasy, as language barriers, physical differences, and cultural habits created both work and social barriers. In the face of widening international trading and commercial associations, the original privileged role of the Manchu gradually declined, and they became increasingly divorced from Mandarin power.

From the treasury, a main thoroughfare led to the South Gate named Sheung Mun Tai and later renamed Beijing Road. This was one of the busiest streets with its terminal gateway housing a water clock comprising four copper water containers cast in 1316.[25] As water seeped through an inclined sequence, this allowed its levels to be registered by means of a float within a certain time period and registered by a keeper who displayed the hourly time on a board.

The wealthier quarters to the west of the city were constructed along wider streets, and mansions were situated in large walled enclaves with delicate pavilions and summer houses strategically situated according to strict feng shui principles around engineered lakes and water courses. Visitors, having entered from the main south gate, were confronted by a large granite

tish forces guarding the Great
st Gate during the occupation of
nton, 1858.

slab aimed at diverting the potentially straight alignment of evil spirits. The main halls of the mansions, including the ornamented reception hall, were furnished for the extended family and guests, with domestic quarters arranged in a hierarchical manner according to the family structure, along with kitchens and school rooms.

The Western city quarter was home not merely to the largest and most elaborate temples, but to many of the *hong* merchants in the eighteenth and early nineteenth centuries who formed the *Co-hong*. This was allowed to conduct trade with foreigners, acting as an intermediary between Western traders and producers of goods which fetched a high price.[26] Family progenies associated with the Co-hong were able to purchase high offices and rose to exalted positions in the mandarinate, such as the family of Punqua whose *juren* degree was conferred on him by the emperor in 1832 for his public benefaction. The garden of his house, Lai Heung Yuen, was one of the most famous in the city, with flocks of rare birds, including mandarin ducks, and animals in caged settings associated with walkways. This became the popular model for the "Willow Pattern" associated with the products of noted porcelain workshops in Canton. In the mid-twentieth century the garden became Liwan Hu Park—now a focus for Chinese opera performances.

A military camp was situated in the northern part of the Eastern Suburbs with a parade ground near to the East Gate, where military procedures and examinations were held. An annual ceremony, presided over by the Prefect who represented the Emperor, was held to bless each agricultural year in order to ensure the correct conditions for a successful harvest.

Early Maritime Connections: East meets West

The Pearl River Delta is formed through a dendritic system of rivers and tributaries, akin to a branching pattern in the south of Guangdong Province, uniting to form the main river corridor that flows into the South China Sea. The Delta has traditionally represented the most fertile part of the Province where established forms of agriculture in the form of rice, vegetables, and sugar cane were sufficient to feed an urban population that continued to expand from the seventeenth century. The delta area has always been well endowed with labor that could be engaged in industrial production. The interlaced system of waterways has also long provided an expedient means of transportation and port anchorages alongside new trading trajectories.

Ships left Canton on what was termed the Maritime Silk Route. Cities began to emerge based on mercantile values, creating not merely a new type of urban condition but a domination of trade routes throughout much of Asia from Afghanistan, Africa, and India to Japan and Korea. Mercantile power and the accompanying growth of trans-oceanic trade led to a rapid expansion of China's trading vessels under the tenth-century Sung dynasty, and new ocean routes were opened up through accomplished navigational and ship-building skills. Sailing vessels could travel for up to a year, with supplies of live animals for food. At the time of Marco Polo's travels to China in the thirteenth century, there was equally little resistance to foreign trade via overland routes. Port cities in China took on not dissimilar cosmopolitan characteristics to the cities with which they traded, which included

Alexandria, Antioch, and Venice. A system of "secondary" cities then began to emerge, closely associated with the established and far-flung trading empire with *fan-fang* or "foreign" quarters diversifying the urban commercial and cultural climate. From the thirteenth century Canton had become the most cosmopolitan port city in Asia, and the premier trading city in China.

This trend was, if anything, accelerated by the Mongol invasion of China in the thirteenth century which, while considerably diluting the sense of Chinese nationalism, massively assisted the expansion of trade routes, and extended the influence of China to other cities under Mongol control, as far as Constantinople, Moscow, and Cairo. The Mongol Empire enjoyed a high degree of religious tolerance, so that certain city quarters, for example in Xian, exhibited Christian and Islamic characteristics as well as those of Buddhism and Taoism, just as they do today. Mosques and commercial quarters in Muslim districts were administered under Islamic law. However, goods were taxed, and the movement of foreign merchants, who at the time were mainly from the Arab world, carefully restricted.

The seven Ming naval expeditions in the early part of the fifteenth century were undertaken on a grand scale with colossal junks, each up to 114 meters in length and with 9–12 square sails, able to carry 2,000 tons of cargo. Each of the ships had on board an astronomer and a geomancer to ensure good fortune. Some of them followed the routes of early T'ang and Sung traders, and later the great Mongol fleets under Khublai Kahn, through the Indonesian and Malaysian archipelagos, extending the empire to the Adriatic. In 1292 Marco Polo recorded four-masted ocean-going junks with crews of up to 300 men. Under the Yongle Emperor the Ming fleet made seven maritime treasure voyages from 1405 that comprised 317 vessels and 28,000 men. It made contact with various towns and cities on the Malay peninsula, Sri Lanka, and India, together with other destinations in Africa and Arabia, many of which sent back envoys to China.

The treasure ships known as *bauchuan* carried precious cargoes of silks, porcelain, tortoise shells, ivory, and pearls, together with items carved out of rare wood. They were accompanied by fleets of supply ships on their voyages between 1405 to 1433 across the China Seas and the six-thousand-mile expanse of the Indian Ocean. However, these were by no means the first craft from China to make long ocean voyages. The Han navy was powered by the shipbuilding traditions of Guangdong, Fujian, and Zhejiang under the moral auspices of Confucianism and the ambition of China's early emperors.

With the death of Zhu Zhanji, the Xuande emperor in 1433, these expeditions suddenly ceased, probably through a combination of the immense costs involved, but perhaps also reflecting the narrow outlook of the Confucian court and the mandarinate with its mistrust of the growing merchant body. Historians have differed as to the precise reasons for this, and why the prosperous trading cities of China fell into something of a decline. Undoubtedly, a contributing factor was the conservative imperial tradition that held that as the capital city was the universal center, the farthest cities were unworthy of serious attention or consideration. What is not in dispute is that the curtailment of trade by sea and the disbanding of its naval fleet had a consequent and

The five-storied Zhenhai Lou on Yuexi Hill was constructed in the 1380s during the Ming dynasty as a guard tower for military surveillance. It was restored in 1928 as the city's Natural History and Art Museum, with the original wooden structure replaced with reinforced concrete. The museum contains, among many older artifacts, the water clock of Canton—one of the most ingenious means of measuring time.

destabilizing impact on Chinese entrepôt cities, although there still remained a flourishing "junk trade" between cities along the coast. Around the same time the imperial tribute system began to break down, and trading profits began to be redirected toward provincial officials and local merchants who established independent markets for foreign trade. With the opening of the Grand Canal the requirement for coastal supplies of grain to the north shifted to barges. This led to a gradual economic introversion at almost the precise time that European cities were gearing up to maritime expansion through the Venetian trading routes to Asia, and through fleets of vessels in the hands of European adventurers.

The Foreign Impetus to Trade

The decline in trading and social contact with western cities on the part of China also virtually coincided with the European Enlightenment, rooted in an urban-based theologism.[27] Its spiritual and cultural expression was based on Christian history and a Eurocentrism in relation to the arts and sciences that viewed the non-European world as semi-barbarian, in much the same way as China viewed the West. This was important in three ways that were to have a strong bearing on future events.

Firstly, scientific knowledge and understanding in Europe began to be increasingly seen, in a progressive sense, as *praxis*—a resource that could be used effectively for beneficial socio-spatial innovation and the public "good." This involved new city building and the export of this experience outside Europe through the parallel expansion of mercantile trade and colonization. The enlightened philosophy that lay behind the transformation of cities collided with the new forces of social revolution in Europe, accompanied by emerging calls for the universal rights of man and citizenship. In turn, this became further shaped by the economic and cultural ramifications of urban-industrial capitalism with its full emergence in the eighteenth century Industrial Revolution, and the consequent drive toward the establishment of new international markets.

Secondly, European cities through the period of the Enlightenment were dominated by the merchant and artisan classes which, through increasing democratic rights, provided the key instruments of social change and economic expansion. By way of contrast, China, with its feudal blend of autocratic rule and rigid social structures, turned a largely introspective eye on the commercial world even within its own trading empire.

Thirdly, a cohesive force in terms of both city and empire building in Europe was religion—in particular the Catholic Church that underscored the European Renaissance. Thus, the first Western expeditions to Asia not only represented flourishing mercantile regimes, but a sense of righteous superiority through Jesuits and other missionaries. This began with the arrival of the Portuguese in Goa, Malacca, and Macau in the mid-sixteenth century, followed at later stages by the Spanish in the Philippines, the Dutch in Indonesia, and the British in India, who were more inclined toward opening up trading routes but nevertheless frequently carried missionaries on their vessels. This brought to the fore strong cultural differences between the forces of Christianity, which is a proselytizing religion, and the more philosophical precepts associated with Buddhism and Taoism.

New Frontiers

The founding of trade between Europe and China began in 1498 through the voyages of the Portuguese explorer Vasco da Gama. Canton has traditionally occupied a key position in relation to an extensive trading network of migrant Chinese communities who had settled in Indochina, Thailand, and the Philippines. Inland waterways extended from the city's immediate hinterland—for example in the eighteenth-century high-quality ceramics from Jiangxi Province, 600 miles away, could be brought to the southern trading center by means of transferring goods from one river to another. A hierarchy of coastal settlements located at the intersection of roads and waterways could sustain a hierarchy of commercial connections with producers across a wide radius, but which ultimately converged on Canton.

By 1511 the Portuguese who had already established a footing in India, took Malacca and within four years dispatched a vessel under the command of Raphael Perestrello to the north of the Pearl River to investigate trading opportunities. Macau, the Portuguese settlement on the main estuary of the Pearl River, was a celebrated port of call for Portuguese ships trading between the Malabar Coast, Malacca, and Japan. The Portuguese territory dated from 1517 during the Ming dynasty, 150 years before the Tartars conquered Canton. This successful overture was followed by a full expedition of four ships that travelled along China's eastern seaboard as far as Ningpo. The Chinese were quite cautious, however, in terms of granting a settlement, and an informal "leased settlement" arrangement in 1535 to erect buildings in Macau was not translated into a more formal tenure until 1582 through the intervention of the viceroy of Canton, without any actual deed of grant,[28] possibly in return for suppressing regular pirate attacks along the coast. From this they began to consolidate trading operations. Three hundred years later, strict controls were applied over ports of entry into China, these being mainly Canton, Amoy, Shanghai, and Foochow, with operations supervised by Chinese bureaucrats, so that only foreign emissaries were allowed to go onward to the capital in order to pay tribute.

The system of tribute missions themselves began to gradually morph into more orthodox trading activity orchestrated largely by Chinese merchants in the late seventeenth and early eighteenth centuries. This slow but inevitable transition from the cultural realm of the tribute system to commercial avenues of trade inadvertently opened the door to a new and more forceful breed of merchant adventurers from the West. These were commonly identified as *Fo lang chi* or "Westerners," purely on the basis that this represented the direction from which they came.

Tribute missions from Southeast Asian countries continued well into the second half of the nineteenth century, generally restricted to a single port of entry. Under this system, tribute and trading concessions were inter-related through imperially appointed brokers who frequently travelled between ports—mainly Canton, Shanghai, and Amoy, to obtain the best market price on imported goods. Tribute missions also occasionally acted as trading partners for other nations, establishing a wider network of commercial possibilities for Western companies just as they affected the coastal trading systems.

China technically exercised control over Macau, which had to pay both customs duties and anchorage dues. However, within 20 years of their arrival the Portuguese were exporting goods directly from Canton with taxes and duties suitably negotiated with local authorities. This was, in effect, the beginning of direct Sino-European trade which, after a somewhat stuttering start, developed rapidly in the first years of Manchu rule. From the mid-seventeenth century various European countries consolidated and expanded existing trading routes with other Asian trading destinations and began to trade with the Chinese ports of Amoy, Foochow, Ningpo, and Canton, although this was eventually restricted to the latter. What is known as the Canton System evolved through a gradual relinquishment of imperial control over the system of customs, which came under provincial administration after 1685 in all cities except Canton.

Fairbank explains this delicate balance of power, as working through a sophisticated system that traditionally underscored the procedural "recognition" accorded to both sovereign and subordinate states and which relied on complicated but generally accepted forms of diplomatic protocol. The extended formalities surrounding the paying of tribute were sanctified by procedures that combined a discreet reciprocal arrangement, tacitly accepted by both parties. In this way tributary states were diplomatically incorporated into an elitisted hierarchy, under an imperial mandate.[29] The accepted process acted to formalize mutual recognition and achieve relative stability, establishing a recognized framework for both expansionism and security, and facilitating diplomatic procedures. In turn this extended Chinese influence abroad through recognized envoy channels, and provided direct and extensive avenues for commercial activity and trade across its land frontier.

By the beginning of the Ch'ing dynasty in the mid-seventeenth century, the form of cities had become increasingly irregular, reflecting both the incremental and spontaneous growth of commercial activities and industry that framed new types of urban quarter. Wu Jin has determined that out of the sixty-four largest cities in China at this time, only fifteen had a formal traditional layout, of which eight were national and regional capitals so that their regularity was largely determined by their political role.[30] A concentration of administrative and ceremonial buildings constrained the development of coherent commercial centers or public open space so that a discontinuity developed between the traditional role of cities and the shifting development patterns associated with growing guild quarters that represented significant commercial power. The extended clan lineages, alliances, and guild system were well organized and influential in providing the operational service necessary for complex mercantile and maritime activities in the port cities of the southern provinces, in particular Guangdong. Groups of wealthy merchants first joined together to engage in trade with Japan, and later the Portuguese.[31]

Port cities began to expand through multiple cores with overlapping catchments that later made the notion of new concession and settlement areas associated with the treaty ports comparatively easy to absorb. These, perhaps unintentionally, introduced substantial urban contrast through invigorated trading and commercial conditions. Differences in administrative, trading, and transportation criteria tended to influence the type of city form that evolved, while a defensible and protective location for a major settlement upstream from the coast often necessitated a first line of defense down river with little agricultural support, so that these small settlements eventually tended to evolve into ports, for example Ningpo, which was subordinate to the Zhejiang provincial capital at Hangzhou.

While Chinese cities formed part of a loose urban hierarchy as seats of administration and military garrison, the main port cities by the early part of the nineteenth century had come to represent complex settlement models related to trading routes, where administrative and market functions overlapped. This fueled their growth and shaped local economic and social organization. However, the tenuous connections between cities and uneven population distribution effectively prevented a cohesive national market infrastructure. G. William Skinner has suggested that by the late imperial period, the notion of administrative capitals had become secondary to a realm of urban centers that had evolved through commercial needs.[32]

The Manchu Qing dynasty that effectively ruled China from 1644 occupied certain key roles and held control of the military, but generally remained outside core Chinese society, forming a mutually respectful but somewhat distant coexistence. The Chinese army was increasingly relegated to a relatively harmless provincial role, while Manchu garrisons were stationed around Beijing and other major cities, including Canton.[33] These and other measures were geared mainly to the preservation of Manchu dynastic power, and it was beyond the imagination of the ruling elite that future threats to national welfare would come not from the landward borders, but from the sea.

By the late seventeenth century Manchu officials and dignitaries still outnumbered the Chinese at court and in the leading state offices. This privileged position occupied by non-ethnic Chinese rulers, engendered an isolated and inflexible social and political structure that had become virtually self-sustaining, and made it difficult to either respond or adjust to rising undercurrents of change, let alone invasive challenges.

Chapter 2

Avenues
of Commerce

**he International Trading Settlement**

Foreign merchants first constructed their factories on river-front sites of around 200 square meters to the southwest of the old city, fronting onto the Pearl River, with plots of between 15 and 45 meters in width. The appellation of "factory" came from the type of joint-stock company personified by the British East India Company, although the area included Danish, Dutch, American, French, and Swedish concerns. It soon became common practice, however, for trading firms such as Jardine, Matheson and Company to occupy factories while also acting as consuls for one or another country. Factories were leased to foreign firms and named after the corresponding nation carrying out business, although trading firms often rented out space, so there were usually far more operators than actual premises.

The first plan of the factory areas shows that this involved Dutch, French, Swedish, Danish, Spanish, and America concerns. Other factories belonged to the Co-hong merchants—Houqua, Mowqua, Kinqua, and Samqua who had been given a trading license by the emperor and were able to virtually monopolize foreign trade and commerce. Old China Street ran through the area, four meters in width and lined with shophouses, while the adjacent Hog Lane quickly became filled with grog shops to serve the Western sailors. Running parallel to the river from east to west was Thirteen Hong Street, which today exists as Shisanhang Road. To the north was the guild assembly hall where the early traders met to discuss matters with their government counterparts.[34]

The Pearl River was the window of the city, connecting the factory area with the port of Whampoa to the east, and inhabited by a massive floating "Tanka" population in various types of Chinese craft, joined in the 1840s by Western steamships. Paintings from this period depict the profusion of river incident, extended by the use of trading vessels as stationary residential quarters that needed constant provisioning during their stay. With the massive growth of industry and port-related uses along the Pearl River during the following century, a not dissimilar outlook could be seen on the river until the early 1990s.[35]

The first factories were grouped in a line about 300 feet from the river frontage. They had a ground floor of blue-gray brick construction with a timbered upper-floor, although these were continually modified and upgraded so that within several years they were substantially re-built, sometimes with a

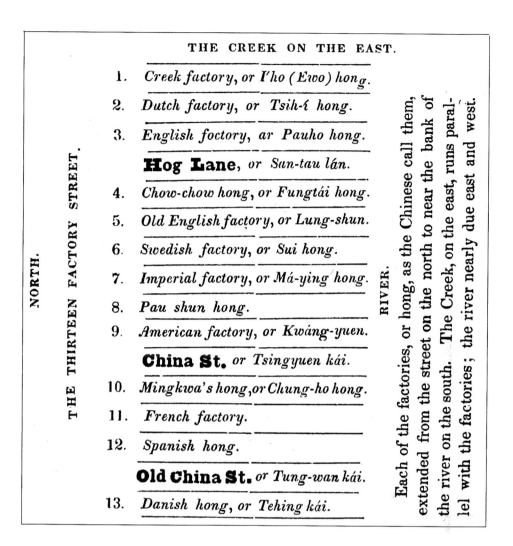

THE CREEK ON THE EAST.

NORTH.

THE THIRTEEN FACTORY STREET.

1. *Creek factory, or I'ho (Ewo) hong.*
2. *Dutch factory, or Tsih-í hong.*
3. *English factory, ar Pauho hong.*

Hog Lane, *or San-tau lán.*

4. *Chow-chow hong, or Fungtái hong.*
5. *Old English factory, or Lung-shun.*
6. *Swedish factory, or Sui hong.*
7. *Imperial factory, or Má-ying hong.*
8. *Pau shun hong.*
9. *American factory, or Kwáng-yuen.*

China St. *or Tsingyuen kái.*

10. *Mingkwa's hong, or Chung-ho hong.*
11. *French factory.*
12. *Spanish hong.*

Old China St. *or Tung-wan kái.*

13. *Danish hong, or Tching kái.*

RIVER.

Each of the factories, or hong, as the Chinese call them, extended from the street on the north to near the bank of the river on the south. The Creek, on the east, runs parallel with the factories ; the river nearly due east and west.

third story. In 1822 when a fire destroyed many of the old buildings, more durable quarters were constructed in brick and granite, with an open market square in front, establishing a point of interface with the outside city. The ground floors were used for storage of tea, silk, and porcelain with rooms for the comprador, servants, and a treasury. Above this were the merchant's residential quarters. Gabled roofs were finished in local tile with ridge ornamentation, typical of traditional Cantonese architecture.[36] As factories were extended or re-built after the fire of 1822 they garnered additional features that offset their individual identify such as masonry arches, large verandahs, and hipped roofs built by local contractors who began to utilize the same features in local buildings.

Ships anchored at the island of Whampoa around twenty kilometers downriver from Canton, and were measured by the Hoppo's staff to determine customs charges that were based on size and volume.

The Bogue forts on the Pearl River, intended to protect Canton, were named after an offshore island, shaped like a crouching tiger or *Bocca Tigris* in Portuguese, but offered only limited protection.

Plan of the factory layout 1830, William C. Hunter (from Bits of O China).

Initial Trading Commodities

The main trading commodity in the early years of the English East India Company, along with the large Dutch and Danish trading companies, was tea. The cultivation of tea plants – *Camelia sinensis* evolved in the Himalayas, and by the ninth century was considered one of the seven necessities of life. Buddhist monks were the first to transport seeds to neighboring countries. Tea was imported into Europe and America by the Dutch in the seventeenth century, and was introduced to England for the wedding of King Charles II in 1662. It was said to ensure a healthy constitution, and its consumption quickly spread to the remainder of society. The Tea Act, passed by Parliament in 1773, effectively allowed the English East India Company to monopolize the tea trade with America. This led directly to the "Boston Tea Party" when chests of tea from three of the company's shops were dumped into Boston Harbour. This was the flame that sparked the American Revolution. It was also the catalyst that sparked the first American trading expedition to China in 1784, via a ship appropriately named *The Empress of China*.

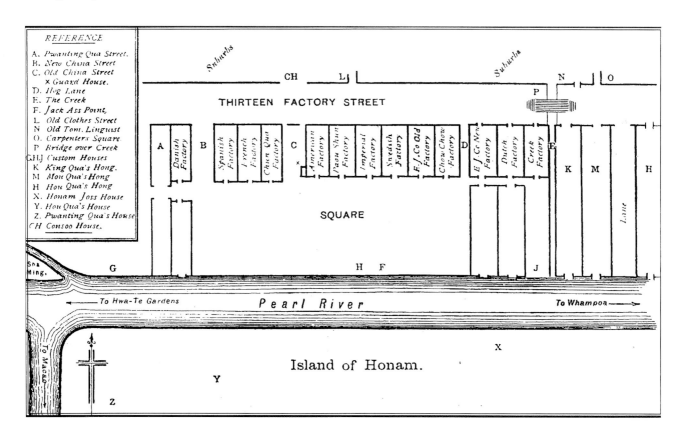

By the mid-nineteenth century, more than forty million pounds of tea were exported to Britain annually. Amoy was the port of export from Fujian Province—the main tea growing area for Pekoe, Bohea, and Souchong, the black teas that were most popular in Europe. When this port was eventually closed, the tea was transported by river and canals to Canton.

Silk was another main item of export to the West, often kept dry on-board ships by tightly sandwiching it between bales of tea. As the area around Canton was a silk producing region, the city became a center for silk goods, clothing, and embroidery. Silk was one of China's most precious exports and one of its most assidually creative art forms. According to legend it dated from 2600BCE having been discussed by Lei Zu, wife of the Yellow Emperor from the *Bombyx mori* – a moth native to northern China. Since that time the practice of sericulture had become a well-guarded secret, and although a number of other countries produced it, Chinese silks were the finest.

The third major export commodity to the West was porcelain, commissioned to order by artists in Canton in a not dissimilar way to the paintings and reproductions undertaken in parts of Guangdong Province today. Other workshops specialized in jewelry production, furniture, ivory carving, fan making, silverware, and lacquerware, while a large number of studios were dedicated to mass-production of "China Coast" paintings of the Canton riverscape, often completed by groups of artists specializing in individual aspects. The city therefore built a reputation not just as an entrepot, but as a center for exquisite craftsmanship that found a massive market in European countries. Artists and craftsmen belonged to guilds that regulated production and monitored quality, and streets were often dedicated to one particular trade. Guildhalls were essentially chambers of commerce and came to play an important role in civic organization. Because of their representational role and wealth, they were some of the most architecturally beautiful buildings, often housing shrines, an elaborately carved deity, and an ancestral hall. However, their chief function was to provide a meeting space together with accommodation for merchants from a particular region.

By the 1830s there was a standard list of "connivance" fees that applied to different goods, and well-established networks through which smuggled goods were imported and distributed. As coastal defenses became increasingly over-burdened, corruption and contraband became ever more insidious, and private foreign traders began to break the monopoly of the large companies, rapidly finding inventive ways to satisfy the demands of international markets. Two important factors contributed to a shift in the trading balance. First was the introduction of shallow draft steamships that undermined the traditional system of control over the entrance and departure of vessels on the West River and past the Bocca Tigris forts; second the expansion of sophisticated tea plantations and processing in other parts of Asia, and the production of high-quality silk and porcelain in Japan and Korea undermined China's traditionally exclusive monopolies in these products.

Top appointed officials had only loose connections with the realm of local customs officers, merchants, and pilots who relied on the system and made it work. While the issuing of credit facilitated the smooth conduct of trade, it also put financial pressure on customs officials to re-classify commodities from dutiable to non-dutiable in exchange for bribes—something that could only be financially sustained through a continual expansion in the overall volume of trade.

The New City

During almost the entire time span of the Qing dynasty after the Manchu invasion, the majority of Chinese lived in the "new city" to the south. Migrants from other provinces, together with the really poor, were from the early nineteenth century directed to the southern suburbs between the city wall and the river in temporary shanties. To the west was the suburban neighborhood of wealthy merchants with spacious mansions and extensive gardens. To the east was the overcrowded labyrinth of narrow streets and basic accommodation of clay brick houses, subject to occasional flooding from the typhoon storms along the Pearl River. In Canton's nineteenth-century street matrix, the less intrepid could summon sedan chair bearers to preserve both their dignity and the hem of their robes. Shops opened directly onto the street frontage so that purchases could be carried out directly from the chair. The intense level of activity at street level coupled with the frequent procession of sedan chairs carried by coolies created various degrees of confrontation, particularly as trades frequently extended outside the shopfront to occupy the public space with both manufacturing and transaction activities. Informally, this frequently gave way to a one-way system of sedan chair travel within the wider street matrix, which allowed the occupants, in particular the wives and daughters of the wealthy, to avoid the cacophony and congestion of the thoroughfares themselves.

In an ingenious but enterprising way, it was common to compensate for dank and potentially dangerous environments by christening them with auspicious names that evoked good fortune such as "Heavenly Peace" and "Everlasting Love." Streets were also alive with calligraphy as carved vertical signs in red, green, and black with gold or vermilion characters competed for visual attraction in order to extoll the virtues of the goods on display. These were often accompanied by large carved images of the products themselves to cater to the illiterate. Some of the best patronized were the pawnbrokers' establishments, several stories high in order to store the pawned objects in camphor-wood chests. The items themselves often consisted of precious clothing from one season to the next, with valuables stored on the top floor.

Buildings were generally no more than two stories in height, constructed from clay bricks with terracotta-tiled roofs. Heavy street gates could be closed and guarded at night, a tradition that came to signify neighborhood or clan associations defined in terms of urban street blocks which otherwise lacked distinguishing characteristics. Within these areas, self-governing committees orchestrated both service and social operations including fire prevention, garbage removal, security control, and religious celebrations.

Establishment of Authority

State authority was administered by the Mandarinate, a collective body of officials that dated from the Ming dynasty. Officials were appointed by the emperor to govern the province, with those of the highest ranks given charge of either civil administration or the maintenance of order and defense. Qualifying examinations were technically open to all males, with certain exceptions depending on social and professional status. Preparations involved intense study of Chinese classical works, as it was intended that participants should acquire an extensive scholastic vocabulary but also absorb moral precepts useful for their working life as administrators and judicial officials. Around 3,000 students took the examination each year with around 500 successful candidates proceeding to subsidized post-graduate study at one of several colleges in Canton. Two of these were the Yuyan Academy, established in the Song dynasty, that later moved to a site on Yue Hill adjacent to the Five-story Pagoda in the early nineteenth century, and the Kwong Nga Academy built nearby, established at a later stage by the governor-general. Those who graduated successfully with a *juren*—degree—were able to take a final metropolitan examination in Peking.

Mandarins were held in high esteem and commanded great public respect. This was assisted by a requirement to perform periodic acts of filial piety, including the ceremony of the kowtow to the emperor in lavish ceremonies where they had to assemble in order of rank, divided by their civil and military affiliations. The nine ranks of officials were distinguished by adornments embroidered on robes and on symbolic signage outside their domestic entrances—exotic birds such as cranes and peacocks for civic dignitaries, and animals for military mandarins. The most senior civil officials had to undergo regular transfers at some distance from their home base to avoid persuasive temptations for corruption. The viceroy was the most senior official in Guangdong Province and its neighbor, Guangxi. From the mid-fifteenth century he was responsible for direct liaison with the emperor and his court in Peking. One of his responsibilities was to review petitions from members of the public that covered wide matters of concern together with appeals against criminal convictions. The imperial commissioner of customs for Guangdong Province, the *Hoi-Pu* or the *Hoppo* as he was better known by foreign traders, was one of the most enviable positions, enabling them to receive an indeterminate percentage of all paid duties. Fifth-ranked mandarins controlled the eastern and western sectors of the city with jurisdictions that included the Whampoa anchorage for foreign vessels, and the foreign factories.

During the Qing dynasty the Chinese governor's yamen, was situated in a palace originally constructed for a Tartar general on what was reassuringly named the Street of Benevolence and Love in the older part of the city. Nearby was the yamen of the treasurer, with its adjoining well-guarded treasury for the storage of silver bullion and copper cash.

Other posts included a grain commissioner who administered ultimate control over government's monopoly of these essential resources that were brought into the city along the river system and stored in warehouses and granaries.

Forceful Trading Trajectories

In 1600, largely as a response to the incorporation of the Dutch East India Company, a charter was granted by the Crown to allow a new English East India Company a monopoly of trade between England and all countries lying to the east of the Cape of Good Hope. Thereafter, the intricate relationship between trading trajectories in India and China became closely interrelated, and in 1637 a British commercial expedition of four armed ships under Captain John Weddell reached Macau via Goa and Malacca[37] under the auspices of the Courteen Association at the behest of King Charles I. Weddell might therefore be said to be the first British subject to establish a trading connection with Canton. After several months at anchorage with little enthusiastic support from the Portuguese inhabitants of Macau, and interrupted by a series of skirmishes with Chinese war junks, a delegation of officers was allowed to proceed to Canton where a petition was handed to the authorities requesting formal trading representation. Seven years after Weddell's voyage the Ming dynasty collapsed and the Qing Manchu dynasty commenced in 1644. It was not until 1717 that trade was established on a regular basis under the auspices of the East India Company, primarily importing tea into England. However, in practice the monopoly of the East India Company, which had been integrated with the Courteen Association, successfully restricted other private merchant traders for more than a century, while the civil war in England enfeebled commercial enterprises to the extent that the Company's own efforts were paralyzed through lack of funds.

The foundation of trade between Britain and China dates from the voyage of the *Macclesfield*, which arrived in Macau in 1699, where its officers agreed terms with the officials of the Board of Revenue for trade and measurement of duty.[38] For a long period, however, the fulfilment of trading agreements continued to be embroiled around the problems of merchant monopolies, trading privileges, and the established convention of extracting bribes.

The first superintendent of marine customs for Canton Province was appointed in 1685 by the new Manchu Imperial court under Emperor Kangxi, who agreed to open four ports for foreign trade. A revival of commercial activity in England in the late seventeenth century encouraged the East India Company to obtain a permanent footing in Canton in 1715, with its growing monopoly of trade controlled by a select committee of taipans. Over the following years the difficulties of policing such a complicated area with its long coastline and waterways, with little co-operation from self-interested local officials, proved to be almost impossible. Finally, it was decided that a more workable solution was to share responsibilities with the provincial governor-general that allowed officials in Canton to manipulate duties from foreign trade through the use of brokerage firms as agents. Fixed sums and some surplus payments were made to Peking and the remainder disseminated through a local realm of officials and middlemen.[39]

The heads of thirteen *Hongs* or Chinese merchants were appointed as official agents of the government where their credentials offered an unofficial license to both supervise and facilitate European commercial relations. The Chinese word *Hong* signifies the place of business of one merchant only, but might well comprise several mercantile establishments. The Hong merchants had to manage large-scale business risks involving massive shipments of commodities, and transportation in-line with sailing dates for foreign ships. Business premises acted as reception points for imported cargo, elevated above floor level to escape the predatory threat from white ants, and cleaned regularly by an army of retainers so that silken goods could be carefully examined, and where tea was weighed and wrapped before being shipped.

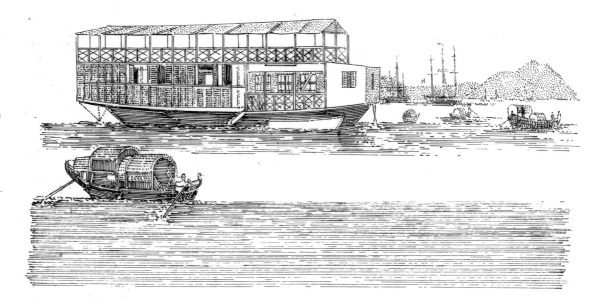

By 1720 the Hongs had transformed themselves into a guild—the *Co-hong*, which effectively managed all the trade, banking, and business dealing with foreign concerns in Canton, including the East India Company. Licenses were granted to twelve Co-hong merchant houses to effectively act as controllers of all aspects of foreign trade including customs payments. The most powerful were the families and immediate descendants of Houqua and Punqua who attained massive wealth and took to discreet displays of the official insignia despite by-passing the imperial examinations.[40] In practice, however, merchants were subject to extortionate demands from the Mandarinate and had to make compulsory payments to the imperial court. The Co-hong merchants could display acts of generosity. Houqua rented a large site for the construction of a hospital to a missionary organization and after 1839 financed its renovation.

Initial competition to the British was from the Dutch, French, and Swedish East India Companies who arrived in the early eighteenth century. The French East India Company established a presence in 1728, the Swedish Company in 1731, and the Danes the following year.

The Co-hong successfully controlled its institutions in ways both legal and imaginative, and obediently paid dues to the imperial coffers while helping to regularize the price of goods. This provided a reasonably transparent basis for negotiation but also put the supercargoes in a somewhat vulnerable position in dealing with what was effectively a cartel. The merchants also acted as intermediaries between foreign traders and the Mandarins who had considerable political influence, so that the process, which effectively regulated the price of goods, acted to secure their affluent position within society. In this way they could publicly observe an indifference to the expanding maritime trade while using their unique positions to prolong an opulent lifestyle.[41] Official policy was to portray a sympathetic attitude toward foreign trade, but with a multitude of prohibitions intended to prevent any kind of cultural

assimilation by foreigners, along with restrictions on Chinese commercial expansion overseas. In order to further control the trading relationship an imperial edict was issued in 1759 that effectively redirected all foreign trade with China to Canton, followed several months later by a set of regulatory controls that, amongst other things, restricted the movement of occupants of the factories during the trading season, and banned them from the city altogether during the non-trading season in winter. Such a situation foreshadowed a completely new and powerful force that was to exert fundamental change in the country.

The allotted foreign facilities along a 1,000-foot shoreline housed both residential and business premises, but had no connection with manufacturing activities, and were technically owned by several hong merchants who received ground rents. The national designations themselves, denoted by the appropriate flags, were somewhat deceiving in that much of the office and residential space was occupied by a wide range of users including private trading groups. The English factory was known as *lung-shun*—roughly translated as "flourishing and amenable" although not necessarily compliant.

The first factory buildings were of simple construction, utilizing the blue-gray bricks commonly used in Canton. As they were periodically modified or reconstructed, some of the more substantial became progressively elaborate with neo-classical facades, attached structural appendages, verandahs, and well-appointed interiors of the private rooms. In the predominantly low-rise city elevated spaces were considered as advantageous, and integrated within the architectural compositions as discreet viewpoints from which to observe happenings in the competing hongs. William C. Hunter,

a long-time resident of the Russell and Company factory, writing in the nineteenth century, stated that the comprador of each merchant house effectively orchestrated its internal order, organization, and economic operations together with supervising servants in addition to coping with the needs of the merchants themselves. In return he secured a percentage fee from each trading transaction, and loyalty to his employers was therefore a necessary fact of life as well as being a profitable concern.

An unusual facet of the East India Company was the practice of facilitating limited private trading activities by the Company's captains under a special license. A scale of allowances was agreed that incentivized trade, and on this basis trading routes were established with various Chinese ports as well as Canton. The China trade was a precarious one, and a combination of violent storms at sea, disease and human-made disasters reflected a risky operational agenda. Marine insurance had been established in England in 1601 reflecting the growing importance of trade, but while it applied to both cargoes and ships, reimbursement of loss to both ship and cargo did not extend to the time spent in port, or to the seamen themselves of which there was often little record. The eighteenth-century trade was nevertheless an essential source of employment for foreign seamen for six months of the year that included a four-month period at the Whampoa anchorage, even if opportunity was countered by disillusionment.

In reply to a memorial sent to the imperial court, the emperor issued an edict that confined trade between Europe and China to a single port, Canton, along with detailed regulations for the control of commerce. However, as a benevolent concession he also prudently commanded that in the future European ships should not be called "Devil's Ships" but "Western Ocean Ships."[42] Thus the stage was set for a prolonged battle of wills.[43]

In the early eighteenth century, ships of the East India Company began to make annual visits to Canton, along with occasional naval vessels, and by the 1740s the factories had assembled large warehouses, loading and unloading facilities, and suites of rooms arranged around courtyards, with spacious dining rooms lit by chandeliers. In 1757 Emperor Qianlong closed the ports of Amoy, Ningpo, and Shanghai, leaving Canton as the only operational port in China until the end of the first Opium War. In 1732 an expedition sent by the Swedish East India Company arrived in Canton, the French *Compagnies des Indes* established a factory in the 1760s, and in 1772 the Dutch Company signed a lease for a factory. In 1784 the first trading vessel, the *Empress of China*, arrived in Canton from the newly independent United States. It brought with it cargo of cotton and seal skins, accompanied by Samuel Shaw who went on to serve as the first United States consul in Canton. By 1802 the flags of seven countries flew in front of the various merchant houses.

William C. Hunter described the area in front of the factories as "the landing place for ships from Whampoa, the place for daily excursions on the river, as well as to Ho-Nam on the opposite bank."[44] Up to a conflagration caused by a serious fire in 1811, the Fankwaes had exclusive use of the square, but after this it became a place of public use for itinerant peddlers and hawkers including tailors, hatters, sellers of tea, congee, pastries, and pickled olives. There were also many beggars including groups of blind men. When things became over-animated the police would arrive from Old China Street and forcefully clear the area.

Control of essential logistics and indeterminacies demanded a high degree of accommodation and tolerance on the part of the Qing government, reflecting the growing importance attached to the trade. Accounts of meetings between foreign diplomatic representatives and Mandarin officers were in fact marked by the greatest courtesy and polished manners of the Chinese hosts. Restraint was used more than extreme force on the part of Mandarin officials, and the politeness of Chinese society were surprisingly successful in achieving compliance through benevolence rather than coercion. Differences were most often resolved through reconciliation, albeit with occasional recourse to the prevailing justice system.

From the mid-eighteenth century, trading patterns began to be increasingly international and interconnected. Great Britain was in the forefront of this new mercantile order through its growing empire and its productive industrial capacity. Sailing ships, including tea clippers, became continually more

streamlined until the advent of steam power after 1830. By the nineteenth century new trading routes were developing around the Pacific and Indian Oceans.

The Dutch East India Company registers from 1762–1764 furnish a wealth of information regarding sea routes for the massive "East Indiamen" galleons of up to 1,300 tons that required large crews.[45] These operated under charter or license to companies orchestrated by the major European trading powers. The early British company ships were tea clippers, but the later English East Indiamen's primary ports were Bombay, Calcutta, and Madras, and often continued on from India to China.

The East India Company's right to trade technically extended until 1834 although several East Indiamen were acquired by the Royal Navy and were made to masquerade as warships during the Napoleonic Wars despite the need for heavy armaments that constrained their commercial trading intentions. Some of the largest were built in India with teak hulls and were manned by Indian crews. These were used exclusively for the China trade, but were also utilized for troop transport, and around the mid-nineteenth century they were replaced by smaller and faster frigates.

The diversity of the private trade, as recorded by Paul A. Van Dyke, very nearly rivalled the company trade.[46] This reflected a necessary part of commercial transactions, in particular the private participation in trade between Britain, France, America, India, and China in the late eighteenth century that blossomed during the following years. Private Portuguese, Americans, Parsees, and Muslim merchants were active in Canton well before the English East India Company. Sino-French trade began in 1698 with the Campagnie, established by royal edict, having a monopoly, but leasing trading rights to private merchants who were largely responsible for French commercial voyages to China. The Chinese places of business were known as *hongs*, run by powerful merchant dynasties such as Houqua and Mowqua, who leased premises to the Western companies.

Private and company trade generally went hand-in-hand with what were known as the "permissions trades" where private merchants traded in luxury or upscale commodities such as porcelain, lacquerware, and artworks. Private traders were responsible for introducing China into the financial sphere of Britain's imperial expansion on the Indian subcontinent, and much early sea trade was carried out under foreign flags of convenience. Servants from the British East India Company began to invest funds in the growth of trade with China, but as Indian revenues were insufficient to fund the trades independently, the need for payment in silver made it necessary to export this from Britain to pay for their investment in the tea trade. Between 1832 and 1835 alone, more than 20 million ounces of silver were shipped abroad, with an increasing burden on the economy, as grain prices became much reduced and landowners had to take on increasing proportions of the crop to sustain their income. In addition, private loans based on money borrowed in India were made to Chinese merchants at high rates of interest but low risk. Most of the larger merchant houses were undercapitalized, and as a result unlicensed traders from India were able to obtain permission to trade in Canton by the Qing government, shipping an extraordinarily wide range of products from other parts of Asia. The result of a continuous expansion of private trade was to progressively draw China into the orbit of the British trading empire, and China itself maintained something of an open-door policy with few restrictions on legal trade to foreign merchants.

While senior officers largely resided in Canton during the trading season, ordinary seamen travelled regularly between Whampoa and Canton to make deliveries, gather provisions, and to assist with loading and unloading activities. They also clearly had to man the small boats in crews of up to eight that carried senior officers and supercargoes between the anchorage and the city,[47] so that there was an almost constant movement of men and crafts in relays along the river according to the ebb and flow of the tides. This was under the constant watch of marine police who tracked their movements, watching out for the smuggling that took place under cover of darkness.

An imperial edict issued in 1760 stated, among other things, that foreigners could only trade in Canton over the summer and that they must reside only with Hong merchants. Despite the potential for increased trade, the Emperor Qianlong wrote to King George III in 1776, stating that, "We possess all things, so that I set no value on things strange or ingenious, and have no use for your country's manufactures." This led to a series of incidents that emphasized the difficulties of conducting trade in the face of constant restrictions. In the light of things to come it also provided an early indication of the essential conflict between ingrained obedience to the commands of officialdom, and equally intransigent interests on the part of overseas trading concerns.

Disputes and Diplomacy

The notion of the "foreigner" as a barbarian was deeply rooted in diplomatic procedures. In Canton foreigners were known as Fankwaes or "foreign devils," partly because the individual Western races could not be easily distinguished, but also quite likely from their alarming and often aggressive appearance that William C. Hunter described as "these uncouth beings, with fiery hair, full of unreasonableness and conceit."[48] Lord Macartney, who was appointed special ambassador to China, brought with him in 1793 such a large mission that the emperor ordered the port of Tientsin to be opened for the fleet of vessels. Macartney arrived in China on the *Lion* that carried an entourage of around 400, accompanied by the *Hindustan*, an armed merchant ship of the East India Company's fleet. Their course lay beyond Canton and through the Yellow Sea. It was reported that as the fleet sailed up the Pei-ho River toward Tientsin, flags on the escorting junks bore the words, "Ambassador bearing tribute from the country of England."[49] The last part of the long journey to the summer palace of Jehol, in what is now Chengde, 150 miles to the north of Peking where the meeting of the Kangxi emperor and the special ambassador was to take place, was undertaken in a carriage specially transported from England.

Macartney's strategy was to impress the 82-year-old Emperor Qianlong with new scientific and technological developments in Britain, including a large planetarium and a hot-air balloon. While the refusal of the ambassador to perform the kowtow in the presence of the emperor has gained popular acceptance, the Chinese Court seemingly did its utmost to show courtesy to the visitors. In fact, the emperor made it known beforehand that the same form of presentation as would be the case before the British sovereign

ipwrights in the fourteenth
ntury constructed a special junk
sign—the *fuchuan*—suitable
conditions on the southern
eans, with a high prow and stern.
eir pointed hulls, wide decks, and
tertight bulwark compartments
de them able to cut through the
ves, and if necessary withstand
ntact with other boats or reefs.
s created the model for the
er treasure ships with a length of
Chinese *zhang* or almost 500
t, as this was thought to equate
h the four corners of the earth,
the "Middle Kingdom" situated
he intersection of the four
s. It is possible to discern the
ginal *fuchuan* style in a number
reaty port paintings from the
-nineteenth century.

would be acceptable. Macartney knelt on one knee and presented the emperor with a gold box containing a translated letter from King George III. In the emperor's reply to the letter from George III, which requested trading concessions at Ningbo, Tientsin, and Chusan, and the procurement of a printed tariff, he re-stated that trade must be restricted to Canton, and no imperial consent could be granted for trade at any of the northern ports. Macartney's party therefore achieved little more than ensuring that Britain had been accepted as only the latest in a long list of tribute-bearing nations. After this the mission departed on a slow two-month journey to Canton via an extensive system of inland waterways, probably in the process offering some of the first glimpses by Westerners of the Chinese interior.

Because of the general prosperity under the Qing dynasty, China's population was in excess of 300 million by 1800, but land under agricultural production was insufficient to meet basic needs. This was compounded in the early nineteenth century by repeated floods along the Yellow River. The result was a series of social upheavals that a depleted and disenchanted bureaucracy, overwhelmed by administrative pressures, was unable to cope with effectively.[50] Fortunately Canton remained relatively isolated from the White Lotus rebellion against the Qing government in the late eighteenth century, which arose out of social and economic discontent in some of the more impoverished parts of China under a slogan, "the officials oppress, and the people rebel." This acted to drain the previous treasury surplus that had provided the financial foundations of the imperial court. The rebellion was not put down until 1803 with the deaths of some 100,000 rebels, and named Shi Yang a new emperor, Jiaqing, the son of Qianlong. The breakdown in the urban-rural balance, exacerbated by social and economic unrest, considerably weakened the country, and, perhaps more importantly, reduced confidence in its embedded institutions. From the outset, the traditional channels of diplomacy within China were difficult to differentiate between the type of formal tribute system that had been followed by previous foreign missions and vassal states, and the new quest for trade expansion on the basis of Western law, but backed up by gunboats.

The imperial court remained aloof from both the administration of trade and missionary activities, and the emperor made little attempt at direct contact with foreign visitors. The commercial interface between the trade at Canton and the court was minimal apart from necessary reported data on the regular amount of duties collected, which had to be sent via messengers on horseback. Evidence suggests that there was considerable under reporting of annual ship arrivals up to 1816, and some manipulation of accounting information according to the gazetteer of Guangdong Maritime Customs the *yuehaiguan zhi*. This suggests that the growing monopoly and increasing influence of the East India Company as a dominant and influential force was underestimated. In this situation the progressive lack of trading competition inevitably led to an increasingly assertive stance on the part of the British in the late eighteenth century. The rapid growth in trade also coincided with the end of the Napoleonic Wars in 1815, when many hundreds of young naval officers sought new colonial opportunities in India and the Far East. These wars also effectively constrained the French commercial drive in China, and American interests were not slow in taking over the French factory in Canton.

A British mission to the Qing court in 1816, 23 years after that of Macartney, was led by William Pitt Amherst, along with Robert Morrison as interpreter, and George Staunton who as a child had accompanied his father on Macartney's original mission and who by this time was the pre-eminent British subject in Canton. The mission was aborted, however, without an audience with the emperor due to arguments over the understanding of ceremonial rites, each side blaming the other for failure of the embassy. One of the repercussions was a denunciation of Amherst's mission from free-trade advocates and moves to abolish the East India Company's monopoly on commerce with China. The main beneficiary was Morrison who represented the London Missionary Society in China. His command of Chinese had brought him a position as interpreter for the East India Company in the British Factory in Canton, while he worked on the first Chinese-English dictionary published the final version of his dictionary in 1823 and completed his translation of the Bible the same year, encouraging the arrival of further Protestant missionaries.

Ship maintenance and repair, along with supply and maintenance of provisions required designated bases at Whampoa in the form of temporary bamboo structures on Whampoa Island, which was also used by ships crews for shore leave. While these were guarded, their storage functions for provisions, in particular the availability of alcohol, ignited an almost permanently disruptive situation stemming from lack of control, sickness, and theft. In order to curb the worst excesses, the East India Company operated a system of armed boat guards to police the fleet, particularly during periods of shore leave.

...rd Macartney's fanciful ...troduction to China in 1793. ...py of an illustration in ...e Beinecke Rare Book and ...anuscript Library, Yale University.

By 1830 more than 100 ships participated in the trading season, with 12,000 officers and seamen. The trading season was from May to November, according to the onset of the hot and humid summer weather and the typhoons. However, the monsoon winds that coincided with the late summer assisted the sailboats in making haste to Europe, particularly those with a precious cargo of tea—a highly competitive commodity. The generally unhealthy conditions and disease together with susceptibility to accidents and strict punishments for disorder led to a relatively high rate of mutiny. Theft was common, not only of supplies but of ship's materials and equipment that could be easily sold.

Crime was, in one or other of its personifications, quite frequent and every attempt was generally made to settle all minor infractions or violations by foreigners of Chinese law without recourse to the Chinese courts. In general, the interactions between Chinese and foreigners were settled or tolerated by the former in a harmonious rather than an unduly firm way, in order to encourage a suitable basis for beneficial exchange, and all parties appear to have subscribed to this. The ships commodores themselves had no reputation for leniency and oversaw events with enthusiastic resource to irons and shackles as a means of keeping order. In any event the generally dangerous and unhealthy conditions together with frequent natural disasters contributed to an exceptionally high death count of mariners, as well as a high propensity of desertion via a foreign ship.

Trials of foreign miscreants were, apart from the most serious cases, carried out under the policy of extraterritoriality under which foreigners were tried and sentenced under their own laws—a process later adopted in the treaty port municipalities. Chinese were tried in local courts presided over by Qing magistrates. One celebrated trial known as the Neptune incident occurred in 1807. Chinese authorities clashed with foreign merchants over a fight in which drunken sailors on shore leave killed a Chinese man. Mowqua, a leading hong merchant, was made responsible for negotiating a settlement, but was caught between the requests of the Chinese authorities for punishment and the insistence of the foreign mercantile for justice. The case was heard in the English factory, and after three trials only one sailor was found guilty of accidental homicide and was later released on payment of twelve taels, the Chinese penalty for an accidental killing. The authority of the Qing court and the lenient punishment nevertheless succeeded in resolving trade disputes well before Westerners imposed their own laws in the treaty ports.[51]

Skirmishes with pirates, and occasionally more serious clashes between the "East Indiamen" and local flotillas, marked the somewhat precarious final years of the East India Company's monopoly. Increasing restrictions were placed on activity in Canton, and exhaustive efforts were made to extend commerce to other ports such as Formosa, Fukien, and Amoy. One of these voyages in 1832 was accompanied by 450 chests of opium, together with the Rev. Karl Friedrich Gutzlaff, a German missionary and naturalized Chinese subject, who was to figure prominently in future events as a translator.[52] Both the cargo and the distribution of missionary literature only managed to convince the people of the eastern ports that in some way these were connected as part of an enterprising but somewhat underhand British commercial initiative.

The introduction of shallow draft steamships also began to undermine the traditional system of control over the entrance and departure of vessels on the West River and past the Bocca Tigris forts. In the meantime, growth in the East India Company's trade was mainly through merchant ships that were often accompanied by convoys, while the Royal Navy also commenced activity in the South China Sea. This was technically outside the civil jurisdiction of Chinese law, but led inevitably to incidents that tested diplomatic relations. On arrival at Whampoa, ships had to undergo a measured survey under the ceremonial supervision of the Hoppo to ascertain its volume on which the port charges were calculated. Further supervision was required of all off-loaded and return cargo that required specialist translation and interpretation undertaken by appointed Chinese linguists.

The relationship between Canton and Whampoa was based on mutual advantage. Whampoa, some twelve miles to the south of Canton and situated in a sparsely settled location, represented an anchorage conveniently distant from the city where incoming merchandise could be offloaded, and outgoing goods exported. The total volume of foreign trade rose from around 5,000 tons in the 1720s, to 40,000 tons some 100 years later. By the early nineteenth century duties amounted to 1.2 million taels so that while benefits were mutual, imperial revenues stemming from trade were of outstanding importance, outweighing most other considerations.

Whampoa was well inland from the South China Sea and secure from the summer storms while offering a substantial deepwater anchorage. The tidal and current movements created compatible conditions for the passage of vessels but at the same time the sandbars that were revealed at low tide required considerable navigational skills and precluded easy access to the massive Indiamen. Here cargoes could be discharged, or loaded on their return trips, by smaller chop boats that transport goods between the principal anchorage and the city. Whampoa was equipped with dry docks and repair facilities, and some Westerners including overseas missionaries lived on houseboats or in local lodgings.

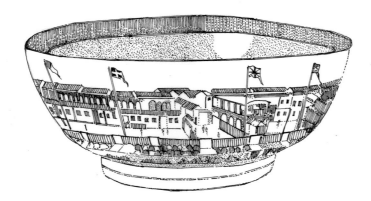

A porcelain punch bowl circa 178[?] showing the foreign factories in Canton built in 1748 with the flag[s] of some of the trading nations, ar[d] gates open to the Pearl River.

Shops were built primarily of woo[d] and blue brick, with residential or storage space above. While Old China Street had a width around twelve feet, the side streets were narrower, creating a seeming visu[al] convergence of outdoor signage.

From 1784, largely through a combination of colonial trading routes, and in particular the role of the East India Company and English military capabilities, Britain had gained crucial advantages over its European competitors. By the turn of the nineteenth century the supercargoes had gained an almost invincible position of influence over the merchant groups, for whom a constant source of revenue was vital to ensure their survival. Trading impositions and cultural differences aside, Qing officials were intent on maintaining a competitive market by means of purposeful restrictive measures and, in particular, to combat irregular and illegal competition. With an increasing number of ships arriving and departing, control of movement was not easy, and maintenance of the ships and crews was largely left in the hands of their captains.

The Bocca Tigris or 'Mouth of the Tiger' formed a defensive position against water-borne intruders, with fortifications embedded within the foreshore of Weiyuan Island overlooking the channel. Smuggling was, if not entirely eliminated, substantially reduced by means of Chinese customs officials who boarded ships in pairs at the Bocca Tigris fort, and on reaching the anchorage attached small boats to the stern of the Indiamen. With correct positioning this technically allowed them to monitor all loading and unloading activities, although it was clearly open to the less than honest inducements and temptations that were proffered in return for turning a blind eye to nefarious activities. The Canton system as a whole was in fact guided by a mix of tolerance and forbearance providing that no questionable activities raised concerns at the imperial court in Beijing. However, the popular saying at the time was, "the mountains are high and the emperor is far away."

The thirteen double-story factories were constructed to the southwest of the walled city so as to retain both a safe and respectable distance, defined on its southern boundary by the Pearl River. The allocated area was gradually enlarged through acquisition of neighboring sites. The East India Company exhibited an opportunist stance, allocating storage space on board the gigantic Indiamen for British merchants to import cotton, spices, and, in the fullness of time, opium from India.

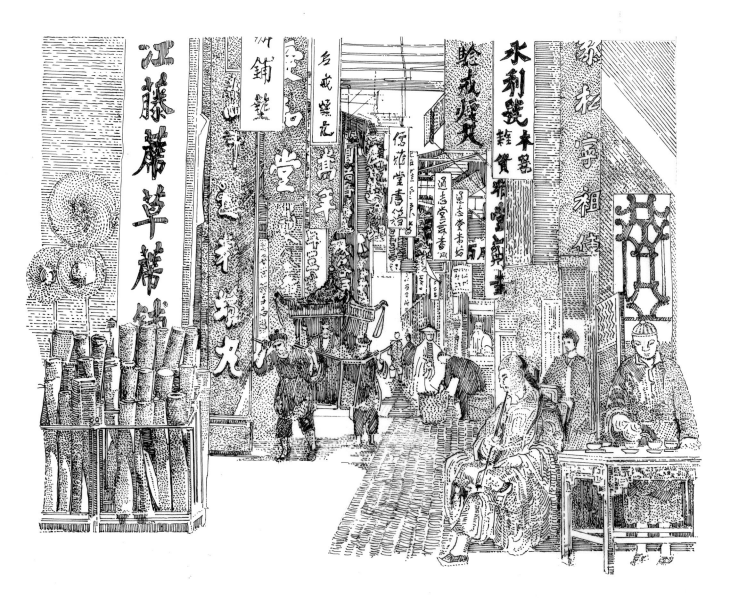

A British parliamentary select committee report on the affairs of the East India Company at this time provides some measure of clarification.[53] It reported that the other Western countries trading at Canton were France, Austria, Denmark, Sweden, Holland, and America, but only at a relatively minor level. A Parliamentary act ended the exclusive trading monopoly of the East India Company from April 1834, while a second statute, dealing with the regulation of commerce involving India and China, provided for "any of His Majesty's subjects to carry on trade with any countries beyond the Cape of Good Hope to the Straights of Magellan." From this point on it became beholden on Britain to pass a China Trade Act that created a new post—the chief superintendent of trade, who held sufficient authority within any part of China and had the ability to exercise judicial functions over British subjects there. It also provided for the Crown to create a system of dues to be levied on British ships. Surprisingly, it seems that no attempt was made to communicate this fundamental change in trading privilege to the Chinese Government, and nor was consent ever sought.

The company of Jardine Matheson, established in partnership with the proprietor of the English language *Canton Register,* became one of the most successful trading and shipping firms in Canton. They were joined by native Indians and Parsees from Bombay who began to assist the British in the 1830s and took up residence in the factories that operated under a national flag, but were frequently rented out to individual traders and missionaries. Some of the taipans became consuls of other nations, such as James Matheson who became Danish consul, and Paul Forbes who served as consul for the United States, thereby cleverly escaping the Company's jurisdiction.

Domestic Commerce and Trade

China had developed a domestic tea industry over almost 1,500 years, with the popular black tea being grown in Fujian for many centuries before it became an international commodity. With the growth in trade, tea was transported downriver to Canton for processing and then examined by inspectors, with prices agreed between a committee comprising foreign traders and hong merchants, before being carefully packed in air-tight chests in order to ensure its lasting freshness. One of the first cases of scented tea is said to have been presented to King Charles II by representatives of the East India Company, and by 1785 fifteen million pounds of tea was being imported from China. By 1830, under the new free trading system, importation had more than doubled, along with company profits. To ensure this situation continued, the East India Company contrived to steal tea seeds and plants from Fujian as well as the necessary processing expertise in order to transplant a similar industry in India that they could control themselves.

Silk was also a major export in the eighteenth century, fetching a high price in the West for both its beauty and rarity. The arduous process for raw silk production in the Pearl River delta could scarcely cater to the constant demand in China. Production involved up to 17,000 workers in Canton weaving the raw produce into luxurious garments. To meet the increased demand in England, items were processed at the beginning of each trading season and packed between crates of tea for the long journey back to Europe. A secondary craft industry was silk embroidery on woven items of clothing produced in the villages around Canton. These were brought to the city for exquisite needlework representations of Chinese scenery and flowers from pre-designed pattern books.

Porcelain was largely produced in the kilns of Jiangxi Province and transported by boat to the large artist's studios in Canton for detailed painting. Extensive sets of dinner services were commissioned in Britain by wealthy and often prominent families who wished to display their coats of arms on the dining table. Personal purchases acquired by foreigners, including crew members, were packed in Carpenter's Square adjacent to Thirteen Hong Street and all goods were then laid out in front of the factories for inspection to ensure appropriate duties were paid.

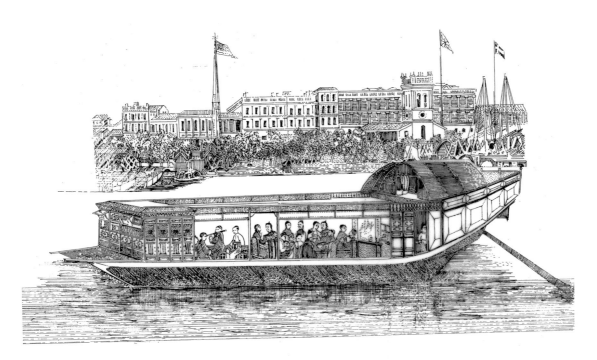

All artisans belonged to one of seventy-two guilds that regulated output, working conditions, quality, and salary. Most craft activities were carried out in small studios and shops located on streets that were largely devoted to one trade. Porcelain manufacturing extended back to the Tang period and was extensively produced in Jiangxi Province, also associated with Foshan through its famous Shiwan kilns. It was then transported by boat to the large artist's studios in Canton for detailed painting. Extensive sets of dinner services were commissioned in Britain by wealthy and often prominent families who wished to display their coats of arms. Personal purchases acquired by foreigners, which often included crew members of trading ships, were packed in Carpenter's Square adjacent to Thirteen Hong Street, and all goods were then laid out in front of the factories for inspection to ensure that necessary duties were paid.

What became known as "export" paintings were produced in large numbers, mainly in water colors and gouache to create an authentic record of the constant changes and adaptations of premises—particularly between 1810 and 1842. The most favored subject was the view of Canton, including the factories seen from across the Pearl River, although views also included street scenes, and the Whampoa anchorages downriver. The work of the most prominent artists such as Youqua, Lamqua, and Tinqua, all active in the mid-nineteenth century, visually documented scenes along the Pearl River with a fine degree of precision, and with a flare that indicated an accurate and exotic sense of place. The export painting studios of Lamqua and his brother Tinqua were situated in New China Street, and combined display galleries and salesrooms. Lamqua painted portraits of Western clients in the manner of George Chinnery,

lower boat near Shamian Island,
Bo.

a frequent visitor. Apart from original works, artists and young apprentices worked in close proximity, often making skillful copies of original works—something that has carried over to the twenty-first century in the Dafen artist's quarter of Shenzhen.

Paintings from the period record both the familiar classical architectural style of European trading premises to the west of the city walls, and the distinctly local array of water-borne traffic in the foreground. The early brick-built factories were situated on an embankment, half a mile in length, and formed detailed compositions that included the decorative aspects of European architecture with projecting porticos, balustrades and semi-circular fanlights. Paintings were transported to London business establishments and country houses, only to be exported back to the Far East more than a century later to be sold in galleries and under auction to local collectors in Hong Kong. For more large-scale studies, which generated a considerable output of similar work on specially treated pith paper, painters sat at tables and concentrated on just one particular subject such as figures, buildings, or ships, working alongside each other as part of a "conveyor" system. This process, together with the use of stencils or standard outlines, explains why many reproduced figures or objects look quite similar.

A copy of Lamqua's oil portrait of the leading hong merchant Mowqua. His ranking as a civil mandarin is indicated by the embroidered gown showing a golden pleasant.

y of a portrait of the Hong
chant Houqua, a partner of
British East India Company
n the studio of Lamqua. The
t was a learned practitioner
tAook over the studio from
grandfather, Guang Zuolin,
carried out some of the first
raits of Chinese merchants
European traders.

One of the most remarkable representations of the entire Canton waterfront was commissioned by the wealthy Drummond family who were stalwarts of the early China trade. The "Drummond Wallpaper" painted on layered mulberry paper was created around the turn of the nineteenth century, and in 1814 was installed in Strathallan Castle in Scotland. Apart from the buildings, the animated life of the river frontage is shown in some detail, with Chinese boat people, food stalls, and entertainers, along with Western figures in colored coats and breeches. The compositions of William Daniell, painted at around the same time, similarly contain details of the busy riverscape and factories.

Other craftsmen were masters of the carver's art, in particular ivory, tortoi shell, and sandalwood, the raw materials often being supplied by foreign traders. Skilled ivory carvers took months to produce intricate figurines from Chinese folklore, while the more ambitious carved long and elaborate processions from an entire elephant tusk. Silversmiths were equally skilled at imaginative concoctions for ornaments and tableware using silver mined in North Guangdong and Dongguan County. However, it was silver imported from overseas that until the early nineteenth century and the advent of the opium trade, was used by traders to purchase goods produced in the province.

Street names offered a brief and graphic summary of what was on offer, and included Lantern Street, Physic Street, Mandarin Cap Alley, Crooked Railing Passage, and Street of Worn-out Clothes. To add to the confusion names were periodically changed to reflect their predominant offerings, so that the early nineteenth century Lantern Street became known as Curio Street and then Physic Street, reputed at the time to be the most fashionable street in the city. Pastry cooks were famous in the city, and William C. Hunter discusses one in Mandarin Cap Alley that sold "skillfully made dragon pastries for ceremonies and dinners, moon cakes for the autumn festival, distilled wine from Macao, dishes of simple or rich food served in Tartar and Chinese style, with every variety of dried and sugared fruit." Hog Lane was the appellation given by foreigners to the more celebrated Chinese name of Green Pea Street. In all likelihood it took its popular name from the animals that wandered around the area, although this might have intentionally embraced the grog shops where Western sailors, on limited shore leave, were sold cheap spirits of considerable potency, leading to credible reports of intoxication. Many Chinese customers tended to choose the preferred alternative option of opium. As a result, the street acquired a deserved reputation for depravity and debauchery.

Golden Lily Street was given over to the sale of tiny "lotus" shoes, embroidered and shaped to fit the bound feet of predominantly housebound wives and concubines—a custom that dated back to the tenth century. The feet of young girls were systematically broken and delicately shaped, and according to anecdote the practice became fashionable through a dancer who became the emperor's favorite concubine at the royal court. This procedure became so widespread that by the Qing dynasty all girls who married into a genteel life, with little need to carry out manual tasks, had their feet bound in a ritualistic but highly painful ceremony that entailed bending the toes beneath the sole. Ironically it was the arrival of Western women in the nineteenth century, particularly the wives of missionaries, who reverently spoke up against the practice during the revolutionary period, that finally made the process unfashionable despite much male resistance.

Signs and attractive displays played a large part in enticing customers, but apart from shops the streets contained fortune-tellers, money changers, and apothecaries. From merchant diaries of the time, all shopkeepers went to great lengths to please, and were recalled as being shrewd businessmen, although value for money was reckoned to be in the eye and occasionally the naivety of the beholder.

The Floating World

The Pearl River was the effective life-giver of the city, but was reliant on securing its main approaches through fortifications, in particular those on two islands—Hai Chu, which contained the Dutch Folly Fort; and Tong Pau on which was built the French Folly Fort. Both were ultimately reclaimed to form part of the river foreshore. These, along with the Red Fort at Honan proved less than effective in withstanding the later naval bombardments, and therefore proved to be quite vulnerable despite their formidable appearance. In 1856 all the forts up-river from Whampoa were taken by British and French forces and their military functions dismantled.

The Pearl River was a complementary extension of the city in terms of its activities and services, and largely inhabited by a floating population engaged with transport of goods, various forms of transaction, and certain types of pleasurable entertainment. It was also for many a place of perpetual habitation. The river itself was described by William C. Hunter as a constant mass of activity from morning to night. This included the Mandarin boats with double banks of oars, decorated with flags bearing the names of individual districts and the titles of officers. The multi-oared mandarin boats, whose primary purpose was to prevent smuggling, could carry up to 70 soldiers—the primary colors were red, white, and blue—a blue hull, red ports, and white oars, with a painted roof. The speed of the oars striking the water against the colorful boat frame was sometimes compared to dragon flies.

The sleek "chop," or cargo boats, were known locally as "watermelon boats" from their distinctive shape and served the Hong merchant's warehouses. The canal or inland river boats that transported cargos of tea from the point where they entered the province to the warehouses, are described as having splendidly varnished hulls with spacious quarters for the supercargo, his purser and passengers. Then, toward dusk, came the occasional long boats, with hands on many oars, carrying in their holds the heavy sacks of opium from Whampoa.

Until well into the twentieth century, much of the river edge was colonized by rows of junks and sampans creating something of a "floating" city in parallel to the growing urban area itself. The main sailing craft were the large sea-going trading junks with their characteristic concertina sails that ventured as far as Malacca, Manila, Singapore, and the northern Chinese ports of Fukien and Shanghai, but also acted as passenger vessels between Canton, Hong Kong, and Macau. Junks and sampans, only fifteen feet long, housed Tanka families and were lashed together for mutual protection in the typhoon season, with families engaged in fishing or the breeding of ducks and chickens. The Tanka or "boat people" were descendants of an ethnic group known as the Baiyue associated with the coastal communities of Southern China, and in particular the waterways associated with the Pearl Delta. These people had for centuries been regarded as gypsies and social outcasts, forbidden to establish colonies on land, and apart from fishing and general port activities lived entirely on water. Duck boats were anchored in shallow bays, with families living in bamboo structures covered with straw matting, above a lower deck that contained cages where birds were raised.

The river itself created a virtually independent residential and commercial culture of its own, through an infrastructure of trading, food production, and transportation networks, representing a special culture based on ancient customs and beliefs. The Tanka boats frequently served as ferries for both passengers and goods. They were operated mainly by women, and were propelled by a long oar at the stern that rested on a pivot, enabling it to move from side to side, while a further operator operated a more orthodox oar at the prow. The bamboo cabin covered with matting allowed entire families to live on the boats when necessary. It was recorded that in 1834 the Canton governor-general proclaimed that the Tanka boats were not to anchor in front of the factories, in order to deter nighttime liaisons between courtesans and barbarians under cover of darkness.

The Red Boats

The Cantonese Opera Red Boats, with their brightly colored banners and flags dated from the Ming dynasty. These transported opera troupes and their accompanying martial arts practitioners around the Pearl River Delta—a tradition that followed the destruction of their land base by the Qing government. It is said that they also provided a discreet cover for those individuals seeking escape from official persecution such as members of nineteenth-century secret societies, bent on revolutionary activities. Opera and other forms of popular Southern China culture drew heavily on local folklore and the politics of the Republican period. From the 1870s around sixty boats were

largely owned by opera guilds and were similar in terms of standardization of design that allowed them to be rented out to opera companies, with crews hired by the guilds for months or even years at a time. Boats were not necessarily painted red, although they displayed red banners, and this might well have indicated a connotation with the colorful character of Chinese opera itself.

The opera troupes formed relatively self-contained communities with actors, musicians, martial artists, and boatmen, along with all their costumes and equipment, travelling together along the neighboring waterways in pairs of boats associated with "heaven" and "earth." Troupes shared a similar social structure, with elaborate organizational management. Their itinerary facilitated travel between temple festivals, much as modern day troupes perform in land based "matsheds," remarkably erected and demounted within several days. Travelling in pairs, known as heaven boats and earth boats, they travelled largely along the sheltered coastline of the Pearl Delta and along its dendritic system of river channels. The pairs of boats could house up to 160 people: a full opera troupe included a crew of actors, musicians, managers, costumers, hairdressers, doctors, stage hands, cooks, and laundry helpers, together with ship's officers and boatmen. Cabins were assigned by lottery at the commencement of each opera season, although were often open to bartering whereby resources could be effectively redistributed.

The red boat groups, enhanced by staging technologies and complex props, reached the height of their popularity in the early part of the twentieth century with audiences that comprised entire local communities where there was little alternative entertainment. They rehearsed on board but performed in temporary halls erected in what were often quite small and isolated settlements. With growing urbanization, permanent theaters were built, dedicated to Cantonese opera with ready and appreciative audiences. According to Barbara Ward the last pair of Red Boats were seen in Macau in 1951.

The mingling of opera and martial arts was intended not merely to enhance acrobatic performance, but to discourage the activities of pirates who plied much the same water channels toward the end of the Qing dynasty. Martial artists therefore presented a strong security presence, and some went on to become armed guards and escorts for merchant companies. This new form of adventurism undoubtedly had an impact on popular culture during a much later period, which has since become established in martial arts folklore. The number of flower boats never exceeded 100, but formed part of a floating world that, along with the red boats and mandarin's craft, created a colorful counterpart to the massive trading junks with their butterfly-wing sails that ploughed the South China Sea.

Dragon boats were not the only ones to be raced on the river. Some of the wealthier foreign merchants brought models of schooners, cutters, skiffs, and sculling craft that were built by Chinese craftsmen. These formed the basis of regular regattas manned by sailing and rowing enthusiasts from the various trading houses, and became a mainstay of social life.

The square itself was a frequently contested space between the predominantly recreational and exercise habits of the merchant groups and the colonization of the space by local vendors and the simply curious.

The Flower Boats

Flower boats were a central feature on the river, decked out in an elaborate way and equipped with musicians and facilities for evening entertainment, usually with reception rooms and smaller cabins, aimed at both the Chinese and Western male society. Their beautiful carving and decoration, lit by colorful lanterns, led to them often being referred to as water palaces or floating birdcages.

The floating world in Canton was related predominantly to well-trained and genteel courtesans that encouraged patronage as part of a pleasurable form of business entertainment that successfully massaged the ego of clients. Costs for hiring flower boats for an evening were expensive and generated revenues akin to a high-class nightclub. The flower boats catered for what was euphemistically known as the "four pleasures," coyly defined as dining, gambling, smoking, and the flirtatious pleasures of female company, and could be hired for one or even several evenings. They were two or three stories high, almost as tall as the buildings adjoining the quayside from which they picked up wealthy passengers for an evening of entertainment on the river. They were luxuriously furnished, and sub-divided into a number of small apartments, a large public room, and a terrace on the top deck.

The boats, which clearly required a slow rate of propulsion, were manned by a team of around four, who effectively used bamboo poles and operated in a similar way to punters who pushed the poles against the water bottom at a given signal to move the craft forward. This had wide usage in the shallow waters associated with coastal communities. To move at a faster rate required oars to be manned from a platform at the prow.

The preparation of food and delivery of meals was delegated to a small type of craft—in effect a floating kitchen that could anchor at the rear of the flower boat and enabled food to be carried ceremoniously to the salon. To accompany the food and entertainment the flower boat was illuminated by colored glass, oil lanterns, or wax candles creating a romantically conductive atmosphere. Other boats provided ships supplies, coal, charcoal, and firewood. Sailing skiffs moved skillfully between them offering essential services such as those of barbers and hairdressers.

The notion of the pleasure "quarter" and the sensual settings of its component parts, whether pavilions, gardens, or boats is a recurrent feature of Chinese literature. The Flower Boat tradition in the Pearl

River delta operated from the mid-eighteenth to the early twentieth century. One explanation of the name is that the girls adopted the demure role of exotic flowers to whom the predatory male butterflies were instinctively drawn, often discreetly usurping the yellow and red silk adornments normally reserved for the emperor. Contemporary references date from the Qianlong period that began in 1736, but Chinese sources date the *hua ting* as early as the Tang and Song dynasties. There existed delicate differences between the welcoming pleasure trade at Whampoa that served the visiting foreign community and that at Canton, which maintained a patriotic dedication to a solely Chinese clientele.[54] It was said that next to quail-fighting, the delights of the flower boats during their peak of popularity, occupied the greater part of a Chinese merchant's leisure time. For the equally susceptible foreigner in the settlement area, however, there was to be little response to requests for the four pleasures, even with the most persistent persuasion. Instead, the more adventurous and promiscuous young traders patronized the red-light quarters of the city, well away from prying eyes.

It was not unknown for the more enthusiastic patrons to arrange the purchase of a suitably demure courtesan who had been trained in poetry and music, and was able to participate in agreeable conversation, as a permanent concubine. This was in fact a favorable prospect for a flower-boat girl, with many opportunities available to make contact with important and wealthy patrons who were frequent guests on the more elaborate boats. The courtship of a high-class courtesan was something of a drawn-out ritual, and formal rules were imposed on clients as to conduct, table manners, and the use of appropriate language in order to avoid a swift reprimand. A rigorous and demanding sequence of events was required to win the ultimate favor, including expensive tea parties and banquets, where participants could engage in preliminary conversation and to which friends of the client were invited following the negotiated transaction. This exhaustive process of familiarization was of course also assisted by necessary gifts to ensure that there was no question of exploitation. The "right of refusal" in the face of a particularly demanding or debauched visitor was in fact an unwritten law of the establishments, and girls were, at least in theory, protected from maltreatment.

Many courtesans adopted an aloof manner, and a popular saying was that smiles, or any other favors from a popular courtesan, were only sold to those who could pay well and bestow great prestige. Paradoxically they enjoyed a rare privilege of publicly deflating the dignity and any pompous behavior of their would-be admirers. As a result of the accumulated affluence and the ability to control their own wealth, courtesans were in turn able to provide for secret lovers, and to patronize famous Cantonese opera actors, or the early cinema heroes. When challenged, the girls of the flower boats were also able to mobilize themselves quite effectively. It is recorded that in 1900, flower-boat owners staged industrial action against surcharges imposed by government tax brokers through an officially registered trade union, and in 1927 hundreds of sing-song girls marched on a police station to demand the release of some of their "sisters" on a trumped-up charge.[55]

The boats themselves were designed in various sizes and degrees of decoration, but generally the vessels incorporated large upper rooms and an elaborate cabin layout. The length of boats varied from 30 to 60 feet with a large saloon opening out onto a deck at the prow. The boats are displayed prominently on many of the "China Coast" watercolor paintings of the period, which provide some degree of reference to both the design and favorable mooring locations. Their artistic décor, ornamentation, elaborately carved and gilded furniture, painted glass windows, hanging lamps, and embroidered silk fittings on the upper entertainment quarters were pointedly aimed at enticing an elite and wealthy following of both merchants and mandarins. This was matched by the garments and make-up of the girls themselves whose staged appearance and elaborate make-up extended to the foot binding tradition, thought to be both attractive and alluring.

Boats usually anchored in lines abreast of one another, held fast by chains and anchored at the prow with wooden planks between them to allow visitors to compare the amusements and services on offer. Boats were particularly susceptible to fire as they were often moored side-by-side. A semi-stationary grouping of flower boats from around 1800 was located in front of the warehouses and enjoyed a ready procession of eminent Chinese officials, ready and eager for nocturnal entertainment. In all probability this is why the boats form part of the picturesque foreground of so many foreign factory paintings, surrounded by a variety of other floating craft. It is estimated that in the mid-nineteenth century more than 2,000 occupants of the flower boats were dependent on this location for a living. A second anchorage was located adjacent to the Western suburbs and its wealthy residents, although the foreshore was eventually reclaimed in the mid-nineteenth century to form Shameen Island—the future treaty port area. The third group associated itself with the many seafarers from Canton and other coastal settlements as part of the coastal junk trade, anchored near the Dutch Folly Fort, Honan Island, or along the river, with a fourth group located to the east near Taishatow Island. In 1908 a fire broke out as a result of a kerosene lamp explosion at the Taishatow anchorage that engulfed some 40 flower boats, and spread so quickly from boat to boat that more than 1,000 people were killed, including 600 girls and many prominent businessmen who drowned in the shallow waters.

By the 1920s the "Flower-feast surtax" had become a major source of revenue to the municipal government in Canton, and by 1926 it contributed around 18 percent of total surtax income. Until 1935 the annual revenue from this amounted to around 450,000 yuan, which was clearly a disincentive to suppression of the industry in accordance with campaigns against social vices. Most Cantonese were generally quite ambivalent and openly supportive of the role and social function of flower boats, at least in part because of their patronage by government officials in a male-dominated society. In quarrelsome and challenging times they presented a beguiling means to relax in a convivial atmosphere that guests were not necessarily free to enjoy elsewhere. However, the most discreet of the customers prudently avoided over-indulgence.

In the Whampoa Harbor to the south of Canton, the flower boats throughout the eighteenth and nineteenth centuries were better known as "Lob Lob Boats" and were of a simpler format, consisting of single-family sampans with one or two girls, open to negotiation with Chinese and foreign sailors alike. The boats were moored in the creek adjacent to the Pazhou Ta pagoda, allowing mariners to visit the area on their regular journeys to and from Canton. Lob Lob boats and sampans also visited the ships at the anchorage under cover of darkness. During much of the Qing dynasty children could be purchased from poor families, or sold for a term of several years, and flower boat owners trained the girls who began working on the boats when they reached puberty. The proprietors paid fees to the Mandarin jurisdictions that ensured that any breaches of the law were discreetly ignored, particularly when hundreds of foreign ships and their demanding crews visited every trading season between August and January. The Chinese who serviced the many requirements of sailors, included barbers who were employed by a foreign trading house or by the visiting ships, and apart from their basic profession also engaged in more enterprising activities as "fixers" with access to important sources of information.

It was from the floating community in Canton, that a young woman named Shi Yang emerged to marry the pirate captain Zheng Yi and help to unite the red-banner fleet of more than four hundred ships and 70,000 sailors. Pirate ships continued to control China's coastlines and inland waterways, with tribute being demanded from entire towns and villages. By 1809 the provincial government had to ultimately offer an amnesty to those who surrendered peacefully. Shi Yang and her adopted son negotiated a surrender of the red fleet, after which the entire pirate fleet joined in government service while Shi Yang herself commenced a long civilian life in Canton.

The Chinese economy, exemplified by the dragon, being slowly strangled by foreign opium trade

Chapter 3

Adventurism and Hostilities

The Foreign Factories

A layout of all the foreign factories was published by Robert Morrison in 1832 and illustrates their extent between Thirteen Factory Street and the river. Immediately to the east of the creek was the aptly named Creek Factory, which from the 1830s was partly occupied by Jardine Matheson and the newspaper office of the *Canton Register* founded by James Matheson.

Proceeding westward was the Dutch Factory that housed the national consulate. The East India Company factory was the most architecturally extravagant, having been almost totally rebuilt after the 1822 fire, with a large coat of arms on its prominent pediment. In 1834, the Company was deprived of its trading monopoly and became known as the British factory. This provided almost unprecedented facilities for both work and entertainment, with furnishings that provided a magnificent setting for unbridled hospitality, including a life-size portrait of King George IV placed at one end of the dining-room.

The Fungtai and French hongs were the center for the prominent Parsi trading community, which formed an increasing presence after 1825, dealing primarily in cotton and opium, the leading merchant being Sir Jamsetjee Jeejeebhoy.

The Swedish factory known as "Suy-Hong" was mainly occupied by American staff, including those from Russell and Company. Number 7 in line was the Imperial factory owned by Houqua who effectively rebuilt the premises and leased it to Magniac and Co., who in turn leased it to other users including George Chinnery. The painter who is buried in the Protestant cemetery in Macau, divided his time between Canton and Macau and completed a painting of the long factory corridor. The pre-eminent factory structure also incorporated the Europe Bazaar and Markwick's Hotel, known to all as the British Hotel.

Next to China Street was the American Factory, which apart from housing the European Warehouse and a hotel, also held regular Sunday prayer meetings for all comers, in the chapel known as Zion's corner. The factory also housed the premises of a regular newsletter—the *Chinese Repository*.

To the west of China Street was Chungqua's hong, standing proud from the remainder of the terraced group—a matter of some concern to the Western hongs. The building incorporated a distinctive rooftop pavilion recorded in a sketch by Chinnery. After the Chungqua dynasty's bankruptcy it was taken over by the Mingqua hong. Because of its prominent position its unbroken ground level wall was used by the central authority to post official notices.

Although there had been long-standing French missionary activity in China, the first French factory from 1803 was short lived because of the war between Britain and France. It was not until 1832 that the Canton Register announced that the tri-color had again been hoisted by the French consul. The factory was intermittently used by a number of Parsi traders.

The Spanish factory next to the recently constructed New China Street was built in a neo-classical style. However, its occupants were largely independent British merchants who traded in opium, including Turner and Company.

At the western end adjacent to the creek, was the large Danish factory compound that housed the popular Canton Dispensary that offered free medical assistance and medicine to local Chinese. It also housed an enclosure for goats from which milk could be extracted for the manufacture of cheese. The Danish factory was the first to be ignited by the second major fire that occurred in 1843.

By 1846 several changes had occurred to the overall layout. Next to the eastern creek new English factories had been extended to Hog Lane, fronted by the English garden and a landing stage. Between Old China Street and Hog Lane the American Garden formed a major open space in front of the factories, while new structures had been constructed in front of the French, Spanish, and Danish hongs.

Danger from fire and floods was never far away. Summer floods frequently overwhelmed the riverside bringing floodwater to the lower floors of the factories. The factories themselves had an immense depth with building blocks sub-divided by courtyards and were therefore less susceptible when compared to the tightly packed street fabric. Furthermore, the line of factories lay adjacent to the river, and stored goods could quickly be transferred to boats in cases of emergency. Fire posed a continuing threat to all parts of the city primarily because of the narrow streets and flammable building material, despite measures that included the integration of water cisterns for use in emergencies, intended to check the spread. The most disastrous fire occurred in 1822, which affected much of the western suburbs and left 50,000 residents homeless. Hundreds of shop premises were destroyed along with all the factory warehouses, with armed forces being sent to salvage any remaining goods. Only parts of the facades of the British and Dutch factories were left standing. However, compensation offered by the governor-general assisted the reconstruction of the factory area, with work carried out by Chinese contractors supervised by a foreman appointed by the merchant houses. It is recorded by William C. Hunter that in 1833 the public granaries were exhausted through a severe draught and after all temple sacrifices had failed to appease the god of rain, several hundred destitute people came to the square for assistance from the merchants. In both 1835 and the following year two serious fires broke out in the New City destroying several hundred houses. While all stored goods were quickly transferred to boats, the factories were saved by the use of fire engines that had been imported from England.

The custom houses enabled the Canton authorities to maintain checks on all goods transmitted between the Whampoa anchorages and Canton, to both enforce regulations and to collect the appropriate

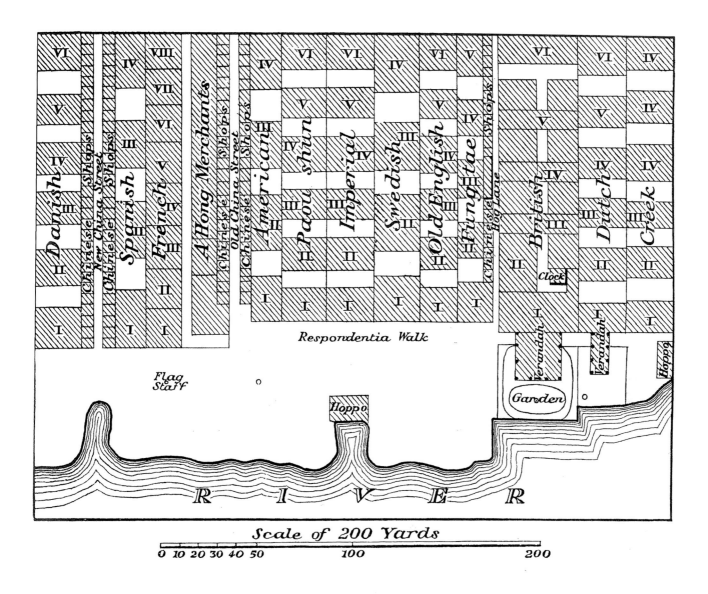

duties. Several were located on the waterfront adjacent to the factories while others were located at Whampoa and various river sites that extended on piles over the water allowing them to easily observe maritime activities. Lanterns and flags visually heralded their essential function.

The Co-hong began to exhibit symptoms of disintegration even in its prime trading period, as it comprised only business agents or go-betweens rather than the imperial bureaucratic organization that operated from Peking. From the beginning of the nineteenth century, Britain had enjoyed the predominant role in China trade, as various other European countries were beset by domestic problems, including the revolution in France, while American overseas adventurism had barely begun.[56] Britain was, on the other hand, on the brink of another kind of revolution—an industrial one that generated a demand for luxury imports such as tea and silk. The United States had meanwhile built up a considerable trade in Manchurian ginseng. As the dominant foreign operator, the East India Company could afford to take a benign attitude toward the Canton trade, but the industrial revolution heralded a more outward trading motivation on the part of the British government—the need to pursue new markets for manufactured goods. New trade routes were initiated along the eastern coast of China to test the demand for British products with the missionary and linguist Karl Gutzlaff distributing copies of Morrison's Chinese Bible en route. This ideological vision culminated in a curious body known as the "Society for the Diffusion of Useful Knowledge" in China, led by Gutzlaff.

The Hong merchants essentially occupied official "licensed" positions as intermediaries between foreign traders and Chinese officials, so that communication was indirect and generally made through petitions. A lackadaisical British policy also helped to precipitate a crisis, by sending Lord Napier, a veteran of the Battle of Trafalgar, as Superintendent of British Trade in China to carry out administration under British law. Napier arrived in Canton via Macau with no official permit, accompanied by two naval frigates that signaled a more defiant and increasingly belligerent approach to the hitherto compatible trading relationships, so that he appeared to be committing an offence against the laws of China. This not only alienated the Chinese but failed to regularize trading dispensations and privileges on behalf of the free traders.[57] His introductory letter of instruction from the British Foreign Secretary, Lord Parmerston, to the Chinese viceroy in Canton was therefore immediately rejected whereupon Napier evidently felt that he had little choice but to recommend to the British government that their interests could only be served by using military power to fully open China's ports.

In August 1834 the Viceroy reasserted that the "English Barbarians" had no public business in China beyond their commerce, and that officers of the Celestial Empire never took any cognizance of the trivial affairs of trade.[58] At the same time the British shipment of cargoes was suspended. Napier was forced to back down and return to Macau, where he suffered an untimely death in October of the same year. This hardened the confrontational aspirations of the merchants, whose immediate level of antagonism was tempered by the more realistic view of the new foreign secretary, the Duke of Wellington, who was no doubt enjoying a more relaxed political life in the post-Waterloo period. This set back the ability to achieve a settlement with China on behalf of all trading nations.

A way around this presented itself through the tripartite trading associations between China, India, and England. Up until the late eighteenth century this had been rather one-way. Eames reports that in 1780 the amount of tea carried in British ships from Canton was over four million pounds, and trade in silk had also reached unprecedented levels.[59] The essential problem was what type of cargo could be sold to China. Private individuals licensed by the East India Company, with particularly close ties to trading companies in Calcutta and Bombay, dealt mainly in raw cotton from

Bridge crossing between Shami Island and the mainland.

India. These merchants and entrepreneurs represented private concerns in London and India that began to extend British interests, not only in trade but in banking, insurance, and shipping, with income gained from both trading profits and commissions for service transactions. Spurred on by Britain's growing nineteenth-century industrial production these activities mushroomed, but were clearly constrained by the inability of even the most enterprising of foreign traders to establish permanent facilities, including warehouses, in Chinese ports. The most striking characteristic of these operations, seen through today's politically correct notions of corporate responsibility, was their energetic disregard for the more ethical side of business, homing the strategic difference between *avoidance* and *evasion* in the name of profit to an extremely fine line. It was almost inevitable that such business ingenuity should find its ultimate potential in the opium trade, that began to seriously compromise the boundaries of mutuality and respect.

The Trade in Opium

The word "opium" is derived from a Greek word *opion* and is referred to by Homer in *The Odyssey* as a means of "quieting all pains." Hippocrates, a Greek physician from the fourth century BCE, was the first to acknowledge the use of opium as a narcotic for treating certain types of disease. The cultivation of opium poppies in Lower Mesopotamia continued through the Assyrians to the Babylonians and Egyptians and was introduced into Europe as a painkiller during the sixteenth century Reformation. Portuguese merchants began carrying cargoes of the drug to Macau around 1600 while the Dutch introduced the practice of smoking opium in tobacco pipes. However, in the early eighteenth century the drug became a commodity of the English East India Company.

During the Ming dynasty, opium's evident attractions were the subject of poetry and literature through scholars who set down their euphoric states of mind in couplets, that might explain the drug's misleading popularity as an aphrodisiac to high society. Until the Qing dynasty it was in fact never seemingly denounced by officialdom and was not actually prohibited. Controversy over the trading and consumption of opium has long been the subject of contention and represented the pivotal catalyst for eventual military intervention. Opium and opiates such as laudanum were widely used in Britain in the eighteenth century as a medicine, and opium was consumed for pleasure in London coffee houses. The discovery that neutralizing opium with ammonia produced morphine, together with its commercial manufacture, opened up its use for medicinal purposes, with large amounts imported into Britain and America from India and Turkey. From the British perspective, trading in the drug had a long history, and it was not until 1874 that the Society for Suppression of the Opium Trade was eventually founded.[60]

Opium was produced in a number of Chinese provinces well before its import as foreign contraband. Its medicinal and metabolic benefits were lauded as being effective during the Sung dynasty, and euphemistically termed "imperial rice" with no mention of pernicious side effects. Its importance in past centuries could well be put down to the ancient process of self-medication as a palliative for relatively minor complaints, without any signs of addiction. In fact, it was widely used to relieve pain.

The importation of opium into China had been prohibited as early as 1764 following Portuguese trade of the drug in Macao. The East India Company had been given the right to

produce opium but did not begin to import this to China until 1773 from Fort St. George in India, and by 1780 a depot for opium was established in Lark's Bay just to the south of Macao.[61] The following year a major consignment was sent to Whampoa in an armed vessel that was exempt from searches and allowed to enter free of measurement duty.

By 1800 the Chinese government was already expressing dismay at the growth of trafficking, and an order from the imperial court forbade its importation. In 1815 a further imperial edict forbid its import to Macau, although the underlying denunciation was perhaps diluted by a threat of potential punishment at the same level as those who promulgated Catholicism in China. Five years later a proclamation was issued from the viceroy that customs officers would search each ship, and that smuggling would lead to the seizure of cargo and permanent expulsion of the ships involved. It was difficult to back up this forceful language due largely to a combination of the clear self-interest of those involved with the trade on both sides, and a constant delegation of responsibility within the wide realm of officialdom. This convinced many that prevailing measures were not intended to actually prevent the trade, but to turn it into an official monopoly. From 1830 the illicit trade was extended to other ports including Amoy, Ningbo, and Tientsin, aided by the use of new "opium clippers" that were both fast and armed. These three masted riggers with large sails and streamlined hulls were originally built for the tea trade, but when this was extended to India and Ceylon, the clippers were used almost entirely for the transport of opium and continued to dominate the India-China trade for the next two decades.

The drug had been introduced initially into China by Arab traders during the T'ang dynasty but opium smoking in China was not particularly widespread until the early nineteenth century. The vicious spiral, caused by imports on a massive scale, is attributable not merely to the direct line of supply, but to several related factors, notably its contribution to the Indian economy and the competition between areas of supply. By 1830, the British East India Company had maneuvered control over virtually all the supply of opium grown in India, although the Company did not itself act as a trader but licensed this, under the Company's stamp, to private operators.

This not only made the Company susceptible to a growing economic dependency on opium, it encouraged private marketing at precisely the time when trade was expanding beyond the old established Canton system of regulation. The subsequent growth in unmonitored trading of opium produced massive profits, but eventually brought about a situation where governments inevitably had to get embroiled.

Mutual benefit from the trade was to be gained by both Western and Chinese dealers that generated a somewhat relaxed and practical attitude toward the process. Although opium was technically illegal, many vested interests were at stake in its trade that was at first carried out in a remarkably civil manner. Smoking opium was quite acceptable in respected circles, and even a mark of status with little real risk of arrest. Paradoxically, at the same time the rising popularity of Chinese tea in England was attacked in London pamphlets as causing bodily harm. Opium itself was freely sold as a medicinal product and painkiller and used as a recreational drug by many members of the English literary establishment. A member of Jardine Matheson reported that, during one transaction, religious tracts were being distributed from one side of the vessel while opium was being unloaded from

the other.[62] The trade intensified through sales in Canton via a less than direct transfer of opium chests to discreet destinations along the coastal waterways from where it was smuggled into the city.

The Trading Imbalance

The spirit of rampant enterprise coupled with the commercial free-for-all and general venality that increasingly gripped the coastal trading communities in China created a potentially explosive recipe, although even the mutual trading advantages between local and foreign merchants could not mask their basic cultural polarization. The ordered and proudly self-sufficient Chinese regime, with a divine ruler at its core that at least on the surface disparaged foreign trade, was inevitably drawn into conflict with a Western power with a strong sense of nationalism, convinced of its own legitimacy.

In 1835 an imperial edict referred to the English as barbarians who had shown themselves to be violent, crafty, and deceitful. In examining the Hongs of Canton through the lens of export paintings, Patrick Connor states that the introduction of steamships was perceived by China as constituting the greatest latent threat when it was demonstrated to the authorities.[63] The most threatening of these was the iron-built *Nemesis,* used during the ensuing conflict. While it was a large vessel, 184 feet in length, it had a shallow draft that allowed it to sail well past Whampoa to the city itself.

On the accession of Queen Victoria to the British throne in 1837, London was the financial capital of the world, and it felt empowered to extend its reach. By this time an important

question concerning the export of silver began to be raised, as the balance of trade that had previously benefited China began to be realigned.

Silver, which was not extensively produced in China, was in short supply, and major commercial transactions had to be undertaken in silver rather than copper cash. Between 1829 and 1836 China sent 100 million ounces of silver abroad as payment for opium cargo.[64] The increasing scarcity of silver was also the result of revolution in Mexico and Peru, which were major suppliers. As silver increasingly became a trading currency, particularly in exchange for opium shipments, the outflows of silver bullion became a problem as it engendered an inflationary spiral against copper coinage, and in turn had a negative impact on the population at large in terms of their tax burdens. This was only mitigated to some extent by the need for traders to also pay for their own imports such as silk and tea. Much of the silver was in the form of *sycee*, lumps of cast silver with an official chop, and its export began to result in a scarcity of silver taels and rising inflation.[65]

In 1836, the viceroy ordered all foreign trading firms implicated in the trade to leave Canton,[66] although the Chinese campaign of suppression was mainly directed at consumers rather than traffickers. Captain Charles Elliott who had helped to bring about the abolition of slavery in British dominions in 1833, had by this stage taken over the role of superintendent of trade and was therefore the major representative of Britain in China. He remained convinced that a renewed sense of purpose in the defense of trading conditions would secure a relaxation of restrictions. Thus ensued a long series of dispatches between the superintendent and the foreign office in London. To a considerable extent, this seems to have been a case of the blind, or at least short sighted, leading the blind, with Lord Palmerston, the foreign secretary, unequivocally ordering Elliott to decline official communications with the Hong merchants while Elliott himself, convinced that the opium trade was to become legalized, continued to advocate a policy of conciliation through a petition to the viceroy. Palmerston, in a communication with the Lords of the Admiralty, appears to have compounded this provocative situation by ordering that ships of the East India squadron should visit China as frequently as possible to defend British interests, with the clear inference that the opium trade should be protected by force.[67]

By the late 1830s the trade in opium had reached a point at which there was little attempt at concealment, with opium openly smuggled into the city from depots along the Pearl estuary. Matters came to a head in December 1838 when bales of opium were seized from a vessel anchored outside the factories, which led indirectly to a crowd attacking the foreign buildings.

On January 23, 1839, William Jardine bid farewell to Canton after a twenty-year career at a well-attended dinner in the old British factory. He was lauded as the most successful British merchant, and in a speech defended the character of the foreign merchant community and communicated his admiration for the Cantonese. Jardine's departure was well timed, as six weeks later the emperor took a decisive step to deal with the opium issue, sending a special imperial commissioner—Lin Tsih-seu, the viceroy of Hankow—to stamp out both the opium trade and its use. He began by initiating mass arrests of Chinese opium dealers, and the confiscation of raw opium. Commissioner Lin, who had been brought up in the maritime provinces, and whose father was a laborer in a porcelain factory, was an example of the open literary advancement available to everyone through the yearly examination system. Accompanied by civil officers and military personnel, he immediately issued an edict addressed to the foreign traders stating that their entire opium stock must be surrendered through the Hong Merchants and destroyed. To underscore this order, foreign residents were confined to their factories until this was carried out, and these were immediately surrounded by a blockade of armed junks. Around 350 British, Americans, Dutch, and Parsis were trapped, with Old China Street as the only means of outside communication.

Elliot, who had been summoned from Macau, arrived in full uniform and assured the recalcitrant merchants that they would be reimbursed by the British government through signed promissory notes. This represented a somewhat single-minded gesture, as the majority of opium was only on consignment to them. In the meantime, the Cantonese authorities had installed a protective barrier of wooden stakes to achieve effective control over access to the factories from the river.

Elliot then ordered the chests to be taken to the Honan shore across the Pearl River where they were destroyed under the supervision of Commissioner Lin, although it was said that at least some found its way into warehouses in Macao. It took almost three weeks to dissolve the residue of the opium, Lin at one stage apologizing to the spirit of the sea which had to absorb it. At the same time

tack on the Bogue forts of
k-kok and Chuen-pi in the
arl River in 1841 signaling the
ening of Canton as a treaty port
Western trade.

the leading Hong merchants were made to relinquish their official rank. On surrendering opium stocks, the siege of the factories was lifted and compradors allowed to return, although the back doors of the factories were closed, and movement of foreigners was restricted.

In a letter to the Governor-General of India Lord Auckland, Elliott requested armed naval assistance and "as many ships of war that can be detached."[68] Possibly with an eye on the massive income that was being earned by the colonial government of India from the sale of opium, this request was complied with. Two ships, the *Volage* and the *Hyacinth*, arrived to commence in hostilities off Chuenpi in November in response to threats to British shipping, which formed the provocative catalyst for the Opium War.[69]

While the restrictions on foreigners leaving Canton were lifted on May 21, 1839, tensions continued to grow. In England, Lord Palmerston, the prime minister, was prevailed upon by all sides, some insisting on compensation and a re-opening of the market, while others reminded government of the questionable events that had led to the situation. With little political leeway, and in a situation where the British government was already in receipt of a large debt left over from the Napoleonic Wars, an armed expedition appeared to represent an appropriate show of strength as a means of forcing China to pay the

indemnity under threat. The parliamentary vote was narrow—271 votes to 262 in favor of dispatching a naval fleet and a rationale for war. This duly arrived at the mouth of the Pearl River in June 1840 with sixteen men-of-war and four thousand British and Indian troops on twenty-seven transport vessels.

Palmerston was advised by William Jardine, by then a member of Parliament, as to the commercial necessity of gaining a concession from the Manchu government to allow trade with the northern ports of Amoy, Foochow, Ningbo, and Shanghai through a blockade of the China coast, accompanied by possession of Chusan and Gulangyu adjacent to Amoy.[70] This advice, in effect formed the basis of a forthcoming military strategy.

The First Opium War

By July 1840 a considerable force of British warships, led by the armed steamer *Nemesis,* had assembled with around 4,000 men, and on January 7, 1841, the isolated forts of Tai-kok and Chuen-pi on the Pearl River below Canton were attacked and many Chinese killed. After a temporary armistice, a number of preliminary settlement terms were arrived at between Elliott and the high commissioner at the Chuenpi Convention, including the secession of Hong Kong, payment of a large indemnity as compensation for trading losses, and the resumption of trade at Canton. These terms were not ratified by the British government, but an imperial edict left no doubt that there was no other course than to seek military retribution on the part of China for what was seen as a deliberate act of aggression.

On February 25, the Battle of the Bogue took place, the British fleet taking the forts together with Sha-kok, and proceeding to Canton so that by March the city was brought directly within a line of fire. In May, hostilities broke out again, the British ships coming under fire from a new shore battery as well as from fire ships. This was followed by a long standoff until Elliott was replaced by Sir Henry Pottinger who was also appointed a special plenipotentiary with full authority to conclude an agreement with China. In August, Pottinger headed an expedition to the north accompanied by thirteen men-of-war and fifteen troop transports. They overcame the weak defenses at Amoy and stationed troops on the adjoining island of Gulangyu, and by October, the forces had occupied Ningpo.

By this time the British force in China had been reinforced, mainly by regiments from India amounting to ten thousand men, including artillery and cavalry, while more than 100 ships of various kinds made up the naval force. In June 1841 the expedition occupied Shanghai, and Chiekiang and Nanking later surrendered without resistance. On August 29, the British demands were formally put before the Chinese commissioners in Nanking and the Treaty of Nanking was signed on board the flag-ship HMS *Cornwallis*, without waiting for the emperor's sanction.[71]

Settlement negotiations were carried out under a mix of military weakness and political uncertainty on the part of the Manchu government, with various provincial governors setting out the dangers of prevarication, fearful that the British were intent on more ambitious conquest, with the colonization of India as a model. The treaty signed at Nanking was the first of several "unequal treaties." Henry Pottinger, the war-time envoy, avoided the issue of legalization of opium as part of the Nanjing Treaty. Its eventual terms awarded Britain its demanded indemnity while denying any complicity in continuing traffic of the drug.

Commissioner Lin Tsih-Seu wrote a letter to Queen Victoria that was published in the *London Times* in June 1840, reinforcing the moral question that would underscore his long-time position as a voice of reason on the subject. His statue stands in several southern China townships and in New York City's Chinatown with an inscription: *Pioneer in the War against Drugs*.

The Governor of Canton Ye Ming Chen refused to sanction the 1842 Treaty of Nanking and for some considerable time the British were unable to leave their factory compound. In 1856 the British consul drew on the seizure of a British-flagged ship as a basis for redress, and when compensation was not forthcoming a British naval force was introduced to storm the city, with the result that the European settlement was set on fire. The following year British and French forces again attacked Canton, transported the governor to Calcutta, and occupied the city. A commission of consular and military officials was then appointed to oversee its administration, with a new Chinese governor instated.

The East India Company's aggressive trading ethos was not the only thing imported from India. "*Loot*" was originally a Hindi term enthusiastically embraced by the British to represent the legitimate spoils of war.[72] In time this came to represent not merely the ultimate outcome of military campaigns, but in some situations became an underlying reason from them. In the process this helped considerably to financially sustain the foundations of colonial power.

Terms of Settlement and the Continuance of Trade

The Treaty of Nanking provided for the opening of trade at four additional ports, an indemnity of 21 million dollars for the opium that had been surrendered at Canton in 1839, and the abolition of the Co-hong trading monopoly. The main ports, in addition to Canton, were Shanghai, Ningbo, Foochow, and Amoy. This removed, at a stroke, Canton's established position as China's only port for foreign trade, while reinforcing its role as an open port. The Treaty also acted to refine the terms under which Hong Kong was to operate. While the treaty sets out something of a face-saving description, essentially defining the territory as "a port for refitment of ships and keeping of stores for that purpose," the then Prime Minister Lord Aberdeen instructed Pottinger, as Hong Kong's first governor, to make it a self-supporting free port, and to raise revenue chiefly by leasing crown lands for the highest possible price. This was something that would ultimately, in circumstances that were unforeseen at the time, contribute to Hong Kong's eventual high density, compact urban form, and the immense price of property.

The agreed arrangements reflected some degree of compromise, considering the realistic capabilities of actually carrying out the terms of the treaty. In setting a treaty port tariff low enough to disincentivize evasion, the British had to acknowledge both the hidden charges that profited local officialdom and the necessity of ensuring an efficient customs agency. The Supplementary Treaty of October 1843 was, in effect, the key to operational workability of the Treaty Ports, addressing numerous difficult aspects such as residence, "most favored nation status," extradition, restrictions on trade, and treaty limits. This was followed by treaties with America and France. Perhaps not surprisingly, certain discrepancies in translations created some subtle differences between Chinese and English versions of the document. The treaties of 1842 and 1843 that were to introduce a new order to relations between China and the West for the next 100 years, could only be regarded as the culmination of events over the preceding century. The situation was exacerbated by the continued stationing of the *Nemesis* as a source of intimidation, reinforced in 1847 by an armed steamship *Pluto*.

With dramatic irony, only four months later a fire broke out in a street close to the Hong factories that burned down the western buildings, leaving only the central group remaining. In response to the changing circumstances, Pottinger put forward a plan for wholesale regeneration of the factory area that appropriated all the space between the factories and the river and proposed the redevelopment of Hog Lane and New China Street. By the following year sporadic rebuilding was underway, including a new transformation—the American public garden that covered four acres and extended along the frontage of the six central factories and south to the river landing stages.

By 1849 the central space between the two gardens was further distinguished by a new British Episcopal church and a parsonage approved by the governor-general several years earlier, on land purchased by the British consul. Its simple form and square tower appears as an identifiable focus on many paintings of the period. Meanwhile, a range of new consulates had appeared on the waterfront including those from Austria, Prussia, Portugal, Brazil, and Chile. To emphasize foreign control over the waterfront, a new clubhouse and boathouse were constructed along with a library, masonic lodge, and numerous recreational amenities.

At the end of the day, the chief advantages of the treaties favored Western interests for one overriding reason—they helped to sanctify commercial priorities. The Chinese side could not entirely envisage what the future trading outcome might be, and the ramifications of this for growth and development. A significant outcome of the two treaties was that of "extraterritoriality" that exempted Westerners living in the Treaty Ports from Chinese law and the granted most-favored-nation status to the foreign signatories, thereby creating a dual system of legal governance. The former allowed the barbarians to regulate their own affairs according to their civil and criminal codes. The effect of the latter was that China could not negotiate properly with other states, as conditions that applied to one would be automatically extended to the others.

One of the first steps taken in implementing the Treaty of Nanking was to legally restrict British trade in China to the five treaty ports, although apart from Canton there were no consular offices, nor an agreed scale of duties or tariffs. Furthermore, Hong Kong was now the official seat of British legal jurisdiction, placing a further constraint on the ability to enforce these provisions. As trade opportunities were clearly being opened up, manufacturers and traders in Britain were increasingly vocal in denouncing the opium trade, seemingly not for ethical reasons but because so much Chinese capital was directed toward opium imports rather than other export goods. Meanwhile, Jardine Matheson and others began to trade under the American flag, utilizing ships from the United States that were already heavily involved in the export of opium from India.

"Unauthorized" trade continued with impunity through a tacit understanding between the numerous vested interests that official permission, and therefore recognition, were "unnecessary." This reflected a diplomatic acknowledgment by both parties that the actual facts of the matter should be discreetly avoided. Britain's foreign secretary, Lord Aberdeen, adopted the interesting but somewhat questionable line that while Britain could not actually prevent the opium trade, it would stop short of actual assisting it. In the meantime, Pottinger took steps to regularize and control the storage and distribution of opium from Hong Kong, while separating this from the legal trade in tea and silk.[73] The Crown Colony therefore took on a role as the recognized port of call for import of opium from India, from where it was transferred by fast cutters and schooners that offloaded opium cases to receiving ships along the Chinese coast. In this sense opium traffic was bound up within a regulatory framework that facilitated expansion of trade overall. Paul Van Dyke makes the case that without funds generated from the contraband trade, the legitimate trade in tea, silk, and porcelain would not have grown so rapidly.[74] Canton itself embarked on a new era of international trade that served as an engine of economic growth.

The New Trading Concessions

According to the Treaty of Nanking, Canton and other treaty ports were opened to British subjects "where they might reside for the purpose of carrying on mercantile pursuits without molestation or restraint." The five initial treaty ports proved to be the coastal gateways for Western trade with China. Canton was officially opened up in July 1843, Amoy and Shanghai in November 1843, Ningbo in January 1844, and Foochow in June 1844. Foreigners were allowed to live in specially established concession or settlement areas. The terms "concession" and "settlement" in a historical perspective represent different things. A concession was an area leased, under the Treaty of Nanking, from the Chinese government for a nominal rent, where foreign occupants constructed buildings and services, and were entirely responsible for their maintenance. A settlement was allocated at the behest of the Chinese government where foreign nationals or firms could lease land from local landowners.[75]

At the time, Shanghai was the youngest of these ports, and not only had a strategically sheltered position on the Yangtze Delta, but a long agricultural history with irrigation canals dating back to the T'ang dynasty. The shallow river was subject to siltation and this had given rise to a market town and fishing port in the Sung dynasty. By the sixteenth century the settlement had become a walled town and an important center for a growing overseas trade in Chinese silk. The first British consul, George Balfour, had to organize the foreign land concession on marshy land to the north of the walled city, adjacent to Suzhou Creek. Separate leases had to be orchestrated for the various foreign governments. Rent was nominal, but roads and jetties had to be kept up and maintained by the concessionaires. The American concession was in Hongkou to the north of Suzhou Creek, and the later French concession in 1862 was built between the British concession and the old city. In 1863 the British and American settlements merged to form the International Settlement.

Foochow was the tributary port for trade with Liu-chu, Fukien, and Formosa (modern Chinese Taiwan). It was situated some 30 kilometers from the sea, and large ships had to stop at Pagoda Island. The city had no concession area, but a settlement for foreigners was esta-blished on an abandoned cemetery, local officials subtly demonstrating their antipathy to the newcomers, as well as an intimate knowledge of local feng shui.

Ningbo, not far from Shanghai but to the southeast of the Yangtze delta was, by the mid-nineteenth century, a major port for trans-shipment of river trade along the northeastern seaboard. In 1843 visitors described the town as, "standing at the junction of two fine streams who by their union form a noble river." They were particularly taken by an ingenious arrangement of boats that were moved at equal dis-tances across the river on which rested a wooden framework that was used as a bridge.[76]

Amoy on the southeast coast was a large island with a harbor partly protected by another smaller island with an interesting topography. In the early years this was used as a British army encampment. Descriptions of the town at the time tell of narrow and insanitary streets, and fre-quent outbreaks of cholera. After the Amoy settlement was opened, it attracted wholesale mer-chants from Britain, Germany, and the United States who handled a variety of goods, including opium, but whose representatives also acted as agents for steamship lines, insurance companies, and banks. Early merchant compounds included Butterfield and Swire, Dent and Company, and Jardine Matheson who had their headquarters in Shanghai. Members of missionary societies and church groups followed soon after, establishing early churches and schools, although many suc-cumbed to illness and death so that the port took on an unhealthy reputation.[77]

In Canton the first foreign settlement in 1849 was on Honan Island, sitting almost oppo-site the original factory sites. It was only after the Second Opium War of 1856 that a foreign settlement was established on Shameen Island—at that time outside the city itself. The British consulate was built there, but the consular residence itself was situated in an old Manchu com-pound within the old city. Streets were wide enough only for two people, lined by single-story houses and shops devoted to specific trades. A number of the original trading firms had by this time left Canton to establish new headquarters in Hong Kong where security, better urban management, and an excellent harbor made day-to-day livability more amenable.

Houqua's Garden

The notion of Chinese "style" and aesthetics, exemplified by the experience of the garden landscape and its inherent dialogue between interior and exterior, was in exotic contrast to the more formal Western-built environment where neo-classical form and a visual relationship with the public realm was more notable. Merchant gardens in and around Canton before the First Opium War, in what was known as the Lingnan region at the beginning of the nineteenth century, were the first indication of refined environmental design. The Chinese garden had its origins in the Ming dynasty, but its nineteenth-century descendent represented the distinct design characteristics of Cantonese features, which differed markedly from those to the north in close proximity to the Imperial court.

Houqua, the leader of the Hong merchants, inherited his position and wealth from his father Wu Guoying who had purchased a large estate on Honan Island to the south of the Pearl River,

almost directly across from the factories, which enabled him to construct a large private garden associated with a private villa built in 1801. The garden of Houqua and the equally refined Puankhequa's garden were located on each side of the Longxi Stream adjacent to the Ocean's Banner Temple. Houqua's mansion and garden were visited only by elite Mandarins and highly placed Western guests with whom the merchant maintained cordial relations. Invitations during the early trading period were in part a reflection of traditional Chinese hospitality, but also a perceptive exercise in cementing courteous relations and business transactions.

The layout of Houqua's garden exemplified the various elements that constituted both a magnificent landscape and a collection of exquisite buildings distributed within the environmental setting. The design axis accommodated a number of shrines dedicated to the god of learning, a tall *Wenchang* structure that acted to maximize the benevolent influence of *feng shui*.[78] Entering through a deliberately simple gateway set into an enclosing wall, the first major building was the ancestral hall, emphasizing the family's long lineage associated with Canton from the seventeenth century. The large ancestral hall situated in the garden was therefore partly to symbolically emphasize Houqua's long relationship with the city where his father was interred.

The entrance to the garden, famously painted by Tinqua, was a lotus pond known as the Half-Moon Pool lined with bricks and crossed by a low zig-zag stone bridge. After this was the "Garden of the Ten

Interior of Houqua's mansion on Honan Island.

Thousand Pieces" or Wansongyuan, for intimate gatherings. The garden, main hall, and adjoining temple acted as the focus for cultural gatherings while the majority of the estate was designed as a natural setting with lotus ponds, streams, pavilions, water kiosks, and low stone bridges bordered by landscaped pathways. A large standing *Taihu* rock was integrated in a prominent position with its distinguished profile selected to evoke the garden's natural qualities. These rocks from Wuxi were famous in Chinese gardens for their elegant shapes and a thin base which appeared to make them float above the ground. The vegetation was dominated by banyan and fruit trees intended "to delight the eyes of visitors," along with fragrant potted flowers such as magnolia, roses, and camellia nurtured in local nurseries. The trees included oranges, limes, loquats, citron, apples, and lichees, and it was faithfully reported that signs were erected to discourage the picking of fruit or flowers in order to preserve the natural beauty of the garden.

The garden of Houqua generated many aspects of decorative detail in its incorporation of screen doors, zig-zag bridges, octagonal arches, ornamental brickwork, and the relationship between architecture and water. The gravel-paved walks, stone grottoes, pavilions, and granite bridges across water features created a setting for bird and animal life included deer, peacocks, storks, and mandarin ducks. The grounds were surrounded by a brick wall, nine feet in height, entered through a massive door of polished Siamese teak. The two-story buildings had light and graceful forms, encircled by wide verandahs, and with rooms separated by open courts. From the upper verandahs it was possible to see the walled city of Canton some five miles away across the Pearl River. The garden watercourses like those in Houqua's garden could accommodate gilded junks in their water basins. A particular feature of Canton's gardens were "boat halls" that sought to visually emulate the familiar Canton flower boats that passed along the Pearl River. The garden contained various fish ponds crossed by arched-stone bridges, with grottoes and seating areas shaded by fruit trees. The ponds were linked by a lock system to the Longxi Stream, allowing genuine pleasure craft with their passengers of scholars, merchants, and courtesans, to enter the garden for special events. It is said that even Dragon Boats and their teams were allowed to enter during the annual river festival in order to parade with their boats on the large pond, with the winners receiving generous rewards.

Groups of visitors arrived by boat and were given tours of the villas and gardens, and those fortunate enough to participate in dinners enjoyed an elaborate parade of twenty or more courses over at least three hours on tables decorated with magnificent flower arrangements. A number of visitors were given to comment on the French wines and the many ornaments of European manufacture that included French clocks and British plates.

A theater for opera situated in the garden could accommodate more than 100 actors. William C. Hunter, writing in the early nineteenth century, mentioned dinners given in the private mansion where, after the meal, the manager of the resident or visiting theater company would submit a list of plays from which a selection could be made by guests—the choices being tragedy or comedy. No vigorous preparation was required, as the orchestra would be in place behind the performers, and actors had only to put on the appropriate costumes. The stage was often an open pavilion on a lakeside location, with changes of scene denoted by large gilt characters on wooden "tablets" periodically suspended from the corner columns. Plays were also staged in front of temples to allow room for up to three thousand spectators. There were neither drop curtains nor shifts of scenery, and as activities such as opening a door were made through hand gestures much was left to the imagination of the audience.

Following the Opium Wars and the abolition of the Co-hong merchants trading monopoly, Houqua's garden gradually fell into disrepair after his death in 1843, and its last traces were erased during the Cultural Revolution. Puankhequa's garden area was given over to a hospital in the 1870s.

Long distance view of the Catholi[c]
Cathedral from the roof of the Su[n]
Hotel, with the Baiyun Mountains [in]
the background, 1906.

Chapter 4

Beachheads of Foreign Influence

Treaty Port Settlement Patterns

The prevailing character of Britain's trading pattern in the mid-nineteenth century, coinciding with the formal establishment of the treaty ports, has been characterized as a long arm stretching through India and the Straits to Hong Kong as a central entrepôt, from which five fingers clutched the Chinese mainland.[79] The ports were not merely served by primary waterways but also shared a similarity through their naval protection and commercial opportunities. In the larger cities the older, walled enclosures were left substantially as they were while the foreign settlements were situated outside. In all cases this arrangement provided opportunities to lay out new development areas and to expand them as necessary. They also provided extensive water frontages for warehousing, anchorages, and defense installations.

By 1844 there were some ninety-five commercial agencies represented in the Chinese treaty ports including British, American, and other European firms, together with nineteen Parsee firms from India.[80] Within a few years the number of Western firms within the concession areas had risen to some two hundred, not all of which were involved in trading, that included such unlikely occupations as Swiss watchmakers and French wine importers. Of the professions, architects were in particular demand. The various consuls were vested with all necessary powers, chief of which was to smooth the path of trade, such as dealing with ship's papers, customs, examination of goods, and enforcement of port limits.[81]

The somewhat uneasy alliance between Chinese and foreign communities was reflected in new patterns of urbanization for the settlement and concession areas. Land speculation initially led to a rapid appreciation in value, with the cost of land escalating rapidly in price after 1852.[82] The design of the British settlement initially drew on Victorian-Indian colonial structures, modified by climatic considerations and the more hybrid building types associated with the established Portuguese port of Macau, familiar to most of the early traders. Continuing growth demanded a mix of commercial accommodation, godowns and arcaded spaces interspersed with ornate public buildings such as consular offices, churches, missionary establishments,

The French Roman Catholic Cathedral was founded in 1863 and took 25 years to complete. It was built on the site of Governor Yeh's official residence, which was destroyed by the British and French cannonade. Unsurprisingl[y] its facade bore certain similaritie[s] to Notre Dame cathedral in Paris. [Its] twin steeples soared above the c[ity] creating a constant reminder of [the] foreign presence and consternat[ion] among local citizens, but also housed various charitable missio[ns]. Constructed of granite blocks an[d] built over 25 years, its towers are 88 meters in height. It is flanked [by] Italianate housing blocks built to house those connected with the cathedral.

and other landmarks. Both traders and newly appointed public officials were often required to move from place-to-place at short notice, so that although the early communities were small, walled compounds could offer large sites within which residences, business offices, servant's quarters, and warehouses could often be located in tandem.

The architectural style became known as *compradoric*, designed to suit the work and living requirements of merchants, but built by Chinese contractors under an operational model supervised by a comprador or Chinese agent employed by the largest foreign firms. Some of the early European buildings in China were effectively prefabricated in Hong Kong, and their components shipped and assembled in situ. Eventually, contractors from Hong Kong and Canton established building firms in the port cities to assist with site formation, construction of embankments, and the buildings themselves.[83] The hybrid amalgam of Western forms with Chinese vernacular ornamental details helped to generate the beginning of a new cosmopolitan architecture in the treaty port buildings, with an expressive interweaving of different cultural values.

There were few Europeans to supervise building works, and contracts had to be prepared in Chinese for the local contractors who developed the design details. Early two-story buildings generally followed the form of those in the Canton factory area. They stood in private compounds, with the residential component to the front with enclosed verandahs. Servant's quarters were set apart but connected by a covered way, and godowns for storage extended down the sides along with offices and domestic accommodation for the comprador and staff. There was also generally a large annex for junior staff with a communal kitchen.

The Chinese comprador played a significant role in the development of expanding trading enclaves acting as a commercial intermediary assisting Sino-Western trading interaction and diffusing actual or potential conflicts. Yen-P'ing Hao notes this "middleman" role as being necessarily developed from traditional Chinese economic institutions.[84] After the Treaty of Nanking the arrival of a large foreign trade community created a focused comprador class. This helped to shape the development of treaty port investment to serve both Chinese and Western interests, both economically and culturally. This also, and more crucially, signified the upward mobility of the urban merchant class that had hitherto embodied a relatively low social status.[85] The widening of economic activities within the main port cities opened up a more gentrified merchant body whose knowledge of "barbarian affairs," international law, and diplomatic skills enabled the rise of a new power and political elite who challenged some of the most traditionally held values.

A number of compradors became sufficiently wealthy to invest in land and build houses for rent, thereby accelerating the urbanization process. In this sense the comprador was an instrument of gradual Westernization relating to both business practices and urban design, and generating the beginning of a new cosmopolitan class in the cities with an increased interweaving of Chinese and Western cultural values. After this time, compradors mainly became independent businessmen and industrialists, particularly in Shanghai, Hankow, and Tientsin, investing in shipping and import and export businesses.

Extended Trading Access

By mid-1845, regular steamship routes between Britain and Hong Kong were opened up, taking about 55 days for the three-stage route from Southampton to Alexandria; through the Suez Canal to Sri Lanka; and then to Hong Kong with a "Peninsular and Oriental" service between Hong Kong and Shanghai. Mail and dispatches between China and India, and even the transport of consulate funds between Hong Kong and the treaty ports were, with little sense of irony, often sent courtesy of the fast opium clippers.

Canton was seen as the head and Shanghai the tail of the treaty port arrangement. The Chinese relationship with foreigners was rooted somewhere between practical toleration and a constant need for

The American-made paddle-wheel steamer was moored at Honan, 1857. It was built in Delaware and owned by the California Steam Navigation Company. The steamer carried passengers and freight between Hong Kong and Canton until 186 when she was put into service on a new route between Shanghai and Hankou.

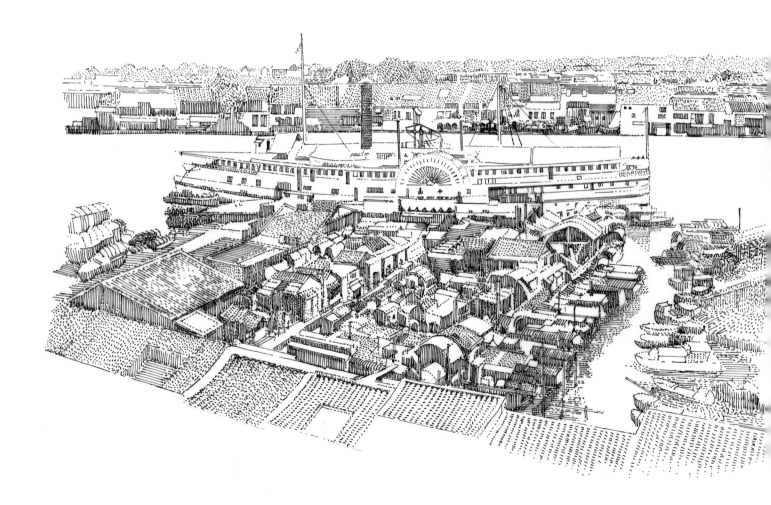

The Canton Factory Area and waterfront, mid-nineteenth century.

reassurance that foreigners had no obvious designs on the imperial dynasty that went beyond mere trade. While Westerners often referred to "oriental inscrutability," a repeated phrase amongst Chinese was *i-ch'ing p'o-ts'e* ("the barbarian nature cannot be fathomed").[86] Both sides clearly looked at the other from not dissimilar and largely incomprehensible perspectives. The general solution was for each to avoid complications or embarrassing incidents by precautionary tactics that ensured, as far as possible, a minimum of absolutist positions that might require direct confrontation. Trade relations proceeded with a high degree of obfuscation, often on the Chinese side through the use of relatively lowly emissaries. A notable exception was Wei Yuan, a nineteenth-century scholar from Honan Province who was one of the first Chinese thinkers to explore how reforms might help China regain wealth and power. Wei was the author of a treatise of Western maritime nations, the *Hai guo tu zhi*, which attempted to recount and describe the chief characteristics and tendencies of Westerners in 1843 as a basis for more cordial relations and as an optimistic means to reduce the barbarian threat.[87]

In general, trading access to the five ports was gained through plenipotentiaries who secured favorable concessions, privileges, and immunities. The United States signed the Treaty of Wanghia in July 1844, and the French later the same year at Whampoa. Further treaties were concluded with Belgium in 1845, Sweden and Norway in 1847, and Russia in 1851. It was stipulated that residents of the ports should be able to obtain proper accommodation for housing and places of business, as well as the ability to lease sites from Chinese on which to construct housing, godowns, hospitals, churches, and cemeteries. This notion of equal treatment for all foreign countries had the unintended effect of consolidating foreign trading powers as concessions granted to one were automatically granted to the others. Both the physical and social texture of treaty ports entailed something of a business separation between foreign concessions but with the same vested interests. In actuality the concession areas became privileged enclaves, exempt from Chinese authority, and with the ability to act as virtually autonomous political bodies. Chinese who lived in the concession areas were equally exempt from imperial authority.

Residence and Jurisdiction

An initial issue that taxed the diplomatic representatives of both sides was that of residence. The British and Chinese versions of the Treaty of Nanking had differences in phrasing as to the housing of merchants within the pre-existing walled cities. While the residential requirements of the consuls within the city had been acknowledged, the Chinese version specified only temporary residence for other bodies, in conjunction with the port anchorages.

In Canton a 25-year lease was signed with six of the former Hongs for several factory sites that were divided into lots for the consulate, and for two British merchant firms—Jardine, Matheson and Co; and Lindsay and Co. Sixteen lots were also rented to other firms including Americans and Parsees. The British Chamber of Commerce was established in 1847 to promote commercial interests and assist with arbitration of trade disputes. It immediately began to press for expansion of the foreign enclave by seeking to displace a number of Chinese shops, erect a church, and procure land for warehouses. Up until this time, the foreign community had lacked sufficient storage facilities, and as a result it was impossible to

Number 4 Fifth Street, owned by a
British company Reiss Bradley & C

ascertain or verify goods in transit, so that the process was open to exploitation. This, together with the issue of foreign entrance to the city of Canton, possibly brought to a head the underlying xenophobia that still lingered from the treaty settlement. Chinese officials who attempted to resolve differences were met with charges that they were compromising national interests and yielding to the threats of over-belligerent foreigners.

Gradually, through British trade with Malaysia, Penang, and Singapore, migration gave many Chinese British naturalization, extending the jurisdiction of British law within the ports. In addition, Cantonese moved in large numbers to the northern ports, using their experience and trading skills to obtain jobs as managers, shroffs, and clerks in the trading offices, and in the new consulates themselves, adding a necessary dimension in terms of local liaison, and extending established trading ties.

Free Trade and Treaty Law

In 1846 a formal agreement was signed that permitted entrance to the walled city of Canton by Westerners, but the actual permission was postponed until such time when "mutual tranquility" could be established. Continued friction led to a British raid on the Bogue forts and Chinese occupation of the Canton factories in 1847, which forced a vague compromise whereby the British were technically permitted entrance into the city in 1849, but in the meantime the city was able to discreetly shore up its coastal defense system. In the same year, John Bowring—a free-trader and supporter of Jeremy Bentham's reforms in Britain—was appointed the new British consul in Canton. However, by this time foreign entrance to the city had become a political issue as Britain felt that it had to re-assert its position in relation to trade, free of political interference, in the wake of less than impressive progress in selling British goods. It was, in all probability, this factor rather than anti-foreign sentiment that forced a deterioration in political relations.

During the bombardment of the city in 1857 the city gates were demolished, which allowed for unrestricted access. Following this Canton became a focus for visitation, and therefore a series of maps were informally prepared to assist wayfinding, with diagrammatic designations of principal streets and points of interest that served as route guides. A further means of conceptualizing the city was ascending the taller structures such as the pagoda, the Zhenhai Lou, and city walls. Various authors prepared guides including Dr. J.G. Kerr, R.C. Hurley, and the Rev. J.H. Gray who was loaned a study by monks associated with the Ocean Banner Monastery.[88] Through these means Gray produced an encyclopedic guide to the city and its surroundings in 1875, interspersed with accompanying discussions of Chinese history. These constituted the means by which visitors could, for the first time, explore the entire city and its maze of streets. In the process this gave rise to a growing tourist experience, albeit one that was largely charted by Western residents, a growing number of tour guides, and teams of sedan chair bearers who met visitors as they arrived by local steamer.

As the trading market in Canton began to decline and became overstocked, imported goods were shipped out for sale in Shanghai and Amoy. A report for the governor of Hong Kong on the potential of the China trade revealed that cotton textile imports from Britain competed with Chinese production

Plan of the attack and bombardment of Canton, 1858, George W. Cooke.

...e October 1856 incident. The
...rcha Arrow was boarded by
...inese forces who pulled down the
...tish flag at the order of the viceroy
...d arrested the crew. The acting
...tish consul construed this as an
...ringement of British sovereignty
...d this led to the bombardment
...Canton, and the foreign factories
...ng destroyed in retaliation which
...ralded the commencement of the
...cond China War.

centered in the Yangtze and Yellow River basins, while China's massive export of tea began to re-establish a greater balance of trade with Europe. The established junk fleets sailed between Canton and Shanghai, out of Amoy to the Straits, and from Ningbo to the coasts of Shantung, Tientsin, and Manchuria. Under the Treaty of Nanking it had been assumed that merchant ships would simply move in and out of a single port, but it later became the norm for ships to call at Hong Kong and at other ports, often in order to find the most favorable market for goods. It was inevitable that foreign traders should turn to sea-borne routes along the coast to rival the Chinese junk fleet with its traditional but sophisticated modes of operation. This led to the domination of the coastal trade by British carriers, albeit often hired by Chinese mercantile interests, which represented an important turning point that is interwoven with development of the treaty port settlements themselves.

The idea of bonded warehouses was introduced so that goods could be properly registered and stored. It was provided for by allowing the re-export of goods between treaty ports, once duty had been paid on the cargo at one port. This principle was then unofficially extended to international trade, but in the process the previously clear distinctions between Chinese and foreign trade began to falter, with Chinese merchants shipping cargo in foreign vessels, and foreign ships trading in Chinese produce. This ambiguous state of affairs was compounded by the repeal of the navigation laws in 1849, which removed the British monopoly on direct tea trade to Britain, and opened it to fast American tea clippers. Inherent in this were several inconsistencies with regard to export and import duties, and the payment of treaty tariffs for foreign trade being applied to Chinese goods traded along the China coast.

Within ten years from its inception, treaty law had virtually ceased to fulfill its original intention, simply because it was impossible to satisfy all interests through its enforcement, and trading opportunities became reliant on more clear-cut means. The first of these was the regulation of customs administration in order to combat corruption and counteract both smuggling and the clandestine trade in opium. Along the Pearl River in Canton this was compounded by the myriad of small river craft, mingling with fishing boats and ocean-going junks, that still brought opium and other goods up the river where cargos were landed at a fraction of the regulated tariffs. However, the problem of enforcing the treaty provisions had, by 1851, begun to point toward the use of force.

The Taiping Rebellion and its Aftermath

The Taiping movement was partly a campaign initiated by peasant families against landowners and their private militias, although it came to represent a certain religious and political crusade against the Manchu dynasty. The rebellion of 1853 that wracked the three southern provinces also reflected the situation among impoverished peasants and boatmen and was exacerbated by droughts, rice riots, and severe inflation.[89] In its ambition to unify military with civil administration, it echoed the ancient *Zhou-Li*. All these created a backdrop to the rise of religious sects and societies, together with the many pirate bands still involved in the opium trade.

After initial military successes, the Taipings were undermined and defeated—mainly as a result of disorganization and infighting. However, in orchestrating new regional military bases from which to overcome the rebellion, the imperial authority unwittingly put into position a new organizational system that was to ultimately open the door to an emerging Han Chinese nationalism. In the meantime, civil war and famine between 1850 to 1864 left up to twenty million dead and established a watershed in modern Chinese history.[90]

The Western powers concluded, in the face of uprisings in Shanghai and Amoy, that the long-term stability of the Qing regime would bring more advantages than its overthrow. In September 1853, an uprising in Shanghai comprising a local band of armed rebels made up of various Fukien and Cantonese factions calling themselves the *Hsiao-tao-hui* marched on the city, seized the treasury, opened the prison, and completely razed the Chinese Custom House.[91] To counteract this an imperial army was sent to besiege the Shanghai city walls, which ended with massive damage to the city.

A new joint Sino-foreign administration commenced on July 10, 1854 and provided special privileges to all foreign nationalities but circumscribed the extent of their administrative influence. Armed conflict commenced again in Canton in 1856 with the seizure of the *Arrow*, a Chinese-owned but Western rigged *lorcha*, after which its British flag was pulled down and its crew taken into custody, on a charge of

smuggling. This was considered to be a deliberate infringement of the existing treaty by the acting consul, and a British naval force was sent to capture the most immediately accessible river forts in the Pearl River that sparked what became known as the Second Opium War, which commenced in October of the same year. By mid-December the most vulnerable factories had been attacked and burned down, possibly representing a preconceived tactic by the Chinese authorities. In response the British navy bombarded the adjoining urban suburbs up to the city walls. In London this unprovoked rejoinder was denounced by Parliament and declared to be unjustified, but preparations began for a further military expedition to Canton.

This incident marked a turning point in political maneuvering, marking the end of the older trading position and the beginning of serious hostilities. The factories along with the church were destroyed, the local suburbs were left in ruins, and Britain and France began to prepare for a military expedition to enforce the stipulation of the Nanking Treaty and the rights of foreign traders. In December 1857 the allied forces under James Bruce, the 8th Earl of Elgin, arrived on the Pearl River and formed a blockade of ships along the already dilapidated city frontage. When the forty-eight-hour ultimatum to Governor Yeh failed to satisfy the invading forces, Elgin's forces shelled the city during the last days of the year. Many of the remaining buildings were demolished, including the viceroy's yamen, and the five barrier forts were captured before the British and French flags were hoisted above the city. Three commissioners were then appointed to administer Canton with the assistance of a new governor. The first era of foreign trade had ended with a military occupation of the city, although it took only a short time before a new one began to emerge.

In June 1858, Lord Elgin signed the Treaty of Tientsin that included important concessions. This was followed by Chinese negotiations with delegations from France, America, Germany, Holland, and Spain who obtained the same terms. Within a year it became clear that China, perhaps unsurprisingly, was being somewhat intransigent in meeting the terms of the treaty. In response, Elgin returned with a military force from Britain and India and succeeded in taking the Taku forts before marching on the Summer Palace, known as the "Garden of Perfect Brightness" commissioned by the Kangxi Emperor and extended by his successors. This contained a series of elaborate buildings largely designed and supervised by French Jesuit priests led by Giuseppe Castiglione in the eighteenth century. British and French troops looted and laid the palace to waste in one of the most questionable acts of military history.

After this the Convention of Peking ratified the previous treaty, which was to have enormous consequences. This effectively allowed British representation in the capital, while foreign traders and missionaries were allowed to travel freely and to receive cooperation and protection. In addition, the southern part of the Kowloon Peninsula, adjacent to Hong Kong, was ceded to the British on a ninety-nine-year lease. The long Yangtze River and its adjoining provinces, including the predominant tea and silk-producing areas, were opened to trade. In addition, a number of cities in the north and south, together with Russia, were able to acquire vast territories and commercial concessions in Manchuria.

Viceroy Liu Ch'ang-you, who covered the provinces of Guangdong and neighboring Guangxi from his headquarters in Canton in 1862. He was responsible for direct communication with the Emperor in Peking and was part responsible for suppressing the Taiping Rebellion.

Sedan chair bearers on South
Sassamian Street.

While the treaties were undoubtedly "unequal" the Chinese saw them as a means of keeping foreigners under some form of control that abrogated the need for further confrontation. However, the Tai Ping rebellion irrevocably altered the course of the Qing dynasty despite being protected by the treaty powers.

Co-operation and Development

Over the following twenty-five years, the ratio of Chinese and Manchu officials was finely balanced, and the period was marked by a number of intelligent appointments to key posts that helped the imperial regime to regain authority. Loans were made by foreign banks based in the port cities, secured by revenues from the maritime customs, and several thousand foreign troops were supplied to assist the imperial army, although mainly in the lower Yangtse region. This in turn assisted development in the port cities, by enlarging the foreign economic base, which tended to slowly destabilize the regime. However, tight financial conditions in Canton prevented major programs of economic development and modernization, and increased taxes hindered the expansion of trade. In terms of law and administration, foreign authority within the concession areas ran virtually in parallel with that of the state, with most-favored-nation advantages extended to many countries. This was the true beginning of foreign exploitation of Chinese territory, with trading rights and new enterprises that established the economic foundations for treaty port growth and development. The expansion of the railway network also began to extend the geographical reach of foreign settlements.

In Canton, after intense debate on whether to reconstruct or relocate the factories and settlement area, the Honan waterfront was considered the most suitable. A group of British merchants had, in 1847, following the Treaty of Nanking, leased part of the island of Honan on the opposite side of the Pearl River from the factories, in close proximity to the long-standing Ocean Banner Temple set among mature banyan trees, and containing large Buddhist statues. The group of temple buildings had been used as a hospitality suite that housed Lord Amherst and Lord McCartney as visiting British dignitaries.[92]

Businesses began to transfer their goods to a series of warehouses that lined the river frontage, some of which were used as army barracks. While the Honan frontage became the new center for commercial and merchant operations, buildings along the waterfront were of a more conventional form than the old factories and of a rather more functional nature. Following the Treaty of Nanking, a growing number of firms had removed their modernized operations to Hong Kong, and there was also a growing trend to separate business and residential property. The tea processing operations also required access to wharfs, and shipping activities increased commensurate with new factories and large warehouse facilities. The firm of Butterfield and Swire, which had established a sugar refinery named after their possession of Tai Koo on the eastern harbor front of Hong Kong Island, opened a new factory on Honan and later constructed a large complex in the Pak Hin Hok area for single-story warehouses, residential development, wharves, and piers, creating a firm foundation for efficient business development and cargo operations.

The Americans largely concentrated on redeveloping the site of the original factories, where vacant lots were gradually developed, and Thirteen Factories Street regained its commercial connection with new restaurants and teahouses. A new steamer terminus was also constructed along with new offices of the Steam Navigation Company.

Shameen Island was, until the mid-nineteenth century, little more than a sand spit in the Pearl River. Stones from the two Barrier forts that were captured by the British in 1856 were used in construction of the embankment of the bund walls, and reclamation was carried out for the new Concession Area in 1859. A canal that became known as the "Creek" was incorporated, that effectively divided the reclaimed area from Shaki Street and the existing western suburbs, so that the island site was linked to the suburbs by two "gated" bridges. The new reclamation was formed by backfilling within the bund, with eighty percent of the cost borne by the British and the remainder by the French, so that land for the new concessions was apportioned in the same ratio.

The island was laid out in the form of a grid of lanes and avenues that provided ten blocks of land and eighty-two building sites with a bund promenade along the river frontage. The French Concession comprised a further twenty-four lots. The Imperial Maritime Customs Service, one of the first major institutional buildings, was set up at Honan in 1854—its Deputy Commissioner Robert Hart later became the

A copy of William Daniells late nineteenth-century painting of the hongs of Canton.

inspector general based in Peking. This contained a Customs Club that provided accommodation for trade officials and customs officers. Six lots on Shameen Island were given over to a consular complex while the remainder were put up for auction in 1862. The Island was subdivided into two main avenues aligned from east and west, with five intersecting north-south streets. This created an efficient layout of street blocks, with land alongside the bund reserved for recreational activities, including tennis facilities that are still in existence.

At first most of the lots, including the British consular complex, were occupied by simple constructions that were later redeveloped into grander, hipped-roof and classically styled buildings with arcaded verandahs. These formed continuous lines of elegant two-story structures alongside the two main avenues, that comprised consulates and company offices encircled by rows of banyan trees. At the rear of the compounds were kitchen gardens that supplied vegetables. The building types were unquestionably European in their design, adapted to the hot southern China climate, and formed models for use in other treaty ports. The first building to be constructed was Christ Church, possibly based on the Hawksmoor churches of eighteenth-century London, with a distinctive three-story tower above the entrance, along with an accompanying parsonage designed by Thomas Kingsmill on a site facing the central avenue.

Some of the early neo-classical two-story colonnaded buildings, including the British consulate, were architecturally derived from the earlier factory buildings but were subject to severe typhoons and were therefore short lived. A Canton Garden Fund was established by far-thinking residents in 1864, and the resulting landscape framework with lawns, recreation areas and avenues of trees, underscored its cultural disengagement from the city itself. In addition, a walled Japanese compound was located at the eastern end of the island. The northern edge was essentially defined by the narrow canal.

Both the British and French consuls continued for a time to live in the old walled city in order to maintain a political presence there. Municipal councils were formed to oversee security and the introduction of gas and electricity services, although the French concession was not occupied until the 1890s. For a short time there was even a dairy farm located in the British concession, along with stables for the horses that raced on the Honan racecourse.

The contrast between the Western settlements and the adjoining areas was pronounced. The major comment from overseas visitors, whose accommodation was improved by the development of the Shameen Hotel in 1888, seems to be that both the setting and the insular nature of the precinct reproduced, as exactly as possible, a pastoral country life. This appeared to fulfill all necessary requirements for a comfortable visitor experience without the need to engage with the nearby city at all. The boat dwellers appeared to be in accord with this as the canal quickly filled up with small Tanka craft.

The most important trading establishments were located on Front Avenue, overlooking the football ground, bowling green, and the tennis courts adjacent to the bund, of which the courts still remain. British, French, and Parsee merchants' business was conducted on the ground floor along with warehousing, and with residential uses above. However, ten of the sites became consulates, and these were joined by financial institutions including the Chartered Bank, Bank of Taiwan, the National City Bank of New York, the Banque de L'Indo China, and the Hong Kong and Shanghai Bank. In general, the architecture of company headquarters and consulate buildings, constructed in the 1920s to replace the older original structures, displayed similar but more elaborate characteristics and features—elaborate roof profiles, deep wrap-around verandahs, and a full range of pediments and columns. Because of the high water table, the lower floors were generally lifted above the adjoining pavements.

By the early part of the twentieth century, economic growth and massive building projects were beginning to change the face of the city, blurring the distinction between the Chinese and foreign business and residential areas. The burgeoning business climate led to the transformation of Shameen Island from predominantly one- and two-story houses to multi-story buildings. The first of these in 1905 was the Arnhold, Karberg & Co. building, having a four-story reinforced concrete structure, the first of its kind in China, with an electric elevator. It was designed with a rusticated facade at ground level and a neo-classical facade above with recessed verandahs.[93] This contained commercial, exhibition, and storage facilities at ground level, with offices and living accommodation above, together with a roof garden. The architects, Purnell and Paget went on to design other structures including the Imperial Maritime Customs staff quarters in the French Concession with its somewhat Victorian-baroque composition, and the Griffith Building of around 1906 with its classical facade and roof pediments.

A new German Consulate was erected on the site of the old building in 1906 although this was taken over for commercial purposes after the relocation of the Consulate in 1920. It adopted the arcaded rhythm of other adjoining structures, with decorative pediments and domed corner cupolas. The Hong Kong and Shanghai Bank Building built in 1920 on a strategic corner site, incorporated a simple classical arrangement of monumental columns and regularly spaced verandahs, with a high cupola on the shaved corner entrance acting as a local landmark. Other buildings built in the 1920s in a stylistically similar vein were offices for Anderson, Meyer and Co., the Chartered Bank of India, Australia and China, and the International Banking Corporation with its monumental ionic columns. The British consulate complex was entirely rebuilt after the severe flooding of 1915, and incorporated three residential wings, all integrated within a simple classical composition.

The location of the new concession area, now known as Shamian Island, was strategically appropriate, secured by bridges that could be used to restrict entrance, with safe anchorage for the new steam ships. To the north of Shamian Island were the Western Suburbs, with eighteen "wards" or urban quarters, set around narrow labyrinthine streets and specializing in particular items—blackwood furniture, ailment remedies, antiques, embroidery, and porcelain. Shops either occupied ground-floor space or extended into the narrow streets from the high enclosing walls of courtyard mansions belonging to wealthy Chinese merchants. Other streets such as Great Peace Street were dedicated to banking and money exchange.

Missionary enclaves were dispersed throughout the suburbs and comprised religious facilities, hospitals, and schools according to particular local needs and requirements. A combination of the Medical Missionary Society of China and the American Presbyterian Board jointly founded the Canton Hospital associated with the missionary compound. A further missionary compound was associated with the Gothic complex of the French Catholic cathedral. New groups of missionaries arrived after the turn of the century including the Church of England Missionary Society. While genuine religious converts were few and far between, the facilities provided under the auspices of missions helped to bring the different communities together, countering the climate of coercion through cross-cultural interaction.

For a time, gunboats from the Imperial Maritime Customs protected the concession area, and Chinese were not allowed onto the island unless they possessed a pass, and even then there was a 9 p.m. curfew. The street along the 900-meter northern edge was called Canal Street, now Shamian North Street, with Canal Road on the opposite bank where sampans were moored. Between these streets was a grand central avenue with five north-south streets forming a grid of lots within the two concessions. More than 100 years later, Henry Fok Ying-tung, a Hong Kong businessman who later became vice chairman of the National Committee of the Chinese People's Political Conference, orchestrated a joint venture with the Canton government to construct China's first international hotel, the White Swan, built in 1984 on new reclamation along the river frontage on the site of the old Deacon's Steps, which demarcated the steamship anchorage. Following its opening two days were set aside for all interested locals to visit and appreciate the beginning of the modern hotel industry in China.

e Catholic Church in the French
ncession area on Shamian
and.

The Guangdong customs was established in 1685 during the reign of Emperor Kangxi and was the earliest of its kind in China. The present imposing customs house, built in 1916, occupies a prominent position on the river frontage and acts as an identifying landmark. Along with an adjoining array of durable civic and commercial buildings, it establishes an embedded memory of the city along the Canton bund. It was declared a protected site for its historical value in 2006, and converted in the China Customs Museum.

The Inspectorate of Imperial Customs was established in 1881, and was, until its termination, administered with a high degree of efficiency, providing the state government with almost a quarter of its annual income. Coastal surveys were carried out, navigation charts drawn up, lighthouses built, ports were managed, and fleets of ships patrolled the coast. The Imperial Customs produced annual reports on trade, taxation, and transportation so that it became possible for the first time to track the precise movement of goods.

Progressive development of the system in many ways served to upgrade and modernize both administrative and supervisory procedures covering a wide spectrum of maritime activities including the production of hydrographic charts, navigation aids, and labor management. Above all it became a diplomatic avenue or a "community of interests" for Sino-foreign relations and set standards of incorrupt public service that replaced the tarnished tribute system of the past. It also established a watershed in the institutional acceptance of the foreign presence, and with it the desire to expand the port settlement—a state of affairs that was regularly exploited to demonstrate military superiority and intimidate local authorities. Some twenty years later, with China increasingly divided into areas of interest, necessitating more efficient modes of travel well beyond the ports, an active railway policy was again introduced by the Chinese government. The Peking to Tientsin line was capitalized by the British, the French built a line from Kunming to Hanoi, Germans built lines in Shandong, and the Belgians financed the Peking to Hankow railway. No individual power was allowed to create a monopoly.[94]

Following the Treaty of Peking, signed by Chinese representatives in 1887 the Western powers continued their support for the Qing government in recognition of the need for a strong central authority to protect trade and strengthen China against future internal rebellions. However, the thrust of economic reform was centered on revitalization of the old political order rather than on firm plans for expansion of financial, industrial, or trading infrastructure.

Treaty Port Expansion and Foreign Penetration

The treaty ports were, by the late nineteenth century, increasingly viewed as the vanguard of greater foreign penetration and influence in China. However, foreign export of commodities largely failed to find major markets. Sir Robert Hart commented in 1900 that "the Chinese have the best food in the world, rice; the best drink, tea; and the best clothing, cotton, silk and fur." It was therefore difficult for traders to put their fingers on a precise commodity that the Chinese were in real need of. Britain and France, the two chief Western powers, were not only looking to expand their trading empire beyond the treaty ports but were actively earmarking certain sections of the country in which to build infrastructure to mine for minerals and other raw materials. While Britain regarded the southern and eastern parts of China as their predominant trading domain linked to Hong Kong, the French stretched their influence in southwestern China, looking to consolidate their Indo-Chinese possessions in Laos and Vietnam. Certain ports therefore provided a convenient means of monitoring rival diplomatic and trading initiatives.

In terms of urbanization of coastal regions, the underlying agricultural and market economies were intertwined. Foreign trade clearly had an impact on the hinterland economy of the southern port cities, although the mercantile capital flows stemming from urbanization of port settlements did not necessarily enter the rural economy.[95] It did, however, lead to a strong commercial banking sector in the largest port cities, together with a ready market for imported consumer goods.[96]

Certain influential Chinese supported a policy of cooperation with foreign powers. Feng Gui-fen, a Qing dynasty scholar from Suzhou, produced a collection of essays in 1861 that formed the basis of the "Self-strengthening Movement." This discussed the importance of reform and modernization in financial, education, and foreign relations, notably accepting that it was no longer possible to return to an isolationist ideology while being adamant that Chinese society should remain fundamentally Confucian.[97] The advocated policy of self-strengthening or *ziqiang* was to utilize Western technology for defense, which led to the development of various arsenals for shipyards, arms, and ammunition factories. However, any ambition to evolve from *ziqiang* to *fuqiang* or "wealth and power" proved beyond the means of the fragile economy.[98] Only the merchant class, and in particular the compradors in the late nineteenth century, benefitted from increases in both home and foreign trade in terms of spin-off from the privileges granted to foreign firms. While the government subsidized certain industries, they also imposed controls that constrained the mobilization of capital and prevented the development of competition so that private investment tended to be put into foreign-owned enterprises. Legal and management expertise and the availability of banking services further enabled foreign business expansion, and in many ways simply extended bureaucratic power and control over the market.

The Chefoo Agreement in 1876 extended British influence and inland penetration. This marked a change in British policy toward concession areas, whereby land could now be rented directly from Chinese owners for building, making considerable savings to the British government on land formation and river protection.[99] It was perhaps also prompted by prudent political considerations given the far-flung nature of the new settlements. Canton in the south had flourishing business quarters, and regular steamer traffic that required almost constant protection from British gunboats to combat piracy.

Until 1883 a series of buffer states on China's western flank—Vietnam, Burma, Thailand, Nepal, and Laos—paid regular tribute to the emperor in exchange for China's protection. However, the Sino-French War ended in the renunciation of China's rights to Vietnam granting France the rights of a protectorate. This represented a further stage in the dismantling of China's empire as the influence of foreign powers grew through a sequence of unequal treaties. Similarly, the defeat to Japan in 1885 resulted in the loss of its protectorate over Korea. Britain annexed Burma in 1886 and opened up Tibet to foreign trade in 1893, and in the same year France occupied Laos. By this stage there were twenty-nine open ports, each with a customs office that brought revenue to China but was arguably of even greater value to foreign traders in terms of a "level playing field," as was the guarantee of personal and property rights through the principle of extraterritoriality over the settlements.

Taxes on commodities or *lijin* in the late nineteenth century tended to confound foreign traders, and to avoid this both foreign and Chinese merchants tended to cooperate in the movement of goods.[100] Commodities that required cheap and light transportation were regularly conveyed on Chinese lorchas, often flying a foreign flag of convenience. At the same time, British traders frequently used Chinese

The former British consulate, now housing the Foreign Exchange Bureau, was situated on a corner site with two distinct elevations, the side elevation accommodating an extravagant marble columned balcony, while the two-story frontage along the bund encompassed an open colonnade. The consulate itself, the rear of the compound, burn down in 1948.

vessels to transport opium. In the late nineteenth century some Chinese traders also chartered foreign vessels on a monthly basis because of their moderate tonnage, enabling them to avoid pirates and to settle duties at the native customs house. By these means, merchants were able to exchange products for goods native to other Asian environments—mangrove bark from the Malay Peninsula was a particular important commodity used to tan sails and fishnets; sandalwood was used for temple ceremonies; ebony in furniture making; and sampan wood for boat keels.[101]

Canton and southern cities enjoyed a remittance economy from emigrant Chinese workers that had a significant impact on the balance of trade. Commencing in 1846, a large number of Chinese emigrated from Canton in what became known as the "coolie trade" between China and the Spanish colonies of the West Indies and South America, orchestrated by Western plantation and shipping interests. Labor was sourced mainly from Canton and the surrounding area, with the majority being recruited from Nanhai, Shunde, and Panyu counties. The main destination was Spanish-controlled Cuba with almost 150,000 indentured emigrants. From 1857, Macao became a major port of embarkation, while Hong Kong became the main port for the more regulated emigration to America and Australia, generally financed by relatives from the home village or motivated by foreign recruiters and brokers who were not always well-intentioned, with inadequate on-board food and sanitary conditions that frequently led to death and disease.[102]

Undercurrents of Reform

Reformist thinking began to gather momentum during the 1880s, which included the expansion of trading connections, encouragement of private enterprise over bureaucratic control, and the reform of education and political change in the face of traditional structures.[103] This was generally supported by the merchant class in the large port cities that were developing their own political strategies. However, the imperial court was vulnerable and to a large extent impotent in the face of foreign influence. This was exacerbated by the Sino-Japanese War. The Treaty of Shimonoseki in April, 1895 forced China to make indemnity payments and concessions that included allowing steamship access to interior cities and Japanese investment in the open port cities. This signaled a new period of crisis that triggered a reconfiguration of imperialist expansion and penetration in China on the back of Western and Japanese financial and industrial strength. However, G. William Skinner identifies the Treaty as a turning point in China's urban development through its encouragement of mechanized industry in the major treaty ports and the initiation of railroad construction that transformed the development of urban coastal regions and their degree of commercialization.[104]

The terms of the Shimonoseki Treaty formed a catalyst to a political movement, known as "the hundred days" reform. Sun Yat-sen founded the short-lived *Xing Zhong-hui* or "Revive China Society" as part of a strategy to overthrow the Qing dynasty but was forced to flee China the following year. The 1,300 scholars who had been gathered in Peking for the imperial examination sent a memorial to the emperor setting out various proposals for reform including a reorganization of national monetary and banking systems, the introduction of a modern educational system, a concentration on modern science and technology, and elected political councils at local and national levels. This led to further reformist ideas and

A distinguished neo-classical building with prominent domed corner cupolas was originally built for the German Consul-General in 1906. After World War I it served as the consulate of the Netherlands before being sold to the Asiatic Petroleum Company.

action. A Society for the Study of Self-strengthening or *Qiangxuehui,* attracted an intellectual following before being closed down, and a number of new reformist journals and newspapers spread the message around the cities to activists and students.[105]

One of the more interesting aspects was a new interpretation of Confucianism from a Cantonese student Kang Yau-wei that purported to show that ancient texts, on which the long-held philosophical basis of society had evolved, was not to perpetuate an unchangeable order but to evoke constant adaptation and innovation as a basis on which to facilitate political change. The "new text movement" pursued a reinterpretation of China's classical traditions upon which Confucianism had been based, and provided a reformed school of thought that was considered more appropriate for the times.[106] This formed an attempt to link Confucian ideology with constitutional change, setting a path toward a national assembly. It essentially failed through lack of popular support, but possibly helped to instill into the minds of the most determined reformers that political change could only happen through revolution. Its most immediate impact was a series of foreign expansionist initiatives that began to provoke a reaction against foreigners within the treaty ports.

A large turret forms a landmark corner on the old Hong Kong and Shanghai Bank building, constructed in 1897 at Number 24, South Shamian Street.

The Boxer Rebellion

The "Hundred Days" reform arose in the midst of great uncertainty as to the prevailing intrigue that permeated the Grand Council and senior officials, coupled with ideas generated from a group of activist scholars—the *ming-shih*—who argued, somewhat superficially, for change, including proposals that China should become a constitutional monarchy. In the wake of the disavowed reform movement, with the empress dowager having assumed the regency, the Chinese court was in disarray with various factions representing serious ideological differences.

These events happened just at the time when an increasing Western influence was beginning to arouse greater demands among the urban population for political change, with the new merchant classes experiencing a growing alienation from the introverted and self-serving state machinery. By the late nineteenth century the growth of treaty ports had fashioned both physical and social change. In Canton, new street patterns and Western-style buildings had begun to formalize the urban structure of the settlements, with gas lighting and water supply, while new trading routes subscribed to the success of commercial, banking, and industrial enterprises. This is turn created new professional areas such as law, education, publishing, and journalism that encouraged independent writers and even revolutionary thinkers. However, foreign technology, an influx of overseas goods and the advent of steamships and railways, had put many people out of work, and a series of natural disasters and economic upheavals had generated significant anti-foreign sentiment. This was vaguely directed at Christian converts, reinforced by a superstitious distrust of missionaries, many of whom had penetrated well into the interior of China and frequently showed themselves at odds with traditional beliefs. Rural communities were alienated in this way just at a time when tax levies were being increased to make up the national deficit following the Taiping Rebellion.

The Boxer Rebellion began in Shandong—a poor and over-populated province—by a group calling themselves *yihe quan* ("the Righteous and Harmonious Fists") from their practice of martial arts and shamanism.[107] The "Spirit Boxers" represented a spontaneous and loosely organized phenomenon that comprised impoverished landlords, young villagers, and farmers who took up arms largely to protect their property, and were incorporated into the elusive movement through indoctrination and ritual.

Much about the brief but catalytic Boxer Rebellion was clothed in misinformation and misunderstanding on both sides. The Boxers blamed foreign occupation for the afflictions suffered by China over the previous fifty years, and received support from like-minded groups who were hostile to the recent modernizations. The Western powers on their part were alarmed that the weak Qing dynasty was vulnerable, putting at risk their own interests. The Boxer affair was manipulated by military commanders within the Manchu "Ironhat" regime as a vague strategy for removal of foreign influences through a campaign of deliberate misinformation. Foreign powers took little heed of the escalating crisis, and failed to interpret events intelligently, while allied commanders took full advantage of a power vacuum at the Qing court and exploited the situation to seize as much territory as possible.

The threat to foreigners was admittedly real, particularly to those occupying remote mission stations in the northern provinces during the initial uprising. On the part of the Qing regime, there were faltering views as to whether to support the Boxers with Imperial troops, or whether to reign in the uprising that ended almost as quickly as it started. In the end, foreigners were subject to a blockade in the besieged Peking legation quarter. Witness accounts suggest that Chinese forces could have overwhelmed the foreign legation at almost any time, and the fact that only minimal fire power was deployed indicated the presence of a restraining hand in the background, although by the end of the three-month siege two hundred foreigners had been killed or wounded.[108] The several thousand Chinese Christians sheltering in a carefully segregated adjoining site and in the nearby Peitang Cathedral during the siege fared worst of all, with hundreds killed or injured. The number of Boxers and Imperial troops who perished was many times that number.

The rising prompted an international intervention that, scarcely surprisingly, ignited even greater hostility on the part of China. The seven allied countries of Britain, France, Germany, czarist Russia, the United States, Italy, and Austria-Hungary, together with Japanese naval forces, sent a force of more than sixteen thousand men and in June 1900 captured the Taku Forts outside Tientsin along the Hai River, and on August 14 entered and pillaged Peking and the surrounding countryside. The emperor, empress dowager, and the court fled the city before troops entered and looted the Forbidden City, lake palaces, and imperial temples of virtually everything of value, including the destruction of the Hanlin Library, which contained the last remaining copy of the *Yung Lo Ta Tien*—an 11,000-volume compendium of Chinese knowledge and literature assembled in the Ming dynasty.[109]

Imperial court policy fluctuated according to a sequence of events that were often out of control and where it was difficult at any time to grasp the overall picture due to poor communications and a possible reluctance on the part of minor officials to transmit bad news. This was also linked, particularly on the allied side, to flagrant opportunism. While there was probably initial support for the Boxer's anti-foreign stance on the part of the Imperial court, this was also just as much to do with deflecting opposition to the dynasty itself. Officials in charge of the southern and eastern provinces took a more pragmatic stance and discreetly avoided any engagement with allied forces. The attack on the Taku forts by foreign warships would, in almost any circumstances, have been interpreted as an act of war. On the foreign side there was also a failure to adequately anticipate the uprising or to comprehend the speed at which events escalated beyond their control, so that their later definition of "relief force" was almost certainly construed by the Imperial court as an "invasion force."[110]

The rebellion represented a watershed in modern Chinese history and acted as a prelude to new reforms and political change. Just as the Boxer episode itself remains swathed in confusion, the historical legacy came to be associated with both anti-foreign and anti-Manchu patriotism that resonated through the revolutionary events of the twentieth century. Much of the news that came out of China to the West during this time was from an entirely one-sided perspective, attributed largely to sources that are now discredited: George Morrison, the Peking correspondent of the *Times* of London who wrote largely fictionalized accounts for the paper; and Edmond Backhouse, a flawed linguist and commentator who was later exposed as a forger. Both unfairly attributed the problems that brought an end to the Qing dynasty to the aging empress dowager.[111] There is no doubt that facts surrounding the event were manipulated by allied interests to justify the invasion and the crippling demands that were later made by the allies.[112] The most immediate result was to hasten the end of the dynasty, and to bring about reforms that had a significant impact on development of the port cities.

The "Boxer Protocol" imposed on China in the aftermath amounted to a massive indemnity to be paid to the invading powers in instalments, while ten foreign powers were awarded the right to station garrisons of soldiers in Peking to guard their legations. Article XI of the Protocol stated that amendments to the commercial treaties favorable to foreign governments had to be negotiated and facilitated. This resulted in enforced foreign loans for such things as railway construction, in order to facilitate the export of Chinese mineral resources and import of goods to serve the strategic interests of foreign "investors" such as the Chinese Engineering and Mining Company of London who paid nothing for the shares and debentures as China's trade balance sank deeper into debt.

The centenary of the rebellion in 2000 was adjudged by both Chinese and Western governments as too sensitive to mark.[113] The iron bell that was pillaged from the Dagu Fort, which guarded the route from the Bohai Sea to Beijing, was ceremoniously returned to China in June 2005 providing at least some closure to this unfortunate and unnecessary event.

Chapter 5

An Emerging Modernism

ort cities became the centers of foreign settlement and trade in China, opening up parts of the country to Western cultural influence just as much as they expanded investment and economic horizons. In a more elusive way, the nature of new "gateways" both into and out of China, transformed attitudes to modernization. Foreign settlement areas, which generally formed separate but planned extensions to established city structures, offered an alternative urbanism outside hidebound tradition and state control. New instruments of change and accompanying institutional adjustments were virtually inevitable in shaping the role of port cities within a rapidly evolving internationalism. This opened the door to investment in the city, and propelled new economic and social trajectories.

The growing development of international trade and the economic influence of the foreign concession areas established both the need and to some extent the model for urban land administration to satisfy emerging modes of property development. The social reform movement promulgated a number of projects in Canton, the chief one being a 1907 city expansion plan that extended the bund district from the western city to the new Canton-Kowloon railway station and the adjoining eastern suburbs, along with the new Honam District to the south, linked by bridges across the Pearl River. While this did not satisfactorily resolve many of the prevailing urban problems, it initiated a ready basis for more comprehensive and ambitious planning proposals. In common with all the main treaty ports, significant changes followed the formation of the new Republic in 1912. In a similar way to Shanghai, the bund along the Pearl River frontage in Canton acted to control flooding, but also initiated investment in new multi-story structures. After a fire had destroyed a number of public buildings, the Customs House was built in 1916 with steamer berths demarcated along the foreshore.

While cities in the West were beginning to be shaped and expanded through a combination of benevolent social ideals, economic investment, and the incorporation of public health provisions that called for controls over layouts and infrastructure, in China's major treaty port cities commodification of the land market effectively established a basis for coordinated and market-led urban development. The system of ownership deeds based on precise land surveys not only introduced clarity in land transactions but enabled urban infrastructure to be properly implemented under new administrative arrangements.

This in turn allowed foreign concessions in many of the port cities to dominate the urbanization process, creating "model" municipal enclaves and stimulating forms of unified city planning.

The responsiveness of Canton to new ideas and interventions partly represented the historical context of the city as conveniently distant from the Qing government in Beijing, while being almost uniquely exposed to late nineteenth and early twentieth century European intellectual reform movements via its long-time trading network. The city's initial platform was the new Republican national restructuring program. Canton had, through much of the nineteenth century, been the principal gateway into China, which was consolidated by its trading relationship with the Crown Colony of Hong Kong and through this with the international community. The newly established Nationalist government briefly made Canton its first capital prior to Nanking, reflecting its relative independence from other foreign concessions. This allowed bold plans to be initiated by the municipality through top-down planning. Given that Western planning ideas of the period could not be wholly transplanted into a Chinese city, their interpretation within Canton's unique context reflected its distinctive political, social, and physical interfaces. This partly involved equating a forceful and ambitious political agenda with new regulatory and institutional regimes so that urban reconfiguration emerged as the successful outcome of optimal land management, innovative urban design, and the resolution of prevailing development problems.[114]

Wider forms of urbanization also began to emanate from the military and political power bases in Canton, Shanghai, and Nanking in accordance with the "New Life Movement," a government-led civic movement in the 1930s under the guidance of Chiang Kai-shek, which aimed to promote cultural reform based on the Confucian ethic of morality as a unifying ideology reflecting prevailing social and political forces.

With American and European trained urban planners and architects returning to China at this time, the new municipal administration in Canton adopted many idealistic social principles that framed a new reform agenda, aimed at rationalizing a new planning approach around improved housing, transportation, and open space. New administrative residential development areas were connected by a hierarchical layout of major avenues and streets that in turn facilitated conditions for redevelopment of older urban quarters. The administrative structure largely followed the American form of city government with publicly elected council members, so planning intervention had to be supported by a range of stakeholders.[115] This in turn demanded new forms of city management and public works, of which road building and street widening formed a key part. The labyrinth of narrow lanes were in many cases replaced with streets lined with shophouses that formed continuous active frontages. The colonnaded ground level provided covered pavement and display areas for the shops, with two or more projecting storys above, combining Western neo-classicist styles with traditional Chinese building features and ornamentation.

The city council was first established in 1918, and constituted various departments including finance, construction, and land registration. The city also became officially named Guangzhou and in 1925 became the first city in China to be declared a "municipality" under the Nationalist government. The organizational structure of the Public Works Bureau provided for survey, design, and construction, which together subscribed to a detailed planning framework for the various administrative zones and sub-divisions in the city and helped to both determine land values and allocate resources. Functional zoning also helped to separate incompatible uses and prevent overcrowding in older areas with their concentrations of manufacturing and poor living conditions. New land administration allowed for a clear distinction between municipal and private land so that compensation could be paid for necessary acquisition, while an effective land market and acknowledged conditions of sale paved the way for systematic planning initiatives.

Cheng Tien-tow, the American-trained director of the Public Works Bureau, was largely responsible for installing new paved roads and dismantling the 800-year-old perimeter wall that extended

some ten kilometers around the old city in order to alleviate traffic conditions.[116] Selected narrow streets were opened up based on their ability to improve traffic circulation, while in parts of the city the ancient fine-grained narrow street pattern based on "gated" enclaves was retained. This was a symbolic turning point toward a new planning-led transformation of the city carried out in phases. In 1920 Sun Ke, the son of Sun Yat-sen, who had studied city planning in Los Angeles and New York, was appointed mayor, along with six city commissioners, several of whom had studied municipal government in the USA. Within several years the city limits had been extended from 9 to 69 square miles, with construction material from the dismantled city wall re-used to construct wide roads in the form of a broad grid layout. The various yamens were demolished and transformed into urban parks, including what is now the central People's Park.

At the heart of the city plan was a civic administrative district designed in 1921 as a formal composition of government offices and public assembly halls set around a central park connected with the riverfront on a north-south axis. The American planner Henry Murphy was invited by Sun Ke to assist with the design of this complex, introducing a formal and symbolic arrangement of civic buildings. Murphy, in a similar way to Edwin Lyutens in New Delhi, attempted to reconcile established cultural and architectural traditions with both rationalized construction techniques and the neo-classical forms that had gained popularity in the West for major public buildings. Thus, the developing city diverged dramatically from the rigid symmetry associated with the old city toward a more baroque notion of long vistas and main avenues radiating from prominent monuments. In this sense, Western design influences infiltrated rather than overwhelmed the city core. Educational campuses proved the best context for an architectural synthesis of Chinese and Western styles. These were notably at Lingnan University by Charles Stoughton, Henry Murphy, Warren Powers Land, and other American contributors. Buildings were of reinforced concrete with red brick cladding, low tiled roofs, deep verandahs, and ornamentation including Chinese tile panels. By the late 1930s Canton, along with Shanghai, represented the most cosmopolitan of all Chinese cities. Canton had in various ways produced certain vernacular typologies—the shophouse street with colonnaded walkways, and certain public buildings that married Western neo-classicism with Chinese architectural elements such as the Dongshan University Campus, Sun Yat-sen Memorial Hall, and Zhongshan Library.

The 1932 master plan for the city retained the civic center layout, along with an extensive primary road grid dividing the city into 30 districts and around 300 street blocks. The plan was intended to serve as an effective blueprint for the regulation of land, the management of urban growth, and the restructuring of the dense inner-city areas. New urban design initiatives along with land use zoning as a basis for development control were based on New York's Zoning Act of 1916,[117] but also reflected new urban layout mechanisms in Hong Kong. This facilitated an ordered program of growth, improved transport, and circulation corridors, and better access to public amenities. An accompanying Three-Year Plan provided for a public works program to be implemented in phases that included new waterfront reclamation along the Pearl River, bridge construction, improvement to the navigation channel and the construction of public buildings and recreation facilities. Along the Bund, new department stores featured the first multi-use high rise structures housing combinations of restaurants, cinemas and roof gardens, made accessible by new electric lifts.

Two methods were used to reconfigure urban street blocks in conjunction with road widening, in order to deal effectively with benefits that accrued to the regularizing of block frontages and the establishment of a more uniform streetscape with direct road access. The first method was through land aggregation whereby both construction costs and benefits from increased land value would be shared by lot owners in accordance with their land holdings. The second method involved land resumption through which the municipal government acquired land for restructuring, with lots leased to developers in order to achieve a more functionally efficient layout.[118] While these approaches were time consuming and often open to land speculation, they largely succeeded in rationalizing much of the older urban districts while creating a framework for new and continuous shophouse and commercial frontage. At the same time, restructuring was assisted by updated forms of land administration and building bylaws that regulated both construction and urban form, including the design of public streets, pavements, tree planting, and drainage works.

The design definition of older streets can be observed today in conserved and upgraded quarters, where uniformity of streetscape in terms of height and connectivity is alleviated by the different detailed characteristics of individual buildings, and where renovated structures house a variety of commercial uses at ground level, with residential functions above. Regulations also required that shop-houses fronting streets with a width of not less than 24 meters required a permit in order to integrate a covered ground floor colonnade—a characteristic known as *qilou* that spread to other port cities.

The result of these systematic planning initiatives was that rationalization of the urban framework, brought about through a combination of regulatory controls and guidelines, produced a street-oriented development pattern with clearly delineated urban blocks flanked by new commercial and residential typologies. The urban structure proved extremely robust, open to various forms of adaptation rather than redevelopment, and responsive to prevailing market imperatives.

Through the 1930s, before the new wave of building was effectively cut short by war, many ambitious and potentially ground-breaking designs were left only half realized while others suffered damage or became radically modified through occupation by invading forces. Surviving buildings of the period represent an increasing simplification of design form and a gradual elimination of decorative devices or ornamentation. While they reflect an efficient functionality, like many European buildings of the same period, they embody a preliminary level of austerity that became projected onto some of the post-1949 structures, particularly public buildings and factories carried out under the guidance of Soviet advisers.

Canton's city-building process was therefore quite distinct from the concession area model that was restricted to Shamian Island. This represented a comprehensive program of urban planning initiatives backed up by clear municipal land management and administration programs that in combination helped to restructure and modernize the city. In the process it created new development value and associated real estate opportunities as a basis for urban upgrading, growth, and expansion. The street-oriented pattern and shaping of spaces has contributed to the present liveliness and contrast in the public realm, and at least to some extent, the continuation of urban trades and traditions in the city.

A New Urbanism

From the turn of the twentieth century there was progressive social and political change in southern China. By the 1920s Canton had become the most prosperous city in the country, and foreign investment was accompanied by large-scale urban development and regeneration. Expanding multinational commercial and institutional enterprises gave rise to extensive building programs, just as they did in other major treaty ports, and new forms of architecture began to transform the city's skyline and its river frontages. British business and banking groups with a firm foothold in Hong Kong and other parts of Asia extended their portfolios of imposing but often eclectic Victorian and Edwardian buildings

to Canton. These were adapted for different climatic conditions, some of them built by Hong Kong
contractors in brick and stone—encompassing the characteristic verandah—wrapped designs of two
and three storys. However, a new modernism was becoming apparent in the city.

The process of urbanization was markedly accelerated during the Republican period. By the mid-
1920s Canton had a population in excess of one million people, reflecting a new urban affluence and
a marked socio-cultural relationship between East and West, exhibited through its residue of commercial and residential buildings. Western architectural design, as in other bourgeoning treaty ports,
was directed toward a range of public buildings, utility services, and infrastructure projects. Economic
progress was buttressed by an acceptance of change that helped to transform Canton into a diverse
and cosmopolitan center of trade where old customs were reconciled with new ideas. It was not that
Western design interpretation outstripped its Chinese counterpart, which had an older and equally
distinguished past, but more that its material progress on the back of industrialization, manufacturing, and Western city building programs in the twentieth century had necessitated a more ambitious
and resolute approach to building construction as it entered the final decades of imperialism.

Modernism in terms of Chinese urban design is not redolent of any unified theory, but an approach that evolved from both a long tradition and borrowed style—the first the result of a rich architectural history, the second through foreign influences that imposed an indelible architectural stamp on early twentieth-century Chinese urbanism. The notion of impermanence that characterizes Confucianism arguably inhibited the progress that might have been expected to accompany the revolutionary changes that embodied a strong Western influence. This is not to assume that the influence was all one way, however. From the eighteenth century, European society had shown a keen interest in the aesthetics of Chinese culture, art, science, and design.

On Shamian Island new buildings included the Butterfield & Swire residential block, the Imperial Maritime Customs staff quarters, and the German consulate building with its distinctive baroque roof turrets. The Hong Kong and Shanghai Bank building designed in a restrained Beaux Arts style with a distinctively chamfered corner entrance, and crowned by a domed cupola, was completed in 1920. Imaginative neo-classical interpretations still survived in the offices of the Anderson, Meyer & Co building, the International Banking Corporation building and the new British consular complex, all constructed in the 1920s.

New planning and design initiatives were introduced to meet localized needs and demands, but also arose in a responsive way through forms of cooperation and joint learning. Modernism was introduced cautiously and incrementally into the expanding port cities, but only partially through the prevailing concession area architecture that tended to reflect the insistent neo-classical interpretations that can be observed on Shamian Island. However, Canton and other port cities were becoming laboratories for an evolving range of architectural forms that mutated through a sometimes-irrational fusion of styles in response to an inspired concoction of early modernist influences, heavily determined by the idiosyncratic characteristics of their predominant national concession holding. This does not connote a direct link with specific treaty port development styles or constraints, which were many and varied, but indirectly there were several contributory factors to the new modernism: the inspiration of young Chinese architects in seeking a new architectural language that might personify the revolutionary changes after 1912; the emerging emphasis on design theory, through expanding cultural and educational links with Europe and the United States, rather than the craft traditions associated with traditional Chinese architecture; and the arrival of architectural practitioners from the West who sought to apply new design approaches and structural advances to the abundant commercial and residential opportunities.

A significant factor in this was the Boxer Protocol, with China agreeing to pay some 450 million taels of silver in reparation. The "Boxer Indemnity," as it became known, was partly utilized by the United States, and to a lesser extent by Britain, for education funds to facilitate overseas study by Chinese students in some of the most important universities, and at the same time financed new institutions of higher education in China. A large number of students from China went to the University of Pennsylvania and Columbia to study architecture or engineering and absorbed the early stirring of Beaux Arts classicism and international modernism. This indirectly fostered a familiarization with the first modern skyscraper designs and technology that were transforming American cities such as New York and Chicago and led to a new architectural professionalism in China. This had a considerable impact on the way architecture and urban design were both practiced and regulated.

Western religious groups, possibly responding to a perception that conversion to Christianity was achieving less than anticipated results, began to concentrate on more secular forms of education through new schools and colleges funded by donations. As many philanthropic donations came from America, architects from the country were generally employed to carry out design work. The Canton Christian College evolved into Lingnan University with a campus layout designed by Charles W. Stoughton, William Powers Laird, and J. R. Edmunds in 1918 at Honglok on Honan. Some of this was distinctly Arts and Crafts in nature, which invoked a synthesis of both classical and Chinese elements. The campus later became Zhongshan University. The later architecture of Henry K. Murphy in the 1930s was more restrained in its output reflecting the increasingly ecumenical nature of missionary organizations, together with international social and educational bodies such as the YMCA and YWCA.

A new spirit of patriotism coalesced with a denunciation of entrenched doctrines and an embracing of new cultural ideologies. These reflected a new society that embodied a suddenly flourishing preoccupation with burgeoning artistic and architectural movements that reflected contemporary Western models. In its capacity to form a transition from past doctrines, this sought to reconcile tradition with a new order that embraced the arts, sciences, and cultural and political theory. Official attempts were made to re-engage younger members of society with the city's history and cultural roots, and in 1934 the Confucian classics were introduced in schools as compulsory subjects. In this sense the Treaty Ports began to reflect the building and technological advances that were prevalent in the West, but at the same time absorbed local cultural traditions. Similarly, the engineering feats associated with land formation, telegraph installation, road and railway building, were creating an expanding infrastructure of connections and communications that went well beyond the spatial boundaries of the concession areas. Initial service installations did not always run smoothly, however—the first telegraph line was torn down by villagers who feared its disturbance to their *feng shui*.

Industrial growth, commensurate with the escalation in construction activity during the late nineteenth and early twentieth centuries shaped the evolving modernism through the emergence of essentially new building types, structural systems and materials. This reflected a combination of architectural and engineering skills, but also the practical skills and experience of Chinese builders and craftsmen. The first cement factory was opened in 1882 at Qinzhou, while steel was produced for the first time in 1894 at the Hanyang steel works.[119] The right to participate in industrial production signaled not merely an infusion of foreign investment and impact of Western machinery, but also the introduction of experienced management skills. It also led directly to a proliferation of industrial plants, warehouses, and utility buildings that began to constitute a totally new and different urban landscape. The use of steel and reinforced concrete began to be used on taller and more

anton Street from 1920 shows
'ou arcaded typologies that
fine the commercial edges.
e upper floors encompass Art
eco styles reflecting Treaty Port
chitectural typologies with
ained glass windows.

The Tai Sun Building, a neighboring structure to the customs house, w built in the early twentieth century, and was the first tall building in Canton. It originally incorporated a modern hotel and department sto with a roof garden.

complicated structures, with designs that effectively marked a transition from the "compradoric" style of the early concession area buildings toward the type of structures that were then being erected in European and American cities, and in many parts of the British Empire.

In Canton the modernization of the city began with the construction of the new Changdi district along the northern riverfront, completed in 1914. This coincided with the large-scale restructuring of the city, and the removal of the remaining city walls. Between 1910 and 1935 this provided the opportunity to install an urban hierarchy of roads to contain motorized transport, including the escalation in private car ownership, the installation of a new electric tramway, and a bus system. During this period, returning Chinese graduates played a leading role in both city administration and city building. While this reflected a certain Western symbolism, the architecture represented something of the international life of the city itself in the late 1920s and early 1930s, emphasized by the eight-story New Asia Hotel and the fifteen-story Ai-Ch'un Building. A number of foreign companies were also involved in construction projects. The Zhujang Bridge was the first to span the Pearl River between the revitalized old city and Honan, and by the mid-1930s 200 buses were in operation. New railway connections included the Canton-Hankou Railway, and the Canton-Kowloon Railway between the city and the Tsim Sha Tsui harbor front in Hong Kong, utilizing both Western and Chinese technology. This promoted a rapid growth in population.

The amalgam of new stylistic forms and transposed typologies designed by foreign or foreign-trained architects created a modernist contrast with authentic Chinese antecedents or cultural traditions. Major buildings still exhibited strong classical characteristics through a range of expressive structures that drew on a wide selection of references. Many architectural students studied in Japan, France, Britain, and Germany in the years before the Second World War and drew on design typologies rich in the spirited design theories of the Bauhaus. A number of architects focused on attempts to fuse traditional Chinese architectural forms and features or *zhongguo guyou zhi xingshi* with modern materials and construction technology—known as *ti-yong* (which translates into a literal invocation of a multi-cultural interpretation). As a result, in some cases the emerging architectural language reached unprecedented levels of flamboyance and complexity.

At one level, buildings displayed different permutations of classical features—pediments, columned porticos, and generally symmetrical facades—but with perhaps one carefully circumscribed feature that puts it in a markedly Chinese context, such as the large floating Chinese roofs that establish the overriding character that might or might not display elements of subtly configured Chinese decoration. At a more extravagantly articulated level are the inspiring block forms of Jimei University, a combination of several colleges founded by the philanthropist Tan Kah Kee in 1913 in Amoy that carried the east-west architectural fusion into an expressive and multi-cultural experience.

The growth and regeneration of Canton and other large cities in the 1930s can be directly linked to the institutional integration of architectural thinking, not merely as a design discipline but one concerned with city planning and urban design. The Chinese Society of Architects established in 1927 stated that one of their objectives was "to render support to the public authorities

in their civic developments and improvement."[120] This was given a further boost by two journals published from the early 1930s, the first *Jian Zhu Yue Kan* ("The Builder") and the second *Zhang Guo Jian Zhu* ("The Chinese Architect"), which established mouthpieces for the emerging profession, and a platform for new and groundbreaking projects.

The reshaping of the city in the years up until the Japanese occupation and the Second World War was heavily influenced by the prevailing functional precepts of American urban development. These were introduced largely through American-trained Chinese municipal planners and advisers during the republican period.[121] The third decade of the twentieth century was a time of transformation, when cities were becoming increasingly industrialized, with an accompanying imperative to make an increasing intensity of development functionally efficient, through wider streets, transportation networks, engineering infrastructure and zoned urban quarters. The loss of traditional imperial authority accompanied by new administrative and institutional imperatives for "national reconstruction," was marked by city-building and regeneration principles, honed in the industrializing conurbations that led to an accelerated program of urban renewal.

As Chinese builders and craftsmen became familiar with the prevailing styles and building materials, the more a mix of Imperialism and modernism with paired-back decoration was applied to landmark civic and institutional buildings in Canton, systematically fashioned from stone and granite such as the Customs House and equally statuesque Post Office.

A consistent characteristic of 1930s urbanism in Canton was, for the time, the relatively high residential density that reflected the periodic influx of refugees from political turmoil in other parts of the country. Low-rise and compact forms of housing began to emerge as a matrix of two-story *li-long* and three- to four-story *t'ang lau* terraces with their interconnected components of narrow lanes, elaborate entrance gates, and small courtyards. At the same time, tall apartment blocks began to permeate older parts of the city, reflecting massively escalating land values. As real estate was widely perceived as the best form of investment, and benefited from already tested forms of steel frame and reinforced concrete construction, this made taller building cost-effective, with the ability to create entirely new living and environmental patterns.

A decorative but subtle vocabulary related to modernist buildings was needed to represent the style of the time to avoid becoming mere ornament. Visual and symbolic patterns can both communicate and elaborate character in a way that is meaningful to the public realm, but in purposely introducing a fusion of modernist fabricated forms with vernacular or "craft" elements this inevitably raises the issue of architectural integrity, however ingenious the solution. It must also be said that, by the same token, the unadorned modernist building invites little cultural dialogue with the urban place other than through spatial articulation.

It is perhaps no coincidence that the typological convergence of Western and Chinese features outside the Lingnan tradition were associated mainly with civic and university buildings that embody culturally symbolic values, while the appropriation of more restrained neo-classical forms for banks during this period was largely adopted as a trademark for stolid commercial sobriety. A combination of stylistic forms became, for a time, metaphors for the new society, but the forces for architectural change remained insistent.

During the Republican years under Sun Yat-sen and during the Cultural Revolution a number of temples and other Buddhist structures were either converted for other uses or demolished. Many have now been restored or reconstructed. The five-storied Zhenhai Lou was restored in 1928 and now forms the city's history museum.

The Dongshan Model Neighborhood

A number of new suburban residential estates were developed that remain as low-rise neighborhoods within the city fabric. At this stage of development, Canton was divided into four sectors. To the north was the administrative area that contained the houses of senior government officials; to the south was the Haizhu industrial district; to the east was the industrial and low-cost housing area, and in the eastern suburbs was Dongshan. This reflected the reservation of most land within the alignment of the old city wall for government use. The plan for the "model district" of Dongshan was orchestrated by Western missionaries who settled in the area because it was the only one where land could be purchased outright. Both the internalized local road system and residential designs drew on Western garden city typologies, in contrast to the more rigid layout of villa developments along the urban boulevards in Shanghai's concession areas. The neighborhood unit model popularized by Clarence Perry in the United States that located residential development within walking distance of communal open space, schools, hospitals, and public amenities was adapted through layouts that allowed the auction of residential lots to fund the integration of public parkland, landscape, and service infrastructure. In order to expedite such developments, the Municipal Authority resumed private land where necessary, but

allowed for the conservation and integration of historical features. Guidelines were produced in order to regulate both planning and design including building setbacks, with a hierarchy of local access and distributor roads that framed the configuration of individual sites.

Centrally located public amenities included schools, library, public assembly hall, and recreation facilities together with local services. Purchasers of lots were offered tax incentives to complete construction within a stipulated period. Road construction was financed by a levy on residential owners, and all streets incorporated tree planting and pavement. The various road configurations created a range of layout conditions, and the Public Works Bureau established a template for four house designs to ensure a degree of architectural consistency. While the layout reflected a traditional demarcation between public and private space employed in courtyard housing, with a clear transition of approach and entrance conditions, the house types were essentially Western in character. In a similar way to the garden city ideal prevalent in England and the neighborhood unit developments in the United States, the concept established a paradigm for residential area planning set around a permeable street network. The "garden" suburb as a whole purposely contrasted with the dense development patterns of inner urban districts in terms of its spatial setting, infrastructure and amenity. Until the late 1930s this provided a model for new residential planning in Canton including the Xichun area with a more rationalized layout for low-cost housing. Dongshan retains its characteristic residential profile as a well maintained garden enclave within the city.

The neighborhood was planned as an almost self-contained suburb that attracted returning overseas Chinese after World War I to fulfill Western and local middle class housing requirements for two- and three-story garden villas. It was inaugurated in 1927 and covered around 90 acres. The range of sub-divisions catered for a number of residential types that included villas, townhouses, semi-detached units, and low-rise apartment complexes on what were once rice paddies, establishing a strong local identity that still survives as an exemplary residential model from the 1920s and 1930s. The area became the short-term home for several prominent people who played a major role in the history of modern China, and for a time contained the provincial headquarters of the CCP.

Civic Design

A number of initiatives helped to foster a new civic awareness, but by the 1930s Canton was a city that also personified the spirit of revolution. To an extent this reflected a series of symbolic monuments that were strategically placed throughout the city. The first of these was the Sun Yat-sen Monument, situated on top of a hill in Yuexiu District on the site of a demolished temple, and visible from most parts of the city. In addition, the Sun Yat-sen or Zhongshan Memorial Hall was completed in 1931 on the site of Guangzhou's presidential palace in the foothills of Yuexiu Mountain, with a statue later erected in front of the main entrance.

Bronze statues of Republican revolutionaries were installed in public parks that highlighted the political status of the city. Other symbolic edifices to modernity included the palatial Canton Municipal Government office complex influenced by modernist principles, widened "model" carriageways, and two new iron bridges across the Pearl River—the first of their kind in China. Between 1922 and 1934 ten public parks were built, influenced by recent city planning innovations in Europe and the United States as places of urban recreation, bringing the benefits of the countryside to serve the city. This acted to improve the environment of the crowded city but also expressed the city's transformative energy.

By the mid-1930s there was a proliferation of Western buildings in Canton, reflecting both their stylistic predecessors in Hong Kong and the new Western-influenced commercial buildings, constructed with Chinese capital, particularly the array of tall blocks along the Pearl River waterfront. While older imperial government buildings tended to be hidden behind high walls, the privatized commercial skyline broadcast a modern business expression of wealth and prestige.[122] Multi-story buildings began to proliferate in the 1930s, in part reflecting the massing of low-rise structures. High-rise buildings for offices, hotels, and department stores not only symbolized design technology, but the incorporation of urban archetypes associated with Western cities, which created

Li Garden was built by an Overseas Chinese from America, Xie Wei Li, and completed in 1936. Its architecture and landscape are arranged as clusters of mansions situated around gardens. It is based on the Grand View Garden depicted in *The Dream of the Red Chamber*, and incorporates ponds, a flower pavilion, and abundant tree planting that embellish the layout with rich foliage. The mansion area consists of six estates and two Diaolou with Western and Chinese architectural features, along with expressive calligraphy and murals. The principal structure is the Panli Building, built in 1926 and characterized by its dominant Chinese roof style and cornice brackets, with western window and door details offset on the balconies by classical columns. Its interior incorporates Italian terrazzo floors and oriental ceilings. The plaster decorations and camphor wood carvings illustrate ancient Chinese stories. Other features are the Wanxiang Pavilion built over the Kuahong Bridge, the Vicui Pavilion designed in a traditional hexagonal form, and the Guanlan Pavilion. The Birds Nest, built in 1931, evokes a simple message that the family's descendants should always return home in a similar way to migrating birds. It combines Western and Chinese design traditions, with roof forms symbolizing the exemplary concepts of intelligence, learning, talent, and achievements associated with the Xie family. Its contrasting feature is the Huateng flower pavilion designed as a huge bird cage and constructed in concrete tracery.

a sense of pride in the Republican city. These have frequently been described as representing a colonial style of architecture but one that progressed from the high Victorian neo-Gothic to a suitable range of forms for industrial city building incorporating refined patterns of art-deco, curvilinear corners and distinctive roofscape.

The twelve-story Tai Sun Company Building constructed in reinforced concrete that opened in 1936 contained a hotel, a bank, a department store, a restaurant and a rooftop amusement garden. This created an ambivalent model for a new and occasionally hedonistic lifestyle, offering the first hint of a consumer culture to those who could participate in its countless offerings. Western styles of music, fashion, entertainment, clothing, food, and even the romantic allure of ballroom dancing gained in popularity as symbols of wealth and social status, particularly for those of a sensual disposition.

Most multi-story buildings were situated along the Canton Bund, for business and government purposes, but also as apartment buildings that could profitably replace the older two-story villas and street terraces. The symbolism of modernity indicated both changing values and status associated with an urban identity but also the cultural superiority of the city. It clearly offered a better material life than the countryside that was still wracked by poverty and inviolable traditions. The concentration of urban intellectuals and higher education facilities created a progressive class of professionals and businessmen, with a refined respect for the rich Cantonese urban culture provided by the city, including its distinctive *Shêng Kang pan*—the Canton opera troupes.

In contrast to the cult of the city through its positive virtues, there existed enclaves of corrosive poverty. Accusing fingers were pointed at the foreign settlements as being representative of a tainted imperialism that had become an undermining force for socio-cultural equilibrium rather than a more proactive one in responding to changing urban forces. The belief that the traditional village and rural lifestyle was accountable for a backward-looking resistance to change, as opposed to being "the cradle of idyllic values" espoused several decades later by Mao Zedong prevailed through the city's association with material progress, industrialization, and free Republican spirit. Official attempts were made to re-engage younger members of society with the city's history and cultural roots, including the introduction of Confucian classics as a compulsory part of the school curriculum in 1934. In the meantime, increasing emigration from village to city had become a precursor to the explosive migration following the reforms some forty years later.

Assimilating Disparities

A degree of anti-foreign sentiment can perhaps be set apart from a mere distaste for imperialism and a resentment regarding its underlying power structure and militant tendencies. The Cantonese attitude—whether toward business transaction or blatant intrusion—was largely pragmatic. From all documentary evidence, foreign merchants in Canton were welcomed by local officials and the population at large, many of whom saw the new situation as presenting economic opportunities rather than impositions. During the British occupation of Canton at the time of the Taiping Rebellion they were generally welcomed as peace keepers rather than a marauding force.

The Majianglong Village cluster is situated to the south of the Tanjiang River under the administration of Beihe, and date back some 30 years. Behind the village is a mountain that local villagers termed a dragon, while to the east is a mountain that resembles a horse. "Majianglong literally means "the horse conquers the dragon" and is said to safeguard the prosperity of th village. It comprises five differen settlements: Yong'an and Nan'an villages associated with the Hua clan, and Hedong and Longjian villages of the Guan clan. Origina named "Fengsuilang" or "good annual harvest" it was renamed Majianglong after 1949, with sev Diaolou and eight villas built in t early twentieth century based o a mix of styles from the United States, Canada, Mexico, and Australia, introduced by returnir Overseas Chinese and merging foreign styles with Chinese decorative details.

In spite of this, blatant foreign aggression brought out, on occasions, its own vengeful but generally short-lived reaction. The Canton-Hong Kong strike and boycott that took place in British-governed Hong Kong and Republican China between 1925 and 1926 was a response to the shooting of demonstrators at the Shanghai International Settlement. This escalated to a similar demonstration in Shamian Island the same year when more than fifty Chinese protestors were killed. In Hong Kong the economy was paralyzed and the British government had to provide a trade loan to prevent the economy from collapsing. However, the policy of extraterritoriality that applied to established settlement areas, whereby foreigners ran their own municipal councils, constructed their own enclaves, and were effectively exempted from Chinese law, created little local opposition. This perhaps reflected a situation where "separation" had certain social advantages in keeping foreign communities out of sight and largely out of mind, reducing any lingering hostility. The larger settlements also established models for a well-managed urbanism with an attractive street architecture and landscape that stood the test of time, and to some also represented a mainstay of livelihood.

Hong Kong, which was itself a treaty port, was also popularly acknowledged as a successful model of modernization, and its generally stable currency encouraged wealthy Chinese residents of Canton to deposit sufficient sums to cover their possible exodus to the territory if

Waterfront Terrace along Dixi Ro Chikan township.

e 350-year-old town of Chikan as established during the Qing nasty and evolved as a market nter that expanded rapidly in e early twentieth century as erseas Chinese returned to the ea. The name Chikan means gh land with red soil." Its growth attributed to the economic mpetition between two wealthy n families—the Guan and Situ. e area incorporates around 600 ou-style terraced shophouses. morial libraries were built by ch family that rise above the ee-story street terraces.

The most prominent architectural features that act to create both consistency and variety are the two-story colonnades, decorated cornices, and balconies. The three-story terrace along the Taijiang River, together with the adjoining streets with arcaded frontages and store fronts at ground level, are also excellent examples of the traditional shophouse and t'ang-lou designs—part business and part residential above. The riverfront acts as a promenade, occupied throughout the day and evening by market stalls selling local specialties, with outdoor cafes reflecting its popularity as a place of high visitation.

the occasion demanded it. Similarly, Canton merchants during the 1920s frequently turned to Hong Kong for legal assistance because of its established rule of law over financial matters, and its comparative stability. Sun Yat-sen in a well-known speech at the University of Hong Kong in 1923 stated that the peace, order, and good government of the territory in the face of the lack of a mature legal system in China, had framed his revolutionary stance.

Lingnan Design

The cultural roots of Lingnan design and ornamentalism are intertwined with the history of the Pearl River Delta—a cradle of Chinese civilization for over 2,000 years. For several centuries this area acted as the gateway for trade between China and foreign destinations and was also the departure and arrival point of the Maritime Silk Road. Growth developed around the river valleys, streambeds, inlets, and harbors, mingled with fertile farmland—a Cantonese saying is that, "water and soil nurture the inhabitants." Lingnan culture is therefore equated with Cantonese culture, and applies to all indigenous groups within the region, establishing the Pearl Delta as a long-time source of design creativity.

The term Lingnan, with regard to design, was initially used for a school of painting that originated in the second part of the nineteenth century. However, this rapidly extended to other cultural and design aspects including Cantonese opera, music, embroidery, pottery, and built form. Its distinctive vernacular architecture from the late nineteenth and early twentieth centuries is distinguished by specific influences stemming from long-standing cultural and commercial exchange, and the absorption of a range of architectural elements from the Tang and Song empires. Its architectural interpretation is notable for its responsive approach to the humid subtropical climate through such aspects as colonnades, verandahs, archways, porches, and natural cross-ventilation systems that allow air to move through building structures. These measures include perforated brickwork, roof pavilions, permeable roof structures, and shading devices. Lingnan architecture also reflects a close association with traditional garden design in terms of building integration, use of materials, planting, ornamentation, and explains its predominant colors—green and white. During the late nineteenth and early twentieth centuries, Lingnan characteristics helped to heighten the sense of regional identity, showcased by ancestral temples, domestic architecture, village terraces, and unique tower forms.

Lingnan means "South of the Five Mountain Ranges," that run between Guangxi and Hainan provinces, and that also encompasses Jiangxi, Fujian, Swatow, and Hainan Island, as well as Guangdong with its sub-tropical climate. Over the years there has been a significant blending and interaction between Lingnan culture and that of the central plain to the north. This has nourished new forms of architectural and urban design expression, with details garnered from both China and the West. Design references were extended from the early nineteenth century through a maritime culture based on trading exchanges with western cities. These influences were combined into building styles such as the arcaded shophouse streets of the Canton treaty port and the Kaiping Diaolou towers, expressive of both East and West in terms of their form and decorative devices.

Emigration from South China commenced during the Sung and Yuan dynasties. Later,

nineteenth-century Chinese emigrants returning from America, Australia, Singapore, and Malaysia brought with them western design styles and decorative devices that were absorbed into local architecture and shophouse streets. Their adaptation to a localized context within Canton demonstrates an intriguing integration with older building traditions, taking into account local climatic and cultural opportunities that showcase a variety of styles.

Diaolou structures are located mainly in the south-western part of Guangdong Province, administered by the prefecture-level city of Jiangmen. This represents the hometowns and villages of overseas Chinese in Wuyi in and around Nanhai County. This area was inhabited by people from the Southern Yue Kingdom during the Warring States Period and was further developed under the Qin, Han, and T'ang dynasties through overseas trading routes. After Arabian traders introduced the teaching of Mohammad into China, certain Islamic architectural features became embedded to an extent in local building styles. Around 1,800 Diaolou structures cover an area of around 8,600 acres, and are associated in particular with Kaiping, Taishan, Xinhui, Enping, and Heshan, and which form an integral part of the Guangdong provincial culture embodied in customs, religion, art forms, and architecture.

Diaolou architecture is associated with defensive structures, villas, folk houses, and other ancient buildings that form a strong and identifiable character, reflecting the social turbulence that was common in Guangdong during the late Qing dynasty. The Diaolou towers fall into three main categories—collective, individual, and security purposed. In terms of structure, they can be made with stone, brick, concrete, and rammed earth in relation to buildings that sit in the midst of hills, fields, bamboo groves, and water courses. Their visual image and impact varies in relation to both urban context and architectural type. Prosperous overseas Chinese families became the target of bandits, and the most financially able built defensive structures as forms of protection against theft of property and kidnapping. Entire villages or groups of families would cooperate to build tall watchtowers to protect themselves from local bandit groups, in both urban and rural situations. These often combined residential and defense functions, integrating a mix of architectural influences. Collectively they were recognized in 2007 by being granted UNESCO World Heritage status.

Ruishilou diaolou in Jinjiangli Village, built in 1927 on farmland in the Xisagang Township.

The Cultural Significance of Cantonese Opera

The vivid nature of Cantonese opera performance is a product of its long evolution. Troupes were largely taught by dedicated practitioners from Canton, and theatrical innovations borrowed from various forms of regional opera through the centuries, sets and props getting ever more elaborate and costumes more flamboyant. Actors continue to play to scripts that can take an entire day to perform with characteristic bawdy and occasionally indelicate vocabulary and that might be seen as quite subversive in meeting the political expectations of the audience. This might not be entirely dissimilar to the British tradition of comic opera, loosely borrowed from tried and trusted sources, in which a mix of predictability, satire, and licentiousness—with a strict moral overtone—somehow produces popular and knowingly fabricated entertainment.

Cantonese opera is a lasting performing art that flourished in the southern province of Guangdong and included purpose-built theaters in Hong Kong as early as 1853. The Cantonese opera performers guild, the Bahe Association, was established in 1899, but many performers fled abroad after the Japanese invasion and ensuing class struggles after the founding of the People's Republic. It therefore enjoyed a dedicated following among overseas Chinese communities. Performers who arrived in Hong Kong led a resurgence of Cantonese opera that had almost entirely disappeared from local theaters. While operas were performed in Cantonese, they were based on the *pihuang* musical form—the same as for Peking opera. Established troupes in Canton included Yan Sou Lin, Kwok Chung Hing, and Chuk Wah Lin.

Full-time playwrights were employed to produce topical scripts, and some companies produced a new play every week, although improvisation was crucial. The *chih-shih pan*, or patriot opera groups of the early Republican period, followed scripts that were highly politicized, extremely popular, and well patronized, using vernacular Cantonese dialogue that tended to ridicule authority, re-assimilating a tradition that stretched back to the Ming dynasty. In later periods plays had a less revolutionary but more moralistic theme such as the "evil" promulgation of foot-binding. In some

cases scenes were censored for promoting excessive violence or obscenity. In most cases virtuous heroes and heroines suffer injustice only to morally avenge themselves.

From the early twentieth century there were more than thirty opera companies in Canton operating out of several theaters permanently dedicated to opera. By this time performances had become shortened to around four hours, with broadened vernacular repertoires targeted at receptive Cantonese audiences. However, the cast of relatively standard roles was purposely repetitive, promoting the characteristics of romance, treachery, promotion of virtue, and filial piety interspersed with music, along the lines of a pantomime, in a form of entertainment that molded its constant popularity. The jester, as in all pantomimes, played an important role in injecting a strong dose of puns and merriment into the proceedings, and was considered to be an essential ingredient in the entertainment. This was reinforced through the use of outrageous stage names that generally reflected the special roles they played. One such actor performed under the name "Footbound Shêng" and specialized in playing female foot-bound roles. While western classical opera focusses on vocal performance, traditional Chinese opera emphasizes the integration of various aspects including facial expression, voice, orchestral accompaniment, and gestures.

Ribaldry and double-entendres were also happily received by audiences, possibly underlining the long-held association of Cantonese with witty and earthy humor through both their androgynous gender identity and expression, but assisted by the noisy and informal nature inside opera houses. Wealthy patrons often occupied the front rows of performances, and their reaction could, to an extent, determine its success or otherwise. On occasions poems in classical Chinese, illustrated on scrolls and hung in front of the stage, were dedicated to famous female artists by scholars. This might have been encouraged by more than 100 all-female troupes, with well-known actresses playing major roles. Women were in fact an appreciative part of the audiences even if, until the 1930s, most seats and standing spaces were segregated by sex. Popular Canton newspapers posted regular columns on operas, with magazines dedicated to photographs of famous actors in theatrical costume, which contributed to their rising prestige, and rivalry. Prominent actors and actresses garnered a fanatical personality cult of adoring followers to the extent that this phenomenon was adopted as the theme of an entirely new opera itself.

Opera scripts did not exclude the Chinese relationship with foreigners and the often open-ended issue of patriotism that generally revolved around the suspected underhand support of Imperialism in the context of the Republic. A highlight for many prominent performers was their participation in Sun Yat-sen's inauguration as interim president in 1921. However, it is faithfully reported that prominent opera actors were followers of Western cinema during the 1930s, and classic themes, including Shakespearian ones, were successfully adapted to opera. In turn, many famous stars published self-important biographical works to both impress contemporaries and prominent officials, and to raise their social recognition. One well-known opera star, Ma Shih-ts'êng, made much of charity toward his siblings and his help to the needy. The 1936 funeral procession of another prominent performer, Chien-li Chiu, passed along most of Canton's main streets, following a ten-mile route lined by crowds offering sacrificial items. Cantonese opera was inscribed onto the UNESCO List of Intangible Cultural Heritage of Humanity in 2009.

The Lingering Impact of Opium

The issue of opium, because of its central role in the aggressive stance taken by foreign powers that led to military invasion and terms of settlement had an enduring impact on Canton just as it did on political events in China over the next century. It is necessary to put into context the extent and problematics of its actual use, and to correct any popular misconceptions.

No reliable statistics exist as to the extent of opium smoking in Canton, but as the center for importation from India it can be acknowledged that the number of addicts was relatively high by the end of

While western classical opera focusses on vocal performance, tradition Chinese opera emphasizes the integration of various aspects including facial expression, voice, orchestral accompaniment, and gestures.

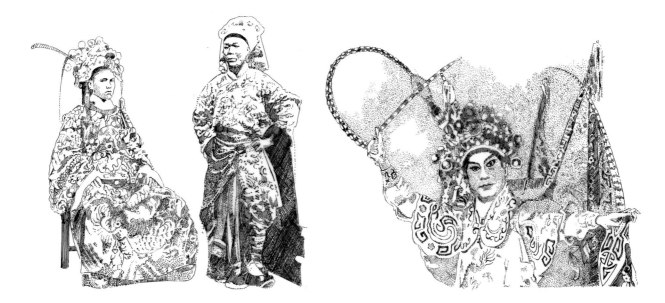

the Second Opium War, and its continued import made the drug easily available. In an 1877 report by the Canton Customs house, a branch of the Imperial Maritime Customs headed by Robert Hart, it was stated that 15,000 *piculs* of opium were imported into the province via Canton, equivalent to 90,000 kilograms or 200,000 pounds, of which ten percent was consumed in and around the city. In 1884 the Canton government announced its intention to tax the sale of prepared opium via a guild of legitimate retailers.

It is estimated that by 1906 there were 13.5 million addicts in China, with 27 percent of adult males being addicted—a level that was considerably reduced after the dismantling of the India-China opium trade in 1910.[123] Only after this was action taken to halt both production and consumption of the drug. Opium dealers were executed, crops destroyed, and addicts forced to submit to treatment. Following this the "Golden Triangle" of the Burmese Shan states across the Chinese border took over as the major international opium producer. By the end of the Qing dynasty in 1912 native Chinese opium had overtaken foreign imports, and the number of shops selling the raw substance had almost halved. Detoxicating institutions were also in place, and the Nationalist Party enacted eye-catching warnings as to the drug's potential impacts.[124]

By the 1920s a large number of unlicensed "divans" had been closed down, although figures from the period indicate that opium was still smoked by ten percent of the adult male population.[125] Surveys of working-class families and boat communities in Canton's Sha-nan area in the 1930s found only a small percentage of addicts, and would seem to indicate that for working people smoking was an occasional pastime. Most users spent only a small amount on the habit, whereas opium divans entertained more affluent members of the community. Authorities in the final years of the treaty port concessions attempted to enforce its prohibition, and opium substitutes, which mingled drugs with other substances such as caffeine, were widely available. However, magnifying the theoretical scale of the problem was a convenient way for a revolutionary government to inculcate negative feeling against foreign occupants, including the Japanese, while those who imported it had every reason to play down its use. In official propaganda it was regularly denounced as a social evil, and Sun Yat-sen's negative pronouncements on the subject were widely repeated.

Physical deterioration and emaciation as a result of opium use were generally linked with overall impoverishment and poor hygiene. It was used extensively by Canton rickshaw men, partly to relieve the exhausting impacts of this strenuous activity, but often at the expense of malnutrition. Its transforming power was commonly called "beating the tiger." However, opium was not merely a drug of the poor. It was served on the flower boats and high-class restaurants as a stimulant and an accessory to both business and brittle conversation.

There was also an artistic side to the habit through smoking paraphernalia, including the pipes themselves that could be carved from expensive elephant ivory or rhinoceros horn. In the most sophisticated brothels in Canton, opium hostesses prepared the smoking pipes as a subtle but markedly docile means of foreplay, which might in practice have acted to suppress the normal enthusiasm of clients.

In 1870 a tael of the best quality Indian opium cost 0.45 of a tael of silver, which was not markedly expensive, and partially explains why its importation enjoyed a steady growth. A further reason was that poppies were not cultivated in or around Canton but in neighboring provinces. At the time of its eventual suppression at the end of the nineteenth century, the price had risen considerably. By the time of the Republican administration in 1911 this had led to an increase in opium smuggling into Canton from other provinces, and over the next decade efforts at eradication failed primarily because of its lucrative benefits that were divided between producers, merchants, and a widespread range of "helpful" intermediaries. Up to the Revolution of 1911, revenue from the opium tax was largely directed toward necessary military expenditure. However, in the early years of the Republic, government enforced a strict anti-opium drive, penalizing those involved and eradicating its manufacture as far as possible. Smuggling routes from the southwestern provinces were at the same time protected by senior figures in the military, using Chinese gunboats that could not be searched by the Maritime Customs. Despite large-scale confiscation and destruction, opium continued to be an essential generator of revenue.

By 1930 most opium consumption was of Chinese origin and prices remained stable, even in the face of political instability, as poorer customers tended to smoke a cheap mix of dross and raw opium, and simply maintained an occasional intake as a stimulant. Locally produced opium and its means of preparation were also said to possess less strength and narcotic effect than its foreign counterpart and was sold at a cheaper rate. It should also be stated that the concession areas of Hong Kong and Macau were by no means immune to legitimate local consumption, and that forms of opium were routinely given to patients as part of Western medical treatment.

Premises where opium was smoked were commonly known as "chatting places" indicating a social or meeting function, where the better establishments, patronized by the well-to-do, were concentrated in the busy commercial districts with well-equipped private rooms helping to maintain a respectable image. Progressive Cantonese opera troupes performed anti-opium themes even as many male opera singers used the drug as a stimulant.

There was something of a hypocritical or half-hearted nature to official suppression measures in the early 1930s as the Canton government not only taxed opium, but also imposed license fees on its associated smoking paraphernalia. In 1934 the municipal government announced the relocation of opium divans to the Western suburbs where business continued to generate income to the government treasury.[126] Fees paid by purveyors of opium to festival organizers also helped to fund the events themselves. Sun Yat-sen patriotically railed against its use, and the revolutionary government established a Suppression Bureau, but in practice this seems to have been used to tax the use of opium, and opium divans were allowed to continue under the ambiguous title of treatment institutes. Eradication failed largely because of its crucial role in raising revenue for military undertakings such as Chiang Kai-shek's Northern Expedition.

It was not until 1951 that the Communist Government began a strong campaign against the use of opium in Canton, closing down more than 3,000 opium divans and seizing large amounts of drugs and related equipment, all of which was publicly burned. In addition, it announced a compulsory registration of drug users and promoted this by banners erected throughout the city.

The Tomb of the Seventy-two Heroes is a monument to martyrs of the 1911 revolution.

Chapter 6

Forces of Transformation

The Compelling Pressure of Revolution

After brutally putting down the Boxer uprising, the Western powers needed to stabilize the ruling dynasty and maintain territorial integrity to ensure a continuation of international commerce. However, it also had to actively discourage future rebellion. The result was the Boxer Protocol, comprising a series of measures that, in their misguided severity, were to stoke a wave of nationalist sentiment and opposition to the Qing dynasty and hasten its end. Foreign legations were allowed to station troops in the treaty port settlements, and forts that had been previously erected to protect Beijing were allowed to be dismantled. In addition, the war indemnity was established at a level that virtually doubled the original settlement terms, and which could only worsen economic conditions in the country. As a final act of high handedness, the civil service examination was suspended for five years, effectively cutting off reinforcement of the Mandarin system from below.

While many at the time believed that the situation would lead directly to the partition of China and national disintegration, the immediate result was a renewed determination and nationalistic sentiment that evolved as a vital force over the following decades. The pace of change in the treaty ports continued to widen the gap between the thriving coastal cities and the Chinese interior, and further incentivized social forces against the Imperial system. New military academies began to produce graduates from an elite class, some of whom would influence events under the Republic. Welfare services helped to maintain social stability that in turn nurtured a growing sense of patriotism.

Continuing commercial and industrial development acted to consolidate an emerging commercial bourgeoisie as a broad meeting point between the old Mandarin and established merchant classes.[127] However, its success required a strong central government, and in this regard the Japanese defeat of Russia over their interests in Manchuria was something of a wake-up call. The decisive Battle of Shenyang in 1905 was the first time an Asian power had defeated a European one. This not only underscored the confidence of Japan that was later to emerge in a more belligerent form in 1937, but showed China that a transformation of the state institutions and administration were necessary to counteract imperialism. One of the most important aspects of this was the introduction of constitutionalism, based broadly on the Japanese model for modernization, which fatally attracted many radical Chinese students at virtually the same time that Japan was consolidating a significant power base in China.

The secession of the Liaodong Peninsula together with extra-territorial privileges permitted Japan to exercise not merely administrative but also planning control over the larger Manchurian cities. In a similar way to the continuation of the German planning and urban design framework in Tsingtao, the Japanese took over the comprehensive planning and urban expansion of Harbin and Dalian. The north-south railway alignment between the two cities facilitated the growth of new settlements which grew into important towns such as Mukden and Hsinking, but a more expansive railway-building agenda also assisted the extraction of natural resources—coal, minerals, and timber.

The deaths of the Emperor Kuang-hsu and the empress dowager in November 1908 dramatically reduced the authority of the court and represented a sudden catalyst for change. Yuan Shih-K'ai who had been appointed president of the Ministry of Foreign Affairs in 1907 was summarily dismissed by the new regent, the father of the infant emperor, and went on to declare himself commander in chief of the armed forces. This created an upsurge in tension between Chinese and Manchus at court.

Elections for provincial and local councils were held in early 1909, but voting was restricted to the higher and educated echelons of society, which diluted its political impact. However, a National Assembly of 200 members met for the first time in 1910 and discussed the establishment of a new parliament, reflecting a groundswell of opinion in opposition to the imperial regime, that provided a largely unintended foundation for the 1911 Revolution. Protests over the nationalization of China's railway system led to uprisings in several cities and, one by one, provinces declared themselves independent of the imperial dynasty.[128]

Foreign investment through the treaty ports continued to grow, with foreign banks financing major infrastructure works. The railway network reached almost 10,000 kilometers by 1911, including the Canton-Kowloon railway, which was geared primarily to the strategic commercial interests of foreign corporations and effectively extended the hinterland of the major port cities. Foreign steamship traffic also made up some eighty percent of the total traffic in the ports, bringing inland markets within their trading ambit. Dockyards and factories developed rapidly in the larger cities, in particular Canton and Shanghai.[129] This had the effect of creating a dual economic structure, with the continued modernization of the treaty ports and development of supporting infrastructure stimulating the economy as a whole, assisted by growing injections of investment from Chinese communities in other parts of Asia, Europe, and the United States.[130] At the same time the rural areas of Central China suffered widespread famine between 1902 and 1911 as the result of natural disasters, leading to a breakdown of the traditional rural social hierarchy.

The juncture of factors that made China ripe for a revolution, with its severe implications for the core foreign settlements, must be seen in parallel, one set of circumstances affecting another. Given broadening international horizons and uncompromising nineteenth-century foreign incursions, the deeply embedded imperial institutions could not, in all probability, have been long sustained. However, the catalyst for modernization came primarily from internal forces for change. Western intervention introduced a new capitalist rationale that, by the late nineteenth century, met with

strong support in the port communities and among the emergent class of merchant entrepreneurs, redirecting a system that had for centuries emphasized self-sufficiency over economic expansion. The unequal treaties, by the same token, gave foreign firms undue privileges such as low tariffs, increased territorial acquisitions, and virtual immunity from official laws and interference at a time when large-scale industrial imports and rapid encroachments into the Chinese interior collided with the resentful ramifications of impoverishment—in itself partly the result of a deteriorating and corrupt hierarchy of officialdom.

British foreign investment in itself was never substantial. At the height of its imperial power, Britain invested only 4 percent of its national income overseas, and of this only one quarter to colonial enterprises, of which India was the main recipient.[131] Niall Ferguson has stated that this was mainly to underwrite measures taken to establish stability, legal protection, and responsive government in areas under British administration, which excluded China.[132] The treaty ports themselves became the primary targets for private investment, and it was around these rapidly growing "frontier" cities, representing gateways to foreign trade and influence, that economic change began to cement the economic and intellectual strands of a new China. This was, however, for obvious reasons, developed outside a rational framework of legal and financial practice, and altogether independent of clearly defined national objectives.

The revolution of October 1911, following the armed Wuchang Uprising, marked the beginning of the early Republican era. This was essentially anti-imperialist, although also directed against foreign powers. However the revolution, while instigating political change, ultimately failed in its mission, as conflicts of interest and intrigue counteracted any real change in the constitutional process. Cumulative disillusionment then began to assume a new and more pointed direction.[133]

Various exiled figures were involved, including several in Japan, which had become a center for anti-Manchu activity, not altogether separate from Japan's own ambitions for extending its empire. The pre-revolutionary movement gained momentum in the port settlements, although much of the intellectual organization was undertaken by leaders and students living in exile, mainly in Japan. Opposition was divided between advocates for reform and those favoring revolution. Sun Yat-sen himself favored the latter, having mingled for some years in rebellious intellectual circles, including the secret societies of Canton and Shanghai, which helped to fuse together different parties to the revolutionary movement.

Sun Yat-sen is credited with the overall direction of revolutionary action, first initiating it in 1893 through the *Xing Zhonghui* or "Divine China Society" in Macau where Sun was based.[134] Sun's wife, Soong Ching-ling, founded the China Defense League to develop his revolutionary cause. Sun was later chosen to head the alliance of Chinese students in Tokyo—the *Tongmenghui*, after being forced into exile. During this time he developed several principles for the creation of a modern China based on nationalism and socialism, which were geared to strengthening the Chinese state. His political philosophy was embedded in his *Three Principles of the People*, and was defined as making China independent from oppression, and both prosperous and powerful. The principles were rendered as

e Sun Yat-sen Memorial Hall
s built from 1929–1931 and
modelled on the Temple of
aven in Beijing. It was renovated
d modernized in 1998, and is
ed as a cultural center for the
rforming arts.

nationalism, democracy, and livelihood of the people through welfare rights, which formed the essence of Republican policy. Sun's democratic ideals were somewhat elusive, preferring rule by an elite group of officials and, somewhat surprisingly, a retention of the civil service examination system.

Sun Yat-sen had lived abroad for much of his adult life and had garnered reformist—some would say radical—ideas along with a revolutionary base through the Revive China Society. In particular, his overseas connections among Chinese in the United States proved both generous and supportive. Many writers of the period, in particular Liang Qichao, were also influential in advocating reform through a new nationalist spirit that called for a combination of traditional societal norms while acknowledged the merits of Western governmental structures and judicial procedures.[135] These were backed up by student newspapers and crusading academic figures.

In early 1912, Sun Yat-sen, having returned from self-imposed exile in the dying days of the Qing dynasty, was proclaimed provisional president of the Republic of China in Nanjing, but with a weak revolutionary base. This was based on the understanding that he would vacate the post at the time of the Manchu abdication.

The final step coincided, somewhat ironically, with official action to introduce constitutional government. Arguments over the establishment of provisional assembles focused dissatisfaction on the ailing dynasty. This led to incidents in many cities and local garrisons were unable to keep order. On February 12, 1912, 268 years of Manchu rule was brought to an end, heralding the birth of modern China, but also a new period of political turmoil and instability that made it difficult to unify the country. However, political order was almost impossible without a coherent structure and organization, and Sun enjoyed little credibility among many of the leaders who, for various reasons, mistrusted his close ties with foreign investors. Within the newly formed Nanjing Assembly there was strong support for a firm leader so that on February 14th Sun resigned, ostensibly to avoid civil war and to secure foreign loans. Yüan Shih-K'ai who had been prime minister since November 1911 was elected the first president of the Chinese Republic, and certain concessions were granted to the remaining Manchu aristocracy at the first peace conference held in December 1911 in the Shanghai International Settlement.[136] However, Yüan's presidency up to 1915 failed in its attempts to solve China's inherited financial problems amidst continuing civil strife.

Inspired by the recent October Revolution in Russia, a group of young participants joined forces to oppose the new feudal order, including then 18-year-old Mao Zedong. At this stage members of different parties formed the Kuomintang which became the parliamentary opposition party. The flag of the new Republic reflected China's multi-national character, its five equal stripes symbolizing Han Chinese, Mongolians, Manchu, Muslims, and Tibetans.

The Quest for a Civil Society

The immediate post-revolution years brought support from the occupying powers—Britain, France, and the United States—who saw political reform as a means of consolidating their key economic holdings in the treaty ports. The Hong Kong Ordinances of 1911 and 1913 provided for incorporation of companies that allowed multi-national combinations of capital and expertise under common

The Sun Yat-sen Library of Guangdong Province constructed in 1933 with funds donated by overseas Chinese in America, designed by Lin Keming.

legal protection. Upon registration in Hong Kong a company could trade anywhere in China under the protection of British law, assisted by local consuls, and British citizenship was given to owners of such corporations. Kathryn Brennan Meyer has suggested that the later British decision to cancel these ordinances and replace them with Orders in Council, which restricted corporate registration to British nationals, breached a key threshold between an interrelationship of interests and political disunity.[137]

After an attempt at a "second revolution" the Kuomintang was outlawed and Sun Yat-sen was forced back into exile at almost the same time that the First World War commenced in 1914. Japan joined together with the Allied powers, thereby providing a powerful foothold in China as a "political and military adviser," gaining major rail and industrial concessions from the government. This, together with the failure of Yuan Shi-kai to resume the role of emperor, led to a struggle for power between rival militarist cliques. Sun Yat-sen again returned from exile and established a provisional government in Canton. Meanwhile, in the midst of social and economic upheaval, the contending powers of the United States, Britain, and Japan made their own agreements on partition based on both individual and mutual interests, tightening their grip in the midst of ferment and constant shifts in power. In response, new intellectual groups emerged that laid the foundations for revolutionary movements aimed at both a transformation of society and an end to forces that continued to impair China's sovereignty.

In January 1915, Japan, strengthened by its association with the Allies in the First World War, presented a list of twenty-one demands to the Chinese government, including the ceding of Shandong which had previously been under German jurisdiction, along with control of its iron and steel industry. Further demands included the right to construct railways, ports and other infrastructure in Manchuria. As Western interests that might have sprung to China's defense were in the throes of the First World War, most of these demands were met. This laid the seeds not only for future conflict with Japan, but for a decade of infighting and intrigue between military warlord factions that looted and collected revenue independently of Beijing, thereby depriving the national treasury of resources. Individual foreign powers during the war encouraged China to move in directions that accorded with their interests and negotiated with warlords from whom they could expect the most favorable outcome. In the meantime, Sun set up a rival government in Canton to the warlord regime that controlled the government machinery in Beijing.

The endorsement of the Japanese seizure of Shandong by the four signatures to the Versailles Peace Treaty at the culmination of World War I signaled not merely a national indignation but a motivation toward self-determination. Thousands protested in the largest cities, sparked by a student body from Peking University. The May Fourth Movement of 1919 marked a significant milestone and an important turning point in the attempted resumption of unequal treaties by allied powers, not so much for its wide support among intellectuals but for its catalytic effect in articulating calls for reform of China's cultural order. Wen-Hsin Yeh identifies the May Fourth Movement and its successful appeal to mass mobilization as the first time that wide political activism was coupled with cultural iconoclasm to bring about a patriotic and ideological response to foreign imperialism, being both liberal minded and revolutionary purposeful.[138] The movement itself spawned a robust ideology, with a new political consciousness turned to the revolutionary Marxist example of neighboring Russia as a way forward against what was perceived as world imperialism. A new leadership began to take shape, based on the gradual assimilation of feudal and working class power. In so doing it called into question fundamental Confucian traditions that were synonymous with the conservatism of the past.

In July 1921, the Communist Party of China, comprising groups in Chinese cities and those studying abroad which included Deng Xiaoping and Zhou Enlai, held its first Congress in Shanghai's French Concession, even as the new warlord government in Peking attended the Nine-Power Pact in Washington the same year. The preliminary struggle was for union recognition, and during the early 1920s China

was beset by major strikes, particularly directed toward foreign or warlord controlled industrial, mining, railway, and shipping enterprises, enhancing the organizational prestige of the new Communist Party.

From 1923 Sun Yat-sen and the Kuomintang were based in Canton. Sun who was not a Marxist but an incorruptible patriot propounded a revolutionary agenda applied to alliances with Soviet Russia and the Chinese Communist Party, and linked to the principal of Nationalism based on the unarguable pre-requisites of equality and support of the masses. The allied government established the Peasant Movement Training Institute of which Mao Zedong was a director, using Russian funds and weapons.

The mid-1920s experienced a significant growth in "cell" organization, bringing about pressure for greater ideological consensus. However, at the time there was no material foundation for socialism as there was little in terms of a unified labor force. Partly to combat this, Sun Yat-sen's Kuomintang in Canton developed a close-working relationship with the Shanghai Communist Party—a process that attracted the participation of a young Mao Zedong who worked with Li Dazhao in the Beijing University Library. This formed the First United Front in 1923, whose impact in both Canton and Shanghai aroused mass activism. In 1924 a new revolutionary government was set up in Canton, with Chiang Kai-shek as dean and Zhou Enlai as political director. In October of the same year, political changes in Peking led to the ejection of the "Last Emperor" Pu Yi from the Forbidden City, who sought shelter in the Japanese concession in Tianjin.

While in Peking in March 1925 to attend discussions that might have led to a peaceful unification of the country, Sun Yat-sen died from cancer. His final testament was to stress the importance of freedom and equality among all nations, to abolish unequal treaties, and to follow plans for national reconstruction. With Sun Yat-sen's death in 1925, a unifying force disappeared and tensions within the United Front gradually escalated into confrontations between Sun's named successor, Wang Jingmei, who held left-wing views similar to Sun, and Chiang Kai-shek, a former army commander and head of the Whampoa Military Academy who held strong anti-communist views.[139] In May the Second all-China Labour Congress met in Canton, representing more than half-a-million workers. In the same month demonstrators in Canton, appealing for a boycott of British and Japanese goods, were shot by troops from the Shamian concession. As a result, the revolutionary base was strengthened and a military "Northern Expedition" was launched in a bid to eliminate imperialist control. The return of the Wuhan concession area was the first such settlement to be recovered after the First Opium War.

The so-called "Canton Coup" in 1926 enabled Chiang Kai-shek to reinforce control over the Nationalists and in the following year the Communists launched the Canton uprising. Shamian Island was turned into an armed camp with blockades and machine-gun positions resulting in a military standoff, with more than 300 marines protecting the concession areas for over sixteen months. Further tension was caused as Chiang Kai-shek and the Nationalist army seized a number of major cities, fomenting fundamental change in the relations between Chinese and foreigners, along with increased demands for withdrawal from concession areas. The Nationalist's ideological agenda became directed toward anti-imperialism and the defense of China's interests against foreign intervention. In January 1927, Nationalist troops attacked foreign consulates in Shanghai and

Nanjing, followed up by purges against the Communists and other left-wing groups. Chiang, with military backing, arrested senior Communist leaders and took complete charge of the Kuomintang and with it control of the Nationalist government in Canton along with the entire armed forces. In April, Chiang's troops raided the Communist Party Headquarters and various union organizations in Shanghai and executed countless members and street demonstrators. A new Nationalist government was immediately established in Nanking. Chiang pledged support for business communities and protection of the foreign community and joined forces with northern warlords for a successful attack on Peking. The International Settlement and French Concession on Shamian Island had to be protected by 20,000 soldiers after being warned that the Nationalists, who had entered the city, were about to abolish extraterritoriality and take over the area. Ironically, on a number of occasions such as the Central Bank crisis of 1927, the city's sense of refuge made it a point of security, while many wealthy Cantonese began to favor the stability of the foreign banks.

By this time membership of the Kuomintang had grown to over five million workers and peasants, but such a mass movement, bent on a transition to socialism, met entrenched resistance from vested interests in government, and from Chiang Kai-shek who connived at attaining personal control of the armed forces. Britain was also aware of post-war stirrings of discontent in some of her Asian colonial possessions, and together with America supported Chiang and the right wing of the Kuomintang. Unrest in the major cities of Canton and Shanghai among workers led to a general strike and raised fears on the part of Chinese bankers and industrialists that led to Chiang's intervention in Shanghai, Canton, and Nanjing. In April, Chiang established his own Nationalist government in Nanjing claiming it as "the legitimate government of China."

The *North-China Daily News and Herald* sought to "correct" a prevailing impression abroad that many cities in China were effectively under foreign control—a view that was in fact partially correct, but somewhat misleading. The questionable rejoinder was that foreign occupants controlled nothing that was not formed or built by themselves. It was pointed out that the Shamian concession in Canton, acquired by the British and French in 1861, was not made up of land, but had been formed through reclamation of the shallow river edge some distance from the older established business center. Similarly, in Shanghai the International Settlement and French Concession had been allocated on low swampy ground at fixed land rents under regulations approved by the Chinese Government, in which the majority of formed land was owned and built on by Chinese residents.

This was also a time of mass popular culture and new media, much of it foreign in origin. Theatrical productions and publications of the period transmitted themes of social injustice, class friction, and women's rights. These themes were to be later remolded by the Communist regime to embrace forms of cultural expression such as storytelling and opera, injected with moralistic overtones as vehicles for propaganda.[140] In this respect it both foreshadowed and promoted a new social climate, as an embryo for the profound ideological struggles that lay ahead—the compromised ideals of Chiang Kai-shek's National government, and the rise of the Chinese Communist Party.

The expansion of newspapers and other forms of publishing, together with the narrative power of photography and new cinematic realism, displayed and articulated the societal contradictions inherent in the constantly shifting intellectual culture that took root in the cities, of which Canton and Shanghai were at the fore. Socialist resilience showed through in programs of physical construction that evolved around clusters of embedded institutional forms: guild quarters, factory compounds, universities, banks, and the cultural and physical residue that remained intact—temples, markets, and remnants of the historical city fabric.

With this, an era that had seen egalitarian and republican notions of self-determination espoused by foreign powers, was pushed firmly into the background to be overwhelmed by emerging political models. Marxist ideas found many followers among Chinese intellectuals, and the battle between ideologies was to have a profound impact on China for the next quarter of a century.

The Communist Party at its Fifth Congress in May 1927 in the city of Wuhan had little choice but to fall back on reinforcement of its social policy and "anti-landlord" movement at the time, which created internal disagreements but also established a long-lasting power base. Chiang meanwhile consolidated power by siding directly with the foreign and imperial forces that required uncompromising military activity. This situation led directly to civil war that engulfed the whole of society.

A major step was taken on August 1, 1927, with the formation of the Chinese Red Army under the leadership of the Party—the forerunner of the People's Liberation Army. Several months later Mao Zedong established the first base of revolutionary state power in the Jinggangshan mountains of Jiangxi Province—the first of 19 such rural bases, well away from the key cities controlled by the Kuomintang.[141] Mao himself insisted that socialist revolution could only be carried out after a democratic revolution had been achieved.

Social and Economic Reform

Conditions of trade, Chinese self-sufficiency, and embedded Chinese mercantile and transport networks all conspired to inhibit the demand for Western products. However, to a large extent, the capitalization of Chinese shipping services were rooted in the wealth of the treaty ports. Essentially, both the economic evolution and urban development of the port cities were shaped mainly by market forces, although indirectly the influences came about through the trading interfaces with colonial operations elsewhere. At the same time new patterns of urbanization and municipal management provided for locally initiated urban redevelopment and capitalization of urban infrastructure.

In Canton the underlying dynamic was tied to both social and economic forces, related to a mercantile economy that evolved somewhat independently of other cities.[142] In this sense the treaty port was, for a time, a stabilizing influence. Many Chinese emigrants to other parts of Southeast Asia had left from the southern ports of Canton, Amoy, and Fujian, but political problems and financial depression in countries such as Malaysia encouraged many to return to these cities in the 1920s and early 1930s, so that much investment capital went into new housing that incorporated both Chinese and foreign architectural features.

e Hualin Temple of the Five
ndred Lohans or "Arhats"
sciples of Buddha arranged in
double bank around the main
ll as life-size gilded images,
corporated in 1861—the last
ar of Emperor Daoguang. It was
nstructed during the Southern
nasties period but was extended
1654.

The complexity of urban culture in Canton had a significant impact on urban places, with parks, teahouses, chambers of commerce, stadia, and theaters all forming a network of locations for political debate and discussion, while city walls became messaging elements for slogans and posters. This was accompanied by the adoption of a more contemporary vernacular writing style, again exploiting the literary vacuum that existed outside the classical form of written Chinese adopted by scholars, thereby enabling more people to participate in written debate. Thus, urban life began to nourish the creative forces of the avant-garde in society, creating new political, social, and cultural models.[143] The cities also represented places of convergence for groups of intellectuals and radicals who built up networks of connections through student movements and societies that transformed themselves into Communist cells with strong influences over other groups in Canton, drawing in many disaffected parties.[144]

In the wake of guild organization came a federation of professional associations known as *fatuan*, chambers of commerce and trade unions, which helped to exert a degree of formalized control over city affairs and local communities. However, cities in the Republican Era also had to deal with a legacy of urban poverty and decay, exacerbated by new industrialization and waves of refugees from war-torn areas. Economic modernizations in Canton and the commensurate rise of bourgeois society also stretched the mutual relationship between urban and rural communities, at a time when the state organization was itself unstable. Nationalism appeared to embody the potential to unify an eclectic collection of guilds, societies, religious dissidents, artists, and social reformers, much as it did a cultural avant-garde, so that there was expanded public debate although little actual social consensus. This largely failed to establish a coherent connection with the divided political regimes, however, something that Mao Zedong was later able to exploit through drawing on a traditional ideal for local affiliations.

The changing relationship between urban and rural society in China during this period, unwittingly underscored in treaty port industrialization and expansion, formed a key tenet of the Communist revolution. As opposed to the Bolshevik Revolution in Russia, founded on classical Marxist theory where dominant urban forces attempted to transform the feudal countryside on the back of an also urban proletariat, the Chinese Communist Party, founded by two colleagues from Beijing University, Chen Tu-hsiu and Li Dazhao, tended to reflect not merely urban but rural discontent.[145] The identification of the treaty ports with foreign imperialism was a key aspect of this. It was argued that if China had, over the past 100 years, been exploited by foreign powers who purported to believe in democracy and egalitarianism but who had to sustain their regimes by means of administrative control, then the Marxist model seemed a more attractive alternative.[146]

Competing Campaigns for Unification

Over the course of a decade, much was achieved in terms of new building, infrastructure, and conservancy projects, and the Nationalist government was able to initially improve the economic situation and partially reform the tax structure, which stimulated the growth of new business and residential districts. However, the Kuomintang proved to be too closely associated with the banking and financial sector, and its efforts to unify the country by military means, and without land reforms, proved to be too extreme for full acceptance by the wider citizenry.

Constant purges of left-wing factions and reformers also prevented the establishment of a broad Nationalist support base. In 1928, Japan announced the movement of troops to Shantung from Tientsin, and three years later invaded Manchuria, establishing a puppet state of Manchukuo with Pu Yi, the deposed Ch'ing emperor, as its titular head. In September 1931, Japan, possibly exploiting Western preoccupation with fallout from the 1929 Stock Market crash, invaded and occupied the industrially developed provinces of Northeast China. Several months later the Japanese attacked Shanghai while Chiang's main concern was the destruction of the Red Army. The latter followed a code of rules laid down in 1928 that governed its behavior—it was summarized by Mao as "the Party commanding the gun, never the gun commanding the party," making it a united force. In January 1932, under the pretext of protecting the 6,000 Japanese civilians in the Chapei International Settlement of Shanghai from Chinese student protests, Japanese marines invaded the area and many people were killed over the next two months through naval bombing.

Economic development failed to be matched by social reform, and as production stagnated, an increasing proportion of national income went toward sustaining the military establishment. Well-connected bankers in the treaty ports helped to finance the government, draining funds that could have been used more positively in financing commercial growth. However, Nationalist rule was sustained through repression, and by 1936 almost half of the Central Executive Committee was made up of military officers who constructed precarious alliances with right wing organizations and occasionally underworld elements, even as Chiang Kai-shek attempted to instill order.

Increased persecution of Communists and great Kuomintang pressure ended with an "extermination" campaign in 1933 that inspired the "Long March" of the Red Army—a 6,000-mile trek to a remote northern mountain base in Shaanxi Province, but with a massive toll on its forces. However, its march through eleven provinces with more than 200 million residents, proved a means of revitalizing the revolutionary cause. The Long March itself became a liberation manifesto. By the end of 1937 it became clear that the larger enemy was Japanese Imperialism that required a united front to support a war of resistance.

The regeneration of the Communist Party was, without doubt, based on both the experience of Mao Zedong and Zhu De in the peasant communities of Hunan, Jinggangshan, and Jiangxi, and the revolutionary philosophical principles that were first formulated there. The Chinese Communist Party had evolved under the strong influence and example of the Soviet revolution and Comintern, with its Marxist emphasis on the essential revolutionary role of the urban proletariat. However, in China, the urban working class represented only a small percentage of the population. Mao recognized that the massive Chinese peasantry, while impoverished and disorganized, represented the backbone of the country, and if properly channeled this force could come to play a critical ideological role. The key factor, particularly after the ravages of the Long March, was grounded in Communist ideology in a concern for the welfare of soldiers and peasants alike through a campaign of courtesy and genuine assistance in dealing with civilians. As a revolutionary Mao was

Chun Yuan (Spring Garden), the former headquarters of the Cent Committee of the Communist Party of China at 24 Xinhepu Roa constructed in 1923. It was the s of the Third National Congress of CPC, with many delegates includ Mao Zedong. In 1993, it was decl a protected site, and in 2006 was restored to its former condition.

nothing if not pragmatic, and realized that the party must have primacy and that military power was, despite everything, the key to success. In this he was skillfully assisted by a master technician in mediation—Zhou Enlai, together with Lin Biao, Deng Xiaoping, and Liu Shaioqi. Together they formulated tactics akin to guerrilla warfare that depended on patriotic and material support from predominantly rural communities. A year later in 1937 Japan launched an invasion of China precipitating a conflict of almost unprecedented ferocity that eventually saw Japan fighting the Western allies in World War Two.

Virtually all coastal areas, including the treaty ports, were occupied by the Japanese early in the campaign, and the loss of these financial and industrial bases deprived the Nationalist government of its main sources of revenue. In July 1937, Japanese troops invaded Peking and Tientsin, although foreign residents in the legation quarters were left untouched. The battle for Shanghai in August avoided the International Settlement and French Concession, but the invasion and accompanying atrocities in Nanking during December heightened the sense of outrage among the public at large. As Japanese forces moved southwards in 1938, the treaty ports were threatened not merely by the Japanese but by besieged Nationalist forces who looted the cities of Canton, Changsha, and Wuhan before retreating to Chungking, the treaty port on the upper Yangtze that became China's wartime capital. By 1939, the Japanese occupying army closed the Yangtze to all but Japanese ships, and began to exert pressure on the foreign concessions, rightly suspecting them of harboring anti-Japanese Nationalists. By this time the Nationalist government had gained control of twenty out of thirty-three foreign concessions as well as the customs service.[147]

The War of Resistance began with an agreed division of responsibilities in terms of designated roles and areas of participation. It cannot be said, however, that the approach and commitment of the two forces shared much commonality, even after Japan's occupation of Nanjing. At this time the Nationalists and Communists were technically in the midst of civil conflict, but while the former were in alien territory, the situation played into the hands of the Communist rural network. The new People's Liberation Army was able to build its vast power base among the peasants while carrying on an armed struggle to such an extent that it was able to offer troop support to Chiang as a Second United Front to fight the Japanese. This opportunity to win over the hearts and minds of the people was grasped successfully by Mao through massive recruitment, improved training, literacy campaigns, and a reformulation of party doctrine, and in this way helped to consolidate resistance to the invading army. In turn this helped to facilitate economic self-sufficiency including, where necessary, forced labor and mobilization of agricultural workers to manufacture weapons and equipment.

Enforced land redistribution and recruitment of village activists formed the embryonic commitment to the core Communist Party principle of class struggle, persuasively mobilizing villagers to adopt a revolutionary path where individual interests were subsumed within a common movement. It was articulated through the conceptualization of certain Marxist principles adapted to the Chinese situation. John Fairbank crystallizes this succinctly by equating the exploited urban "proletariat" under Marxism to the landless rural peasantry in China through

e Haizhu iron bridge was the
st to span the Pearl River in
nton. It was completed in 1933
th a span of 198 meters by an
merican contractor, Markton. It
ns between the Haizhou District
d the Yiuxiu District. It was
maged in 1949 by retreating
dmintang forces.

a term *wuchan jieji* or "propertyless class."[148] This political shift from an urban to a rural revolutionary base embraced a subtle equation between the feudal landlord and the Chinese merchant class in the cities, and in particular the treaty ports.

Military Occupation and a Return to Civil Conflict

In December 1941, Japan declared war on the United States and Britain, and the Second World War was brought home to China, with Chiang Kai-shek for the first time openly declaring war on Japan. In Shanghai, Japanese troops seized control of the International Settlement and French Concession. In 1942 the leaders of the business community were rounded up and imprisoned.

America entered World War II immediately following the Japanese attack on Pearl Harbor. After completing a series of victories in the Pacific, Japanese naval and air power was overwhelmed by American forces. In China the impending victory belonged to the Communist Party who grew in strength and support, multiplying in numbers and influence, directed from Yan'an where members of the Central Committee were quartered. By 1945 the Party's membership exceeded one million, gradually liberating territory from Japan, but by the time of Japan's surrender its following amounted to almost 100 million people, which formed the foundation of both military and economic strength.

A Sino-British treaty was signed in Chungking that resulted in the return of all remaining foreign settlements and concessions. A similar treaty was signed simultaneously in the United States by the Chinese ambassador and the U.S. Secretary of State. When surviving foreign internees were released at the end of the war in 1945, they found the treaty port extraterritoriality had gone. In fact, the essential purpose of the treaty port apparatus had become progressively unnecessary as there was increasing scope for business and trading development outside the foreign enclaves.

After Japan's capitulation, in the face of the atomic bomb attacks on Hiroshima and Nagasaki, the U.S. possession of nuclear weapons acted to deter those forces who were waiting in the wings to participate in any post-war settlement, including the Soviet Union. The American-backed Coalition Government was essentially confounded by a seemingly unofficial agreement between the Nationalists and Japanese to regain territories held by the Communists. Arguably only the national liberation movement stood in the way of imperialist rivals, who were reluctant to see the Japanese army surrender to the PLA, and arranged for this to be carried out by Kuomintang forces under Chiang Kai-shek. In return the Sino-American trade treaty of 1946 facilitated unrestricted access to the Chinese market for U.S. products—an arrangement that was interpreted as fostering increased U.S. intervention. Despite the intervention of the United States to broker an accord between the two sides through General George C. Marshall, and the economic and military supremacy of the Nationalist regime, the respective ideals of the Nationalists and Communists were too far apart for any kind of reconciliation. This formed a prelude to civil war. Marshall's report to President Truman prevailed upon Chiang to pull back from Manchuria—an action which possibly marked a decisive moment in the civil war.

This allowed the Communists to establish a secure base on the Soviet border, with its extensive railway links to Russia, Soviet occupied North Korea, and Outer Mongolia, which provided the capability of transferring new arms and artillery through the existing rail system. Russian military training, the transfer of abandoned Japanese aircraft, tanks, and artillery, together with the transfer of thousands of Japanese prisoners of war, including trained pilots, was of crucial importance to the Communists. A further factor was the in-flux of 200,000 Korean soldiers from Soviet-occupied North Korea, and a "friendly" 800-km border allowing the Communists to use North Korea as a vital link between Manchuria and the east coast.[149]

After 1945 the Nationalist forces held most of the provincial capitals and the main ports in South China, including Canton whose remaining monetary and industrial assets were requisitioned. Systematic corruption and a lack of proper fiscal policies that were necessary to stabilize the situation led to a forfeiture of public confidence. In addition, the agricultural economy was crippled, which led to widespread starvation in the countryside.[150] The PLA withdrew from many cities, seeking a consolidation of support, but the Communist's continued advocation of land reform had become a symbol of resistance and socio-political change, even to the professional and merchant class in the southern cities. Although many of these were not necessarily Communist sympathizers, they saw no sign of political, social, or economic reform under the auspices of the Kuomintang and with economic collapse came social disorder. By the spring of the following year the Communist forces, financed and armed by Russia, had become sufficiently transformed under Lin Biao, so that the Nationalists began to experience a sequence of defeats in the military campaigns, in no large part assisted by the growing defection of key Nationalist commanders. In December 1947, the PLA crossed the Yellow River and began moving south in an offensive to liberate the cities. Within a year Northeast China was liberated, followed by a similar campaign in Shandong Province resulting in the capture of massive quantities of armaments and tanks. In January 1949, Tianjin and Peking surrendered, and in April PLA forces crossed the Yangtze River.

The Communists had built from the bottom up, based not so much on radical social reform as on transforming itself into a vigorous social movement.[151] For several months Canton served as the capital of the Republic of China after Nanjing was taken by the People's Liberation Army. As part of the Nationalist retreat they blew up the Haizhu Bridge across the Pearl River. The final confrontation between the two sides was at Huaihai in January 1949, which ended in a Communist victory.

Mao Zedong forces entered Beijing two months later in captured American tanks to face what was arguably an even greater battle. On October 1, 1949, in Tiananmen Square, Mao proclaimed the People's Republic of China. This was announced as an alliance between all classes, led by the proletariat and orchestrated through military administrative regions as a means of uniting the country and rekindling the economy.

Now our enthusiasm has been aroused. Ours is an ardent nation, now swept by
a burning tide. There is a good metaphor for this: our nation is like an atom…
When this atom's nucleus is smashed the thermal energy released will have
tremendous power. We shall be able to do things that we could not do before.

—Mao Zedong, 1958

Chapter 7

The Socialist Planned Economy 1949–1976

The Political Transition

To be revolutionary is to understand the past as well as forging a route that could repeatedly transcend itself for the greater good of society. By 1949 the Sino-Japanese War followed by the ensuing civil war had left most Chinese cities in a degraded condition. Only 10.6 percent of the population was urbanized and the country was in dire economic circumstances, exacerbated by a U.S.-led embargo. Communist China had to substantiate the superiority of socialism and deal with military threat before it could adequately develop and legitimize the forces of production, even as it reinforced a necessary austerity policy. This had, at some stage, to evolve into a strategy directed toward the effective reorganization of various factors that shaped the production and consumption processes. These in turn held important implications for new organizational models, albeit influenced by prior Republican initiatives, and based on national five-year plans that controlled the rate of urban growth.

While this ostensibly signaled a unified China, the immediate difficulty in establishing political legitimacy was challenged by a less than supportive international environment, through the wide perception of the CCP as an armed revolutionary party. Mao Zedong chose to side with the Soviet Union, one of the three signatories of the Yalta Agreement, in response to an urgent need for both assistance and some degree of acceptance for its policies—a model that was also supported by other socialist countries. This resulted in the eradication of virtually all Western influences, although a number of nations, including Britain, India, and various Scandinavian countries, began to explore opportunities for diplomatic relations. The outbreak of the Korean War in 1954 effectively interrupted this process as did disputes over the future of Taiwan, with Mao and Zhou En-lai retaining absolute control over foreign affairs.[152]

The acceptance of Communism in China, which on the surface seems alien to the country's deeply rooted hierarchical social traditions, is at least partly explained through a state orthodoxy that for centuries was widely respected and obeyed. It must also be stated that the egalitarian ideals of socialism were clearly welcomed after decades of conflict. The transition to a Communist government was expediently handled by the Chinese Communist Party by taking over all civilian institutions. For a time, city governments functioned as normal, and with them the urbanizing regimes that initially invested, if only modestly, in infrastructure. At the beginning of CCP rule over Canton and other port cities many of the economic reigns were still privately held, and both urban industries and commercial operations, at least initially, were maintained. The economy had for a number of years been mismanaged, and massive corruption had led to hyper-inflation with a considerable reduction in gold and foreign currency reserves. Inflation was immediately brought under control by linking essential commodities, such as grain and oil, to income, while corruption in the private business class soon began to be targeted by the new regime.[153]

After 1949, because of the unfavorable international trading environment, the country traded only with Communist Bloc countries, effectively constraining the inherent locational advantages of Canton, and its status was deemed to be "semi-open," but strictly controlled by central government. Urban development from 1949, following the founding of the People's Republic of China, and for thirty years thereafter under the Socialist Planned Economy, was reflected by a plethora of utilitarian landmark structures under the banner of "People's Architecture," which generally represented a fusion of deliberately immense forms with an otherwise subdued identity. Such an approach was intended to display a deliberately restrained national character that lingers on in the residue of public buildings and military headquarters built at the time on prominent sites in the main cities. Thus, over a period of less than 50 years, urban design underwent several transitions, redolent of Western influences but with a reinterpretation of imported styles, and a gradual pairing back of the superfluous. In themselves these established a mixed urban legacy that came to represent China's prolonged absence from the world stage.

The already rudimentary legal system gradually became hostage to Party policy, and the 1950 campaign against supposed "counter-revolutionaries" turned to a harsher form of suppression, honed by Mao during the civil war and termed *lao-gai* or "reform through labor."[154] Party committees were set up to ensure pervasive forms of control through a sequence of campaigns ostensibly targeted at inefficient bureaucratism, but really aimed at achieving high-visibility repression of "class enemies"—a fundamental feature of the proposed *zhengfeng* or thought reform. This was carried out through group discussion and "reformation" of embedded ideas directed toward mass campaign movements aimed at consolidating the ideology of the State, but which gradually became less than discriminate in the identification of counter revolutionaries.[155] The administration was reinforced by large numbers of Soviet advisers, and slowly a systematic "cleansing" of the Nationalist old guard was introduced. The withdrawal of foreign warships from Shanghai, and American forces from the only remaining base in Tsingtao, effectively ended a Western presence in China for the next thirty years.[156]

In 1949, around 40 percent of the total population and two-thirds of total industrial output were concentrated in seven coastal provinces.[157] Virtually all remaining Westerners were expelled, ostensibly to reduce Western influence that had become ingrained in the modern educational institutions. America and Britain alone had financed and operated 31 universities and specialized schools, 32 religious educational establishments, and 29 libraries in China, as well as 2,699 schools, 3,822 religious missions, and 147 hospitals.[158] However, as China became gradually sealed off from much of the outside world in the aftermath of war and famine, it was short of educated and skilled people

Some individual neighborhood[s] made up of street blocks beca[me] semi-private enclaves divided internally by interways—narrow pedestrian streets identified by distinctive gateways, such as those in the Li Wan area—whic[h] announced the name of each district.

eighborhood associations in
anton were defined in terms
urban blocks. Within these
eas, self-governing committees
chestrated various operations
ch as fire prevention, garbage
moval, security control, and
igious celebrations.

to run the cities and their institutions, so that modern schools, universities, newspapers and religious establishments that had largely been founded by Westerners and educated Chinese began to close down. The intention was also to radically curb the liberal Chinese intelligentsia, even at the expense of the experienced personnel necessary to maintain these urban institutions.

Kam Wing Chan's assessment of the urbanization process in post-1949 China divides the period between 1950 to 1977 into various components of growth in terms of both urban demographic increase and rural-urban migration. The first period between 1950–57 coincided with a phase of rapid industrialization, which attracted millions of rural workers; the Great Leap Forward in 1958–60 involved an outflow of intellectuals to the countryside but a massive rural to urban migration of around 15 million people; the period from 1960–1965 led to an overall loss of 18 million workers; while between 1966–77 during the Cultural Revolution there was again a net urban migration of around 11 million.[159] By this time a large proportion of the labor force had been organized into urban worker cooperatives, with an emphasis on employment in heavy industry.[160] Capitalist management and most forms of private industry were replaced in the cities, and a form of collectivization was applied to the state management of industry based on a somewhat questionable interpretation of the Soviet model. Part of this policy was to deflect industrial development away from the traditional port cities, including Canton, which were regarded as bourgeois centers of corruption, to the interior of the country. Of 156 new Soviet-aided heavy industrial plants, all were located in inland cities such as Wuhan.[161]

The Changing Nature of Urban Space

After 1949, Soviet planners who had been invited to China began to import some of the urban development notions that had been tested in the Russian socialist cites, which at first led to an emphasis on large-scale industrial production, with new urban design vocabularies that resulted from a series of five-year plans. The dense residential street structure that represented much of Canton's older morphology, and which traditionally ensured a minutely articulated relationship between the private realm of internal organization and the public realm of the street, became progressively sub-divided. Multi-family occupancy caused public spaces and courtyards to become progressively filled in to create additional "temporary" accommodation known as *dazayuan*— literally "crowded courts," within many of the older neighborhoods.

People's communes were intended as a means to construct a controlled socialist society that set out to eliminate rural-urban distinctions under collective units where private ownership was abolished, and which brought together industry, agriculture, and education. Urban planners and architects were mobilized to develop orderly layout designs. All property, land, and tools were pooled, and older villages were reorganized into larger residential compounds that could contain many households. Communes were divided into production brigades and mutual aid teams, which embraced both political and economic functions to support Mao's Great Leap Forward campaign.

Through a network of worker dependencies came forms of social control and a commensu-rate reduction in individual autonomy, transformed into physical dimensions through living and

work compounds termed *danwei*, accessed only through restricted "gated" entrances that represented an attempt to collectivize labor and revolutionize social relations. These affected almost every aspect of life and represented dispersed and carefully demarcated enclaves as "protective territories" constructed in a standardized form, with integral community facilities and essential services. This effectively minimized investment in anything apart from the most basic form of accommodation, albeit in a situation where many peasants possessed little at all after the destructive civil war. Urbanization therefore became, almost entirely, a process of rationalization. Privatization of urban space has a long tradition in Chinese city building, but from the beginning of the 1950s, private land and building became nationalized under a utopian ideal that lauded public ownership as necessary for a harmonious society. Community services extended to institutions such as universities, hospitals, and government ministries so that *danwei* came to resemble the ancient walled environments, with their status geared to a complicated hierarchical model of power and administrative convenience. The lack of local infrastructure and public space outside the compounds equally emphasized the notion of self-containment, but also isolation.[162]

Urban work units were built according to functional zoning plans, with a close association of workplace and residence within a regularized and ordered form, which accommodated around 90 percent of all urban housing. The work units orchestrated both collective production and consumption, including laundromats and nurseries, so that these served as the main urban reference for social life. Because residents dined in communal halls, residential units were constructed with no kitchens. Women were urged to work on an equal level with men, creating a need to build childcare facilities as part of work units as part of a basic welfare system. Housework, normally the domain

of women, was also operated under a collective system. As a result, incoming revenue had to be balanced with controlled expenditure but was largely unable to extract surplus value in accordance with national economic plans. One notorious example was the attempt to produce steel in "backyard furnaces," which not only failed but diverted farmers from agricultural pursuits, leading to scarcity of food and then to severe famine. In the early 1960s the industrial emphasis was redirected toward agricultural production, and its revolutionary focus began to fade. In Canton the urban communes had a singular success in extending mixed uses and services into the city's old neighborhoods.

Housing blocks were four or five stories high and generally constructed from rough bricks with no surface treatments. Communities themselves operated brick kilns, firing bricks in massive quantities and orchestrating sequences of self-build operations. Most existing houses were requisitioned and sub-divided, with rooms distributed first to the homeless and workers. Soviet aid facilitated the rebuilding of essential public buildings such as hospitals.

Mobilizing large numbers of people for manual work compensated for the lack of available construction technology, but also reflected revolutionary goals. Housing blocks had shared kitchens, bathroom, and toilet facilities, and all services together with maintenance and repairs were included in the low and affordable monthly rent. At the same time schools, welfare offices, workshops, and other public buildings were allocated to facilitate decentralization. Apartments and houses were planned to accommodate between three and five families with a common living area and kitchen.

Government control over urban land meant that uses could be designated irrespective of normal market forces, and city quarters were re-structured as independent communities, each with a different emphasis, rather than forming an integrated texture. As a result, during the post-1949 period, streets gradually lost their active character and social role within the city. Piper Gaubatz has identified three prominent characteristics of older city environment brought about through the *danwei* system: a high level of urban organization in addition to the development of functionally mixed but distinctly egalitarian districts; standardized three- to five-story developments but with wide social differentiation in terms of quality of housing and facilities; and the persistence of the "walking-scale" city with little in terms of transport infrastructure.[163]

Massively scaled road systems acted to demarcate zoned areas for public buildings, and government and military complexes, that reflected the functionalist landmark structures of the socialist state. Equally significant was the use of public space for important political events and pageantry, with a flanking array of stark public buildings. Canton followed a city planning model representing the new political and social order that was matched by a restrained level of public architecture, high in symbolism and prominence.

The Urban – Rural Divide

In essence the post-1949 period underscored a deepening division between cities and the countryside. Heavy industry received the majority of State investment funds, while collectivization and compulsory State procurement of agricultural products discriminated against rural development. Growth of existing cities became circumscribed, and large numbers of their existing intellectual elite were assigned to countryside communes in an ultimately futile attempt to construct the new China on its rural base. At the same time, the expansion of urban services and infrastructural development in the older port cities, including Canton, was suppressed, which meant that these cities were relatively "under-urbanized" compared to their actual populations.[164]

Radical agrarian reform was introduced in the 1950s aimed at the redistribution of land holdings confiscated from landlords. The collectivization of agriculture was controlled within a hierarchical structure of village production teams, brigades, and communes, and crop prices were regulated so that the state not only procured but distributed food supply. This form of systematic organization and brokerage between teams and brigades, was essentially an officially sanctioned but more purposely orchestrated version of traditional authoritarian procedures. Although the process did not unduly act to increase production it was regarded, under the preliminary five-year plans, as being necessary to long-term reform and development in the cities.[165] In practice the campaigns directed skills away from commercial activities, and banks began to reduce lending as industrial production began to fall. By 1952, 80 percent of heavy industry and 40 percent of light industry had been nationalized, and government controlled almost all finance through the People's Bank. In addition, state companies handled almost all imports and exports.[166]

By the following year, 90 percent of agricultural holdings in the country had been transferred, emphasizing the strength of the central authority, and paving the way for a campaign that was supposedly focused on rectifying social and economic problems in the cities, but in actual fact became directed at nationalizing private property and businesses.[167] This finally exhausted the ability of private businesses

to function, and effectively put control of industrial development into the hands of an increasingly totalitarian government. It has been estimated that during this period 61 percent of the national budget was dedicated to military and associated arms and equipment—some seven times the spending on education, culture, and health.[168] This led to the eventual nationalization of commerce and industry in the cities.

Restrictions on Urban Development

The "learn through manual labor" process was instituted firstly because of a reaction on the part of authorities toward the latent reactionary forces inherent in city culture, and secondly because of the traditional lack of urban autonomy. At the same time cities were widely perceived by Mao as harboring sources of foreign influence and endemic corruption. It was therefore both easier and more expedient to redirect urbanization toward the rural heartland and smaller urban centers, where the communist revolution had initially taken root. The main policy instrument that restricted rural to urban migration, and therefore city expansion, was

the *hukou* system of population registration. This effectively controlled population mobility, as it tied people to just one urban or rural location through restrictive access to such necessities as foodstuffs and housing. During this period no urban planning was carried out as there existed an embargo on city expansion, and the strict demarcation between urban development and the rural hinterland created a situation that was to unintentionally encourage urban sprawl during the massive city expansion programs some 30 years later.

The second five-year plan centered around the means to expand agricultural production in line with major growth in industry. This was, in effect, the catalyst that inspired the Great Leap Forward between 1958 and 1960, announced at the Eighth Party Congress in May, 1958. Its idealistic goal was the effective mobilization of the entire population toward achieving economic advancement, on both an agricultural and industrial front, as a basis for self-reliance and ideological correctness. Social re-ordering effectively curtailed the attention needed to deal with the complex dimensions of city fabric, both physical and social, with street blocks turned into "People's Communes" of overcrowded accommodation focused around industrial centers and the activities of production brigades. At a time when the natural forces of production, trade and transaction should have logically led to an increasingly cosmopolitan form of city environment, planning reinforced the regularized urban patterns associated with physically separate quarters, but devoid of their inherent finesse and traditions. The wide streets of administrative centers were lined with stand-alone buildings and monuments within walled compounds, while construction units and housing estates formed stereotyped symbols of standardized production. From the early 1960s, Canton and other coastal cities were subject to a double burden—investment was deflected away from China's main sources of productivity, while the state became ever more dependent on these cities as sources of industrial production and economic return.

The vandalization of urban monuments during the Mao years was in fact not a new device to subjugate the will and confidence of the population at large. The destruction of the Summer Palace by the Earl of Elgin in 1860 to hasten the compliance of China with the Treaty of Tianjin was a not dissimilar situation.[169]

Housing and Urbanization

Development of the Socialist Planned Economy was geared to public ownership, both through resumption of private property and through prioritizing public building.[170] Zang Jie and Wang Tao in examining the impact of this period on built development have identified the most salient issue as being the adopted strategy of "high accommodation and low consumption" in order to facilitate the development of heavy industry. Housing during this period was effectively state controlled, becoming in effect a welfare commodity, including provision by institutions such as worker's villages and factory enterprises. The majority of growth occurred not in the port cities but in and around the regional satellite cities in close proximity to resources. Design at both an architectural and urban level took on a rudimentary and standardized form.[171]

Separate social and economic structures were enforced for urban and rural areas. In the port cities, including Canton, urban housing continued to serve the most basic needs and formed part of the overall welfare system that was tightly controlled and linked with work units, managed by local authorities. Worker's "villages" were built adjacent to factory areas, and the designs, although essentially standard low-rise block forms, had a significant influence on urbanization patterns, which under the first five-year plan continued to multiply. Toward the end of this period as part of a gradual transition to the socialist system of public ownership, existing private units were transferred to the public sector which then controlled both production, consumption, and distribution.

In Canton the social and political turbulence of the Cultural Revolution created a state of urban stagnation. The Provincial Planning Commission was mainly concerned with production of essential food, including quotas for grain and rice with prices tightly controlled. Neighborhood collectives were planned to be as near self-sufficient as possible, with allotment areas to grow vegetables and grain. Communes had to operate in a virtually self-contained way, growing their own food, producing goods, and running schools.

New urban housing in Canton often consisted of parallel terraces, but in general had better internal facilities than older housing. A significant proportion of the construction budget was used to improve or install urban infrastructure, in particular piped water supply. Different families would often share accommodations, which often conflicted with environmental criteria due to a lack of ventilation and daylight. In the interests of economy design ideology shifted away from extravagant gestures toward more rationalized methods of mass production. The impact of inspired "social realism," led to formalistic architectural compositions for public buildings that merged a hybrid classicism with austere facades that imparted an imposing urban identity.[172]

In practice the political ideology both slowed down and redirected the pace of urbanization. Planning was based not so much on facilitating the essential functioning of cities but on re-calibrating their institutional and administrative agencies, by eliminating the economic and social differences between urban and rural areas. The port city of trade and commerce gave way to the socialist city of poverty and uniformity reflecting the nationalization of the land and housing market, and spatial equity in urban development.[173] Urban planning entailed a division into neighborhood zones, each of which contained industry, housing, agriculture, and community facilities, with the communes forming a basic organizational structure for each area.[174] People's communes, with populations of around 2,000, were based on both self-reliance and self-sufficiency emulating the established rural village ideology.

Between 1958 and 1965 the extended people's communes began to exert a strong urban design influence on the form of city growth, with new satellite communities creating an intense utilization of land for predominantly low-rise development. By 1960, around 77 percent of China's urban population were living in communes. Minimalist forms designed to save on building materials reduced design standards, but also utilized terraced configurations with concrete wall panels dividing accommodation into single one- and two-bedroom units, according to local conditions. Housing and dormitory blocks were of the most basic brick and concrete frame construction and remained unclad.

The Cultural Revolution

The turbulent period that commenced in 1966 began paradoxically as an attack on the existing political culture, exemplified by what was deemed to be a necessary purge of Party bureaucrats. In practice, the violence and utter destruction created a veritable reign of terror brought about through a protracted propaganda exercise that emphasized a Great Leap Forward, under the authorization of Mao Zedong. Through his deeds and reputation Mao Zedong had a strong hold on the predominantly rural and subdued population, akin to iconic status, that continued to be associated with his patriotic role in countering national exploitation and long periods of oppression by foreign powers.

Mao had to face increasing calls for change from prominent members of the party apparatus who now occupied privileged positions in an expanding bureaucracy. In turn, Mao called for a "cultural revolution"—ostensibly to "correct" the growth and consolidation of the urban-centered elite and

its multi-levelled officialdom at the expense of revolutionary egalitarianism, political reform, and class struggle. This involved an attack on cultural norms as representing an elitist class with pre-revolutionary values, associated with wealth and privilege whether through the arts or education. A determination to engender a new "proletarian culture" was linked closely with the perception that a permanent state of revolution and change was necessary to keep these values alive, reinforced by the purges of 1966. Wall posters sent out propaganda "messages" and were used to mold public opinion, reinforced by Red Guards—groups of students invited by the Central Committee, who zealously propounded the overthrow of all cultural elites including bureaucrats, teachers, and "capitalist roaders." The slogan was "Smash the old; build the new," that in turn evolved into a move against Party cadres themselves. Traditional art forms that remained concentrated in the cities including music, theater, and opera were banned as feudal or capitalist pursuits, although "reformed" cultural models were introduced to symbolically express revolutionary activism. The Cultural Revolution itself was a systematic attempt at smashing established cultural icons, so that heritage buildings were vulnerable simply because they were in the firing line, both literally and figuratively.

The gatherings in Tiananmen Square in late 1966, attended by an estimated twelve million young Red Guards, was a dramatic means to induce support for a "Better China" and a direct appeal for confrontation against the lingering bourgeois classes, intellectuals, and "rightists." This struck a responsive chord, and Mao's apparent willingness to purge those who resisted quickly led to the country surging out of control as students became increasingly radicalized. Tao Zhu, the Party leader became a vice-premier in 1966 and head of the Propaganda Department in Beijing, but was later taken into custody by the Red Guards and died in prison in 1969. He was replaced by Zhao Ziyang who himself underwent various public humiliations before re-emerging in 1973 and becoming Party general secretary in 1987. Other leading Party officials in Canton were forcibly paraded through the streets, and Zeng Sheng, the former mayor of Canton, spent four years in prison isolation.

From the mid-1960s political chaos emanating from the Cultural Revolution overwhelmed any coherent programs of urban development. As the growing urban populations could not be effectively employed, Chinese cities entered a long period of social turbulence. In 1966 the third national five-year plan reflected an investment emphasis directed away from the established coastal conurbations toward the inland areas, which in turn acted to inhibit the urban tertiary sector.

In 1967, virtually all government establishments were occupied by Red Guards, supported by the army, and many officials were expelled, never able to return. An infusion of younger members into the revolutionary groups, led by the children of peasants as well as those from intellectual families, were reinforced by thousands of Red Guards from the North. Many top cadres were effectively protected, however, and in Canton they were detained in the military barracks on the outskirts of the city. Others less fortunate were subject to house confinement and regularly searched for incriminating material. Meanwhile, different Red Guard factions began to acquire weapons while others seized guns from storage facilities that led to armed clashes.

At Zhongshan University a number of professors were lynched and left hanging from trees, and in all tens of thousands in Guangdong Province were killed in confrontations. It is recorded that in late 1967, Zhou Enlai received representations from different Red Guard factions in Canton to intervene, which acted to bring the situation under control. More formal Revolutionary Committees were established for both Canton and Guangzhou Province in 1968, with more than one million students sent to work in rural areas or on state farms, while many were assigned to work in factories. The State Housing Administration was effectively wound up and, as municipal facilities were not maintained, buildings in Canton fell into disrepair, with new housing generally confined to small lots in the older urban quarters.

In Peking and Nanking large parts of the ancient city walls were torn down together with historical monuments, temples, and tombs, while new public buildings such as the Great Hall of the People were built in the bland Russian style of the period. In Canton, old temples, including the Banner Temple at Honan, were torn down or vandalized. It was estimated that more than two-thirds of the almost 7,000 historical monuments in Peking were destroyed during

this period, while many heritage buildings were closed. Even the ancestral home of Confucius in Shandong Province was desecrated.

The long period of time after the Great Leap Forward, when no reliable information was available, posed obstacles to any empirical assessment of what was actually happening in China during this time. This led to the many ideological statements on the success of the new urban growth model being accepted at face value. In reality, the conflict between traditional and bureaucratic authority, and between political factions themselves, essentially reflected a struggle to realize a modernizing technological model.[175] It might be said that labor-intensive industrial activities during this period, in part, facilitated the later modernizations through an emphasis on an inexpensive but productive labor force rather than expensive technical infrastructure, as a necessary precursor to new forms of industrialization.[176] Politically induced egalitarianism, in the sense that all people had equal rights, was probably more attributable to the decline of urban income rather than a growth in wealth through collectivization.

Factional clashes continued until 1968, representing an era of social and economic convulsion that seriously disrupted urban life. Student organizations were disbanded and it is estimated that more than 16 million young people from the cities were sent to remote villages and state farms, thereby eliminating dissent while relieving the problem of unemployment. Productive workers in large, capital-intensive industrial enterprises were well looked after by the state, while at the same time cities were subject to daunting programs of collective housing. Older and more substantive housing remained the prerogative of the cadre elite.

Following Mao's own initiative, several hundred cadres were sent to state farms to combine physical labor with study of the profound thoughts of Mao under the keen eye of the military, with many not returning until 1975. Only after virtually all opposition to Mao had been purged, was the Ninth Party Congress in 1969 convened to formally recognize the reconstructed Communist Party. The irrational use of state-sanctioned persecution and destructive violence left in its wake profound disillusionment at all levels for a misdirected program that clearly failed in its most fundamental purpose. The end of the Cultural Revolution marked the opportunity to return China to the international community on the back of a broken economy and a seriously fractured society.

The Cultural Revolution considerably curtailed foreign trade and had to meet a centralized policy that emphasized rice production at the expense of other products. The Foreign Trade School in Canton was closed along with branches of foreign trade corporations, and their members persecuted along with those connected with foreign funding of investment projects. As the implications of this became clear to Chinese communities abroad, remittances declined dramatically, the only exception being shipments of medical items. Only through the intervention of Zhou Enlai was Canton's trade fair allowed to continue in a much-reduced form, reflecting the necessary priority given to local requirements rather than import.

Large statues of Mao began to emerge in public places and outside major public buildings from around 1967. They generally showed Mao in an overcoat with right hand raised as if acknowledging acclamation. At the same time, billboards carried Mao's quotations along with political slogans.

一切想着毛主席 一切服从毛主席
一切紧跟毛主席 一切为着毛主席

From around 1970 a restrained policy of "revolutionary diplomacy" began to present a more benign face to the world, and in 1971 Beijing wrested China's seat at the United Nations from Taiwan. Mao's most successful and lasting foreign initiative was his discreet overture to President Richard Nixon, orchestrated by premier Zhou Enlai. The Chinese regime's diplomatic overture turned a crucial corner in terms of China's standing on the world stage, and arguably Nixon's visit to Peking in February 1972 set a fragile basis for the "open door" reforms that were introduced some six years later. The United States-Chinese Communiqué at the conclusion of President Nixon's visit to the PRC in 1972 established something of a watershed. As part of diplomatic recognition, the U.S. offered immediate entry to the United Nations, supported the "territorial integrity" of China, and offered access to Western technology. In the wake of the visit, more Western countries began to recognize Beijing while China also donated scarce currency to provide foreign aid to Third World countries that it had previously attempted to subvert to Maoism.

Mao was particularly sensitive to the remnants of the foreign concessions on the toe of China, namely Hong Kong and Macau. Technically, the taking of both small enclaves would have been easy, as both were dependent on China for water, but Hong Kong in particular was a vital strategic gateway to and from the West, generating hard currency and acting as a conduit for Western technology and equipment. While mobs were induced to attack foreign embassies and consulates in China during the Cultural Revolution, the two concessions were spared invasion.

It is often said that China effectively lost a generation in terms of both people and time, that was not replenished until the early years of Deng Xiaoping's reforms. Family alienation, that formed a constant recurrence during the Cultural Revolution, became a central theme of literature in the following years, covering an era of painful separation and resultant anguish. In the meantime a new state constitution was drafted and Lin Biao, Mao's designated successor who conveniently died in an air accident, was held up as the scapegoat for all past excesses.

Deng Xiaoping, a veteran of the Long March, was eleven years Mao's junior, and had as a young man lived and studied for several years in France. Also trained in Russia, he was part of the top echelon of command during the Sino-Japanese war. Deng was reinstated in 1973 and appointed army chief before establishing an informal alliance with premier Zhou Enlai. With slow deliberation he began to unravel the damages of the Cultural Revolution, even before Mao's death. The urban population had increased over the previous twenty years, and Deng was gradually able to exert more influence as increased levels of investment slowly began to have a positive impact on housing, health, and education. It was not until 1974, when Zhao Ziyang took over the Revolutionary Committee, that Guangdong returned to civilian leadership. Later rehabilitation of many officials was regarded as a form of liberation, and an essential prerequisite for both a restoration of reputation and national re-assessment.

By 1975, the Chinese leadership was increasingly polarized, and with the incapacitation and imminent deaths of both Mao and Zhou Enlai two antagonistic groups emerged with fundamentally different views on national interest. One sought to extend the radical thrust of the Cultural Revolution with power centered in the Politburo. The other comprised a more seasoned group of military leaders and veterans of

做人要做这样的人

将革命进行到底

the Long March who shared a concern for party reconstruction and modernization. This group included Deng Xiaoping who had previously been condemned in 1969 as the "number two capitalist roader."

In 1976, shortly before the death of both Zhou Enlai and Mao, Deng Xiaoping was officially rehabilitated. As a noted pragmatist who had been purged during the Cultural Revolution, Deng began to introduce steps to counterbalance the power of the People's Liberation Army. The death of Zhou Enlai in January 1976 triggered outpourings of public grief, and Mao's own weakening health led to his death on the morning of September 9, 1976. This effectively closed a mournful chapter on modern Chinese history, but also induced a new beginning.

Cultural Production and Symbolism

Cantonese Opera troupes had performed in Guangdong Province since the sixteenth century, although it faced a ban of fourteen years for sedition from 1854 when a leading actor led others in a revolt against the dynasty. The clown's role, characteristic of Cantonese opera, gained prominence in the 1930s through the spoken drama portrayals of Ma Shizeng.

Under Mao all cultural and artistic production was used as propaganda, repudiating the Western concept of entertainment aligned with an educational undertone, and instead reflecting a revolutionary ideology. Music, theater, dance, and literature were ingeniously directed toward conveying a political message that reverberated with the temper of the time. The arts drew on the prevailing inequalities of the masses, with an underlying emphasis that this could only be countered by the Communist Party whose deified figurehead was Mao. While folk art and music had their roots in the population at large, theatrical and opera groups were under the jurisdiction of the state. The Cultural Revolution dramas placed their essential emphasis on class enemies and socialist heroes, which represented the only permitted form of theatrical performance.

During the 1930s, Chinese traditional folk music assumed a revolutionary aura, culturally deployed to bolster the revolutionary rhetoric and hardships associated with the Long March. "The East is Red" with its evocative bell chimes continues to connote a national imaginary, equivalent to a patriotic narrative. Representative imagery is equally subtle—Children's release of doves and the holding of candles symbolically alludes to a desire for peace while an array of minority nationalities, colorfully costumed, offer righteous salutations directed toward the red PRC flag, invigorated by authority.

Urban change during the Cultural Revolution can be usefully discerned through the ideological commodification of cultural modes that have taken on an allegorical association with this period.[177] The contemporary commercialization of the revolutionary model through symbolic imagery marks a curious connective transition from past to present through theater, film, and artistic representation rather than as a unified entity. While the notion of "cultural" practice between 1949 and 1976 could be seen as a contradiction in terms, its roots lay in the tradition of Cantonese and Peking opera coupled with the ambiguous political undertones that embody changes in both popular culture and traditional identity. Such an ambiguous cultural emphasis partly reflected an intuitive rejection of the past while at the same time instigating the power of artistic and design expression for revolutionary purposes.

Modernized "reformed model performances" were based on re-worked classical themes, but gave way to considerable innovation in Chinese operas and operatic "ballet." These combined revolutionary fervor with a transformative realism in operatic works that involved a combination of scenes from contemporary life of the times, even as authoritative views were becoming more puritanical. In fact, Chinese heroic tales abound with the *wu-hsia hsiao-shuo*—a tradition of fantasy built around chivalry, linked to a moral creed of inner truth, although not necessarily tied to Confucian bureaucracy.[178] While the importance of agriculture was honored in imperial ritual many of the peasants struggled on a subsistence income or under forced labor. The dream of social mobility therefore ran through stage performances from tragic to comic.

The model operas were based primarily on Peking opera but related to the Red Army, military campaigns, and peasant worker heroism that were part of an enduring romanticism whose basis lay in traditional drama. *Taking Tiger Mountain by Strategy* was refined over four years of performances including the Maoist anthem *The East is Red,* while another opera *A Surprise Attack on the White Tiger Regiment* included the *International* to underscore the international revolutionary movement. *The Red Detachment of Women* with its theme of heroic struggle was based on a popular film. The other main revolutionary operas and ballets were *The Red Lantern*; *On the Docks*; *Song of the Dragon River*; *Fighting on the Plain*; and *The Azalea Mountain*. The continued acclaim of these operas stems from their established repertoire and a suitably refined input from noted musicians, poets, and writers of

Revolutionary Culture: The politics of revolution in China can be encapsulated in its cultural models or yangbanxi that comprised ten operas, four ballets, two symphonies, and two piano pieces. They are popularly ascribed to Mao's wife Jiang Qing who redirected traditional Peking opera with its more comfortable themes of nobles and concubines, toward a more revolutionary program. While opera and ballet references the political ideology of the times they reconciled xenophobia with an artistic transformation, redirecting the basis of Western dramatic traditions toward a new and radical focus. Film versions carried these works to all parts of the country, in pursuit of a dominant and politically contrived discourse to conform with Maoist thought and the notion of continuous revolution that became part of a socio-political model.

the period,[179] but their association with revolutionary chic undeniably plays an important part in their contemporary popularity.

The dominant principles relate strongly to the political and visual rhetoric of the revolutionary period as a model for proletarian liberation and class struggle that has mythologized the Cultural Revolution. However, the appetite for heroic sacrifice and the perennially popular struggle of good against evil tended to borrow from ancient myths and historical themes that made them identifiable to the masses and was shrewdly appropriated by the CCP leadership. As authentic cultural references for this period, they have also been sustained and memorialized in a commercialized iconic form that arguably belies their real intent.

From 1949, while artistic production had to represent a political context, it also challenged traditional and spoken drama in its opportunities for propaganda. As the political framework was unstable it offered a more favorable cultural environment than the preceding periods of Japanese occupation and civil conflict that were still fresh in the minds of the population. By the mid-1960s all theater troupes had become nationalized, and content was subject to close inspection to ensure the removal of feudal or capitalist ideologies, which included the traditional cast of emperors and imperial officials unless they stood for benevolence and justice. This left the most fundamental features of the performance, such as choreographed stage presence, singing, and costumes intact, to be cleverly translated by experienced actors according to the underlying emotions of the story. However, the hardline ideology of the Cultural Revolution, together with its chaotic side effects, led to many aspects of traditional culture being banned or prudently side-lined, with some actors suffering at the hands of Red Guards. During the Cultural Revolution Cantonese opera performances were, for a time, halted entirely and it took until the 1990s to recommence commercial performances.

Theater also had to comply with the constraints of the Mao Era and had to communicate the right kind of political message under strict conditions and limitations. It was popular, however, assisted in part through compulsory attendance. It is recorded that in 1954 theater groups in China played to predominantly industrial worker and military audiences amounting to 62 million. However, from the onset of the Cultural Revolution until its demise in 1976 only the eight personally approved model operas could be performed. They were not only presented as theater but were made into films, shown throughout the country. Their representation and continued symbolism have been resurrected in new productions in the early twenty-first century as a charismatic form that can be appreciated on its own terms by contemporary audiences as the epitome of revolutionary melodrama.

The post-Mao Era from the end of the 1970s, brought the revival of opera into competition with other forms of media entertainment so that Cantonese opera became increasingly directed at rural audiences at times of festivals. These were performed in temporary venues, usually erected in front of an ancestral temple or a park, and constructed by specialist contractors in bamboo. This nurtured the return of legendary exploits and morality tales that best resonated with the audiences. The six role types incorporate quite standard characteristics allowing for similar demonstrations of specialized skills and make-up according to expectations, but also embody a creative ability to bring the genre up to date. Cantonese opera is now on Unesco's list of Intangible Cultural Heritage. Both opera and film in contemporary China is a means of using the past to influence the present in terms of role types such as those that show off martial arts skills. Traditional theater has many regional forms such as Cantonese opera, and all forms of Chinese theater incorporate percussion as a means of emphasis while the narrative is accentuated by the skills and complementarity of singing, movement, and stylistic gesture rather than the story itself.

Modern Xiqu performances embrace new adaptations of classic novels, with themes that merge comic techniques with contemporary issues, and experimental opera that combines traditional techniques with new stage technology, exotic backdrops, and projected images. This has subsequently promoted the development of Cantonese opera theaters as representing a cultural art form that has evolved and transformed itself through challenging times. Shrines for a particular theatrical patron god are set up, and offerings are made before each performance. A further custom is to write the Chinese character for "luck" beside the shrine to ensure a blessing of good fortune from the patron god. Cantonese opera troupes also actively participate in community, charity, and social relief work.

During the 1980s, theatrical performances underwent a revival, challenging established norms. During a visit in the early 1980s I was taken to a small theater to see a play called *Woman with Three Husbands*. The provocative title was not entirely accurate, as the pretty and suitably unworldly heroine was being pursued by three suitors—the poor but honest boy next door, a self-absorbed army officer, and a shifty-looking fellow from Hong Kong. The enthusiastic suitors appeared in turn on stage to present their credentials, but it was the arrival of the Hong Kong representative, who arrived complete with a pencil-thin moustache and draped with cameras and (in those far-off days) tape recorders, that had most of the Mao-jacketed audience on their feet in hysterics. I looked around rather sheepishly, hastily decanting any similar examples of ostentation before the itinerant scoundrel from the colonial enclave was revealed as a smuggler and shunted off-stage by the army representative. The heroine's romantic future was of course a foregone conclusion all along.

The End of the Beginning

At the Fourth National People's Congress in February 1975, Zhou Enlai called for a drive to implement four modernizations stating that, "by the year 2000 our national economy will be advancing in the front ranks of the world."

Following this, a unified export production base with designated procurement stations was established that formed the basis of direct foreign trade trajectories for the "open policy" reforms initiated in 1978. This led to the opening of almost one hundred ports to foreign vessels by the following year and led directly to a gradual re-opening of the country to overseas Chinese and returnees. At the same time a decentralization of the foreign trade system from Beijing to the provinces actively stimulated foreign exchange reserves. The Guangdong International Trust and Investment Corporation was later established in 1980 to represent its provincial interests and to utilize foreign exchange reserves for necessary raw materials and technology.

Mao's death was the signal for an internal power struggle between forces loyal to his appointed successor, Hua Guofeng, and the so-called "Gang of Four" led by Mao's ex-wife and revolutionary colleague Jiang Qing from their Shanghai power base. Their arrest and subsequent trial not only brought to an end a turbulent and volatile era, but paved the way for a new outlook. After a decade of political turmoil the new leadership took on the task of unifying the county as a foundation for socialist modernization and development. Deng Xiaoping announced the launch of a modernization program as the main priority in moving forward at the Third Plenum of the Eleventh Party Congress in 1978. Following this many thousands began to return to the cities, including Canton.

The new leadership under Hua and Deng was understandably cautious, and reforms were based around the Four Modernizations of industry, technology, science, and agriculture. These were carefully introduced under the guise of extended Maoist teaching until an increasingly confident Deng Xiaoping felt able to broadcast a strongly reformist "Open Door Policy"—a second economic revolution that would carry China forward and awaken the "Sleeping Dragon."

By this time the economy and per capita income were on a modest upsurge together with industrial investment. A serious problem in Guangdong Province was the long neglect of road, rail, and power infrastructure, together with the degeneration of housing stock. However, the most monumental problem was in human resources and the lack of both administrative and professional knowledge. Those who had reached adulthood during the Cultural Revolution became known as the lost generation.

The socialist transformation had stagnated, but Deng Xiaoping was in a position to push forward reform. Standing on a southern hillside on August 26, 1979, he made an announcement that was to transform both the economy and the geography of Canton and Guangdong in the years to come, with a famous commitment to establish four special economic zones in the south of the Province. The new policy of "reform and opening up" was termed socialism with Chinese characteristics.

Deng's speech and the debate and furor that surrounded it set China on a new economic and social trajectory. This blended inherent state socialism with an emerging state-controlled capitalism—a seemingly contradictory combination, but with a successful infusion of the elusive "Chinese characteristics" that have been gradually able to transform the nation's relationship with the global community.

The Changing Status of Women

Women Hold Up Half the Sky
—Mao Zedong (A Chinese proverb, 1968)

Both *Dualism*, which advocated a philosophy of opposite and complementary entities, together with *Confucianism*, remain as ideologies of balance that have governed Chinese society for centuries. These have been taken to advocate the subordination of women with the commensurate growth of a patriarchal society, reinforced through many rituals and practices. For centuries, women's roles

were restricted to the private domestic sphere while the process of foot binding for Han women purposely confined them to restricted roles.

The proletarian socialist revolution, inadvertently or otherwise, metaphorically created a specific great leap forward in the form of women's struggle to transform their previously oppressed role in society on an ideological plane. Arguably the first step to emancipation in China was their participation in social labor after 1949. In Mao's *Little Red Book* it is stated that, "In order to build a great socialist society, it is of the utmost importance to encourage the broad masses of women to join in productive activity. Men and women must receive equal pay for equal work in production. Genuine equality between the sexes can only be realized in the process of the socialist transformation of society as a whole." This was taken literally, in the sense that the state did not enforce emancipation laws, but instead focused on the class struggle against bourgeois values.

Article 6 of China's Constitution states that, "women should enjoy equal rights with men in political, economic, cultural, educational, and social life." Gender representation based on occupational roles suggested an improvement in the status of women, and female labor participation was at almost maximum capacity between 1958 and 1978. However, parity of income tended to give way to the predominant emphasis on class struggle. During the Cultural Revolution schools were closed, and the Red Guard pressure acted to erase femininity in the cause of creating a revolution, with women often being forced to renounce their parents as Rightists or Counter Revolutionaries. In posters from the period women were depicted as having similar physiques, hairstyles, and clothes as men, although this did little to elevate their status, and femininity was regarded as reflecting bourgeois values. In most accounts of the Red Guards during the Cultural Revolution, young women made up more than half the "foot soldiers," with a seeming ability to be just as brutal as their male counterparts as and when necessary. This undoubtedly created ideological opportunities for women's progress, but these values failed to be sustained in the calmer economic, social, and political climate of reform. Liberation therefore succeeded only partially.

The commune system itself was insistently patriarchal, although later land reform technically reallocated land regardless of gender. In practice, however, most land remained within the patriarchal system. The one child policy introduced in 1979 resulted in an imbalanced sex ratio of 115 boys being born for every 100 girls. The rural-urban migration that began in the 1980s was dominated by male workers, although the second wave during the following decade was largely made up of both young men and women. The first five-year plan was successful in terms of ensuring an education for girls and an increasing percentage went on to higher education, and in the following years the role of women in national economic growth has been immense.

However, under the 2021 population census announced by the National Bureau of Statistics, of 12 million babies born in 2020, these were 111.3 boys for every 100 girls, underscoring the prevailing desire of Chinese families to have sons rather than daughters. In addition, it is estimated that up to 40 million more males than females were born in China between 1980 and 2020.

Our people face the great historic mission of comprehensively modernizing agriculture industry, national defense, and science and technology within this century, making our country a modern, powerful socialist state.

—Deng Xiaoping (Speech at Opening Ceremony of National Science Conference, March 18, 1978)

Chapter 8

Reforms, Challenges, and Resurgence

Initial economic advances, guided by the Communist Party leadership after 1978, were several steps removed from a free market economy. The planned reforms had to overcome both the challenges associated with the restoration of a degraded urban environment, but also the more enigmatic emotional and psychological residue of the Cultural Revolution, compounded by widespread poverty, imposed collectivization, and state control. While China required inspired political leadership on one hand to set responsive long-term goals, it also needed bold thinking in response to the economic challenges. A serious problem in Guangdong Province was the long neglect of road, rail, and power infrastructure, together with the degeneration of housing stock. By 1978 less than 10 percent of all housing was in private hands. However, the most monumental vacuum was in human resources, and in particular the lack of higher learning that created a shortage of administrative and professional experience and managerial expertise. More than three decades of sacrifice to the revolutionary period had also inculcated a deliberate avoidance of individual responsibility.

A crucial turning point in terms of both political and city development came at the Third Plenum of the 11th Central Committee when Deng Xiaoping forced through the ideological goal of a socialist market economy with Chinese characteristics. This was encapsulated by the Four Modernizations: agriculture, industry, defense, and technology. In stating this he used what has become a well-used phrase, "feeling for stones to cross a river, one step at a time," which also implies a need to prudently change course when occasion demands it in order to reach the stated destination safely. This created acceptable conditions for land that had been repossessed by the state to be sold and transferred to individuals or corporations. It also acted to generate substantial income to government while ensuring that large-scale redevelopment was able to increasingly focus on privatization rather than assignment or subsidization by work units.

China's reforms from 1978 did not unfold as part of a grand design but as a tentative experimental approach, where each stage was determined by the economic dynamics of its predecessor, which carried the seeds for a concentration of labor skills and diversity of the industrial base. Management also tended to be diffused and decentralized, often built around shifting coalitions between party, provincial, and other power centers. At the commencement of reforms the Inner Delta Pearl River encompassed a population of around 9.5 million people but was still predominantly rural, with communities centered around agricultural production, and products mainly transported to the large markets of Canton and Hong Kong. While small amounts of coastal reclamation had been carried out, investment in engineering and service infrastructure had been negligible.

However, new administrative infrastructure also helped to gradually reform the state sector. At the commencement of reforms, Canton had a close relationship with Beijing and was cautiously granted a high degree of administrative autonomy. Marshal Ye was a highly ranked member of the leadership and his son later became governor of Guangdong. The most important incentive was a special fiscal arrangement that allocated almost full budget control to the Province, putting it on a path to rapid industrial development through small-scale state enterprises.

Market reforms were carried out in two stages: the opening up of China to foreign investment, and the privatization of much of the state-owned industry together with the lifting of protectionist policies. Opening up inevitably began with consolidation of closer ties to its nearest neighbor, Hong Kong, a city made up predominantly by Cantonese migrants and their descendants, and one that was symbolic with international business. In fact, it was, at the time, the world's only industrialized colonial settlement. For many years China had held steadfast to the Treaty of Nanking, and in turn had benefitted from the Territory as a source of necessary supplies, technology, and access to foreign currency through a mix of political prudence and facilitation of joint interests.

For some years after the reopening of Guangdong Province and its border crossings, the differences between the two sides was quite pronounced. Hong Kong had been pictured during the Cultural Revolution as a place of capitalist oppression and exploitation, and this concept could only be broken down through proactive joint-venture programs. Certain well-connected businesspeople donated considerable sums to China for new educational institutions and foundations to support professional training programs along Hong Kong lines. This was echoed and even reinforced by many mainland organizations such as the Xinhua News Agency, and investment corporations that stationed Communist Party officials in Hong Kong intent on achieving China's long-term goals.

Industrial reforms were gradually introduced, but development of industry was still tightly controlled through central planning. However, Deng Xiaoping was in a position to push forward reform. On August 26, in 1979, he made an announcement that was to transform both the economy and the geography of Canton and Guangdong Province in the years to come, with a famous commitment to establish four special economic zones in the South. The new policy of reform and opening up was termed "Socialism with Chinese Characteristics." By offering incentives of cheap land and labor along with tax concessions, these areas together with the later addition of Hainan, promoted growth by attracting foreign expertise and investment.

Beginning in 1980, Guangdong was granted a large measure of financial independence and increased authority in managing new investment and commercial activities, and some of China's most long-term and experienced leaders were lined up to work in the province as part of Deng's

xed-use quarters include
stinctive streets with courtyard
uses, arcaded shophouses, and
amboo barrel" dwellings—narrow
uses that create deep strips
thin the urban fabric along Beijing
ad. These areas help to sustain
strict living and commercial
tterns.

The Hualin Temple. Popular temples have traditionally been associated with markets. A templ itself might house the patron deit of a local guild organization, and might at a certain point become a meeting place for guild members The space in front would be used for public ceremonies or regular markets, and temple dues would be collected from traders. City god temples that were closely associated with official rituals we also the sites for markets. The jac market precinct informally relate to the temple courtyard so that both commerce and religious rite flow together through a causal transition of spaces.

reformist agenda. This included Xi Zhongxun as first Party Secretary and later Ren Zhongyi who helped gain public support for necessary agricultural and collective enterprise reform, reducing the role of state planning through a division of responsibilities between government and party officials. By the 1980s, new revenue quotas and the availability of loans led to some counties submitting petitions to become cities, such as Zhongshan in 1984 and Dongguan in 1987. While economic growth in the Inner Delta began to center on industrial development, the market for agricultural products expanded exponentially. These rural enterprises were officially classified as operating under township or village collectives, financed and run by local rather than state ownership, and enjoying a large degree of flexibility in attracting migrants who flocked to the expanding urban centers.

At virtually the same time, rural reform during the early 1980s simultaneously released surplus labor from the agricultural collective system, and acted to free up a "floating" labor market for the growing body of work in the cities. In all, around two-thirds of new jobs were in the industrial and construction sector, although it took a further decade for tertiary services to become a major form of employment.

Immigration from rural parts of Guangdong Province continued through the 1980s, some of it absorbed by Hong Kong's busy manufacturing economy and supported by a massive new town and public housing program. On the back of an almost inexhaustible supply of labor, many workers in Guangdong were increasingly employed to process goods for Hong Kong manufacturing businesses. As the stagnant aftermath of the Cultural Revolution began to wear off, new policies

began to spark growth within the Province, based on the gradual reform of systemic problems that were blocking progress.

The urban restructuring process was accelerated through a commercialized approach to real estate development, so that within ten years private housing became the principal component of construction, establishing this as the focus of economic growth.[180] In the process this broke down one of the greatest obstacles to city development—the over-dependence on quasi-government enterprises for housing in the cities, which, over a thirty year period, had become a form of welfare. In the process this began to change the spatial order of cities, with a considerable shift in their social and economic attributes.

Ren Zhongyi, a victim of the Cultural Revolution's excesses, and a native of Hebei Province, became First Party Secretary of Guangdong Province between 1980 and 1985 at the time of the reforms. He was an experienced and pragmatic politician, well capable of articulating long-sighted policy, and open to innovative ideas that made him a pioneer of free-market economic reforms. He was also an advocate of establishing limits on political power along with other such reformers as Hu Yaobang and Zhao Ziyang, who had the confidence of Beijing and enjoyed considerable leeway for policy making. Ren quickly realized that creative solutions for Canton and the Province as a whole were reliant on improving infrastructure, which represented a critical key to enterprising investment.

He and others worked to secure central funding but also outside investment from Hong Kong. This systematic approach coupled with a keen vision and use of strong personal and political affiliations also helped to establish a degree of certainty and assurance within the new government system that became increasingly capable of guiding and monitoring progress.

Despite an enterprising start to reform, neither Canton nor the province as a whole had achieved an open labor market. However, an important door had been imperceptibly opened to the would-be private sector. In particular, Hong Kong's professional expertise in sophisticated engineering, urban renewal, transport, planning, and development control formed the initial knowhow for large-scale infrastructure projects coupled with loan packages and financial management. As younger people returned from compulsory spells in the countryside, an increasing number discovered latent entrepreneurial leanings and set up small businesses and joint enterprises with government bodies. State organizations on the other hand were generally inefficient with low productivity, in part because of state pricing policy and lack of trained specialists.

The dismantling of the commune system and its replacement by civic administration was a stimulus to increased rural productivity, especially in marketable agricultural commodities, and the promotion of township enterprises. It was also assisted by the designation of Canton as an "open coastal city" in 1984, which attracted both domestic and foreign investment in industry. In the space of two years this increased the built-up area by more than 10 percent, and in turn attracted new waves of migrant workers.

Changes in political economy transformed both the administration and the form of Canton. As the city became economically more autonomous it evolved an increasingly direct, if ambiguous, relationship with its hinterland, creating rapid change in land use and urban space. Canton had technically retained much of its older fabric from the 1930s, but in a run-down state. However, in a short space of time cultural and religious buildings began to return to their original functions, while the highly regulated and self-contained work units or *danwei* rapidly gave way to specialized commercial concentrations and new housing areas that slowly introduced more dynamic economic and social interfaces.[181] Restrictions on labor mobility encouraged the extension of work unit dependencies, although this gradually gave way to a more diversified range of small-scale industry with a high female participation in the labor force.

During the early reform period Guangdong Province was to a large extent dependent on Hong Kong as an export market, while other producing nations, the "Little Dragons" of Asia such as Taiwan, Singapore, South Korea, as well as Hong Kong, were refining their export sectors. The province received a strong measure of support from Beijing through two senior figures: President Yang Shangkun and Party Secretary Zhou Ziyang who had themselves accelerated trading initiatives. However, tighter credit policies were laid down for new investment projects. At the end of a decade of reform, the population of the province as a whole were undoubtedly better off, but further development of a market economy would require the acceptance of a more open and internationally oriented society, rather than a lingering revolutionary ideology. Almost two-thirds of Guangdong's total exports were to Hong Kong and Macau, but a reinvigorated Customs Administration acted to tighten the growing trade domination of the province. The dual exchange rate system introduced by Beijing with the aim of stimulating exports was widely adjudged to be unsuccessful, particularly in relation to the spiraling U.S. dollar, and lasted only four years.

Special Economic Initiatives

In accordance with Deng Xiaoping's stated commitment, the State Council and the Communist Party Central Committee announced the establishment of three "Special Economic Zones" for Guangdong, the main one being Shenzhen, adjacent to the border with Hong Kong and situated on the east bank of the Pearl River estuary. The designated area was 327.5 square kilometers—around 30 percent of Hong Kong's total land area and more than 20 times the area of the Zhuhai SEZ near Macau. Other SEZs were announced in Shantou and Xiamen in Fujian Province. These represented the first time that China had voluntarily and strategically designated areas for foreign enterprises as opposed to the nineteenth-century treaty ports that had been opened for foreign trade through military force.

Shenzhen, known as Shum Chun in the early part of the century, had an interesting history as a new station on the first Kowloon-Canton railway established in 1911. In the 1930s several casinos were opened there in order to expand the provincial tax base, catering primarily to gamblers from Hong Kong, a mere 35-minute train ride across the border with trains departing from Kowloon every hour. Social pressure finally forced a reduction in gambling activities, and in 1936 operators decamped to Macau. In 1937, Japanese forces targeted Shum Chun causing an evacuation of the remaining population to Canton or Hong Kong. Through the war years only two trains a day were able to make the journeys to Canton, but after the war the population began to grow owing to the convenience of the KCR, and the town became the center for the Bao'an County government.

Deng's calculated experiment in 1978 was aimed at testing both the economic reforms and the accompanying "open door" policy. Shenzhen has, from its inception, had an enormous political and economic significance. It celebrated its 40th anniversary in 2020 with appropriate plaudits for its achievements in introducing both capital and technology, and becoming an international hub of research and innovation with the third largest container port in the world.

New development sites in the Shenzhen SEZ were allocated a considerably lower overall floor area ratio and with more flexible building regulations than Hong Kong, creating an opportunity for more imaginative design. Architectural committees examined development bids for important sites, and building contracts included penalty clauses for construction delays. In various ways Shenzhen served an essential purpose in enabling modern design technology and management practices to be diffused throughout China at a time of intensive growth and development. It was also important to generate effective liaison between Shenzhen and Canton within the province, as the former had been made an independent planning unit under the auspices of Beijing, giving it a low tax rate and a high rate of earned foreign exchange.

By 1984, fourteen coastal cities had been opened for foreign investment together with Canton. Three years later 27 Chinese provinces and a large number of municipalities had opened offices in Shenzhen as an alternative to Hong Kong with its more established access to international markets. This stimulated technology transfer to inland industrial centers with continued political support from Beijing. The difference in prevailing systems with regard to procedural and contractual matters was, in part, resolved by increasing border controls allowing for proper customs inspection. In 1985, twelve counties in the Inner Delta were grouped together as the Pearl River Delta Economic Development Zone which included four cities Zhongshan, Dongguan, Foshan, and Jiangmen.

By the late 1980s over 90 percent of foreign investment was from Hong Kong, via industrial operators who lost little time in transferring their existing factory operations to the SEZ in order to exploit the low land and labor costs on offer. Altogether around one thousand foreign enterprises signed industrial contracts, along with additional ones for export processing, industrial production grew rapidly as more efficient means of production were introduced. At a more discreet level, Shenzhen was a test case for Beijing to evaluate the suitability of Western business practices, and the success or otherwise of political reforms. This enabled administration and management to best meet the needs of new enterprises, along with ways to generate capital from urban land use in a similar way to Hong Kong.

In the process this has provided an effective context for new planning and housing mechanisms applied to Shenzhen's ten urban districts after 2010 when the State Council expanded the SEZ to the Qianhai-Shenzhen–Hong Kong Modern Service Industry Cooperation Zone. This was an underlying acknowledgement of the important economic cooperation with Hong Kong in terms of capital resources and management experience. Shenzhen's population continues to grow by 200,000 to 400,000 per annum, and its GDP has swollen 15,000 times since its inception. In 2018, the city's GDP reached 2.42 trillion yuan or 363 billion USD, overtaking that of Hong Kong, and it is on target to double this by 2035 through prioritizing areas related to artificial intelligence, biomedicine, and integrated circuits. Shenzhen is home to some of the biggest names in China's technology industries and accommodates about three million enterprises. Between 2012 and 2015 the Shenzhen government spent four billion yuan to support 75,000 micro, small, and medium-size industries, and industrial land accounts for about one-third of total building land.

This has been a driver of population growth in the Shenzhen SEZ from the initial projections of 400,000 to an estimated 2021 population of around 13 million people, with an economic and technological trajectory all its own. The almost continuous growth in per capita GDP reflects a steady inflow of investment in the city from diverse domestic and foreign sources.

Provincial Infrastructure and Reconstruction

At the outset of reforms, housing, urban infrastructure, and industrial operations were run-down in the face of negligible capital investment. To travel by road from Macau to Canton entailed five separate river crossings on a vehicle ferry. The city, which lay at the center of a large metropolitan region, was also weighed down by several tiers of bureaucracy and a lack of revenue, together with a vacuum in terms of production capacity. The old government quarter in the central part of the city to the south of Yue Xiu Park, dating from the Ming dynasty, had been expanded toward the east, and remained as the political center of the Province.

While much of the street fabric, including that constructed during the treaty port period, was substantially intact, its condition had unsurprisingly deteriorated. No new housing had been built since 1949 apart from dormitory accommodation in factory compounds, as housing responsibility as a whole had been appropriated by the state after this time. Antiquated factories had been built in the southeastern sector of the city across the Pearl River.

A not inconsiderable advantage at this time was the large number of Cantonese who had emigrated overseas during the preceding century, but whose families maintained strong lineal and cultural links with both the Province and the city. This of course included Canton, and after 1978 an Overseas Chinese Affairs Office began a program aimed at improving city facilities for overseas visitors including new hotels and cultural attractions. This contributed indirectly to the context for the annual

ansha Marina and Yacht Club
reflecting the line of fortifications
* Bocca Tigris across the Pearl
ver.

Trade Fairs that had been initiated in 1957, and with a site which had become reinvigorated with new exhibition facilities and an expanded railway station. The first Canton Fair attracted some 1,223 foreign businesspeople from 19 countries and continued to increase its continuing visitation despite a worsening political situation and the commensurate collapse of Sino-Soviet relations. By comparison, the 127th session of the Canton Fair in 2020 attracted over 25,000 Chinese and international exhibitors.

The process of urban reconstruction grew at a rate of 11 percent per annum over the next ten years, with much of the commercial and housing construction financed through bank loans, and new public buildings orchestrated through the state budget. As road construction increased and new highways began to form webs of connections within the province, particularly to the south, Canton experienced a transformation from a city of bicycles to one of cars, trucks, and motorbikes. While many of the traditional two-story shophouses and three- to four-story t'ang lou were retained, regeneration included programs of taller apartment buildings to reduce overcrowding and allow for a gradual increase in the occupancy rate per person under successive five-year plans.

Canton's long-term expansion strategy called for consolidation of growing development centers, creating the basis for a growth corridor between the city and Hong Kong, propelled by highway and rail alignments. In 1984, Canton contained 20 percent of the provincial population, and plans were prepared for a new economic and technological development zone to complement the more commercial manufacturing processes in Shenzhen, located in conjunction with the remodeling of

Huangpu Port, 35 kilometers from the city center. The zone offered advantageous tax and customs charges, and within three years 82 sites had been taken up by foreign companies.

Increased investment in its road, bridge, and transport framework, together with new service infrastructure in Panyu and Zengcheng, stimulated increased development in and around the Inner Delta area, generated by phasing out the last remains of the collective system. This together with new job opportunities attracted increasing numbers of workers. New road connections led to a decline in water transport but a marked increase in the use of buses between major conurbations and smaller rural counties, and in 1988 the first superhighway was constructed linking the economic zones of Shenzhen and Zhuhai with Canton. Most population concentrations were located alongside the extensive system of rivers, and a major program of bridge building created a connective framework, facilitating the wider transfer of goods and reducing price differentials.

hen Clan ancestral temple
Liwan District, which now
erves as the Guangdong Folk
rts Museum. The temple was
mpleted in 1894 and consisted
nine halls, six courtyards, and
neteen buildings. The Juxian Hall
the center of the symmetrical
ssemblage was originally a
ace for the family clanspeople
assemble and is now the
ncestral hall.

In the late 1980s some of the prefecture-level capitals in the Province were subdivided. Outside the seven capitals in the Inner Delta, which comprised Canton, Foshan, Jiangmen, Shenzhen, Zhuhai, Haikou, and Tongza on Hainan Island, the other more distant ones were traditional centers of water transport. These comprised Huizhou, Zhaoqing, Shaoguan, Maoming, Zhanjiang, Shantou, and Meixian. Some were linked to the Inner Delta while others at a greater distance offered a base for regional development.

Of these, Huizhou was located closest to Hong Kong and Shenzhen, and was an old Song dynasty capital. The city benefitted most from the new superhighway, as did nearby Dongguan, and both benefitted from plants established in the 1980s from Hong Kong enterprises. Zhaoqing, located on the West River which allowed large ships to pass into neighboring Guangxi Province, benefitted from the construction of nearby ports and grew into a light industrial center. It was also a popular visitor center with magnificent scenery.

Shaoguan, to the north of Canton, was a wartime refuge for the provincial government, and during the 1980s experienced accelerated growth through a transition from heavy to light industry. Maoming, well to the west of Canton, benefitted from its oil-refining facility dating back to 1955 and around which the city developed, supported by central government. Zhanjiang possessed a fine natural harbor and was the main port for southwestern China, acting as a base for oil exploration and naval operations. Along with the area around Maoming it was also a center for rubber, sugar, and fruit production, and had a thriving fishing and food processing industry. Shantou, situated on the Han River to the northwest of the Province, directly across the straits from Taiwan, was the most dense prefecture by 1988 with a remodeled port that could accommodate ships of up to 10,000 tons. It also had strong overseas Chinese affiliations that contributed to new educational and cultural establishments, and introduced the potential for investment of high technology. Meixian was the poorest of all the prefectures, with a largely indigenous Hakka community—an agricultural minority originally from northern China.

The prefectural capitals became the focus of new commerce and industry, with investment in new technology fueling economic expansion that in turn facilitated the development of essential infrastructure and industrial plants. This was central to administrative reorganization in 1988 where metropolitan regions, independent of government, replaced prefectures. Yangjiang and Shanwei, the leading port cities in the west and east, became capitals of the new metropolitan regions along with Qingyuan and Heyuan, because of their strategic locations associated with new road and rail corridors.

The remainder of the Province, being predominantly mountainous and with isolated settlements, comprised 47 counties, each with around twenty townships that contained around 34 percent of the provincial population. A significant proportion of land was state controlled, and contained reservoirs, mines, farms, and forest preserves. The preliminary approach to rural reform largely involved the sub-division of land together with an extensive reforestation program in order to satisfy the need for construction material. Appointed production teams were designated to oversee private land that had been collectivized into new land entitlements, with households granted a percentage of income from timber production on collective land, but subject to tightened control.

明勁第

The program was assisted by the introduction of both state and collective tree nurseries, with large-scale planting schedules to which both cadres and students were required to contribute in terms of erosion prevention.

As the county capitals became better connected to the wider delta area through improved transport links, commercial activity began to catch up with that in the larger cities. Under the new reforms, the mountain communities remained as heavily agricultural economies, but with a growing concentration on the production of construction materials, largely to serve the requirements of industrialized settlements in the Inner Delta. However, the rate of economic output and new wealth, while being significant, lagged well behind the average of the Province as a whole. By the late 1980s it was estimated that several million construction workers from the mountain counties were working on sites in the major cities and economic zones under the auspices of county construction bureaus. The seventh five-year plan for 1986 to 1990 set out a strategy to eliminate lingering aspects of a stagnant rural economy through an improvement of productive capacity and new infrastructure in poorer counties along with taxation adjustments. Young provincial officials were assigned to coordinate these new initiatives, which slowly began to have a positive effect on the wider economy.

Major reform of the retention system for foreign exchange led to resurgent export growth. Between 1985 and 1987 Guangdong was the leading province in China for exports, while imports soared on the back of foreign exchange that in turn reinforced its industrial and development strategy. This acted to induce foreign bank loans for such heavy items as railroads, power installations, and telecommunications, although limits were set on the value of projects. By 1988, around nine hundred firms had established foreign trade rights, while many others remained unregistered. However, in the service sector, regularization resulted in increased competition for business. Hong Kong experienced major growth during the period that contributed to Guangdong's export drive, while some 85 percent of foreign investment originated in the territory.

A further fourteen open cities around the coast of China were designated in 1992. The majority of these were former treaty ports, so that the very cities previously subjected to perceived exploitation by foreign powers were symbolically transformed into the very agents of China's economic recovery, as gateways through which flows of investment and technological resources could be filtered and selectively utilized. In return, the inducement to foreign capital was a range of "concessions"—cheap labor, serviced development sites, and significant tax benefits with access to international markets via Hong Kong. The open cities essentially became testing grounds for experimental policy initiatives geared to planning and urban management, and for the integration of specialist infrastructure to serve new industrial zones and other investment environments. This enabled city government to increase the share of financial revenues that could be allocated to urban infrastructure, commensurate with greater urban autonomy. Zhi Wenjun has compared the "micro-urbanism" found within the SEZ model to the notion of the old "concession area", which allowed for foreign occupation of specifically demarcated territory within the framework of an established conurbation, with its different form of administration and economic base.[182]

The Qianhai Business District located adjacent to Shenzhen, which only began planning in the early 1990s, now covers 607 hectares. In September 2021, it was announced that this area is to be extended by more than 1,000 hectares, and, as a result, Hong Kong's Policy Address that followed shortly afterwards announced a new Northern Metropolis in Hong Kong that involves upgrading several existing projects linked to the enlarged Qianhai economic zone. Two problems, which have remained over the past three decades, are the accommodation of constant population growth and the issue of land tenure with its inseparable rights of ownership. The outcome from the first reflects the difficulties associated with coordinated land-use planning in the face of strong private development initiatives; and from the second a situation where revenue could be generated from the sale of state-owned land to seed further land use change and growth, often through ad hoc rather than regularized development patterns.[183]

While urban planning and implementation are now generally carried out by the cities themselves under the auspices of planning bureau, plans must still be approved by the State Council, which also imposes strict policies over the use of rural land. Given the economic impetus over the past 30 years the developing city model, whether in the form of clustered urbanization patterns in the Greater Bay Area with its interconnected service structures, or the expanding coastal cities with redeveloped cores, must increasingly accommodate the same generic urban components. Evolving typologies for large, homogenous, and self-organizing development types found on the fringe of Canton, such as industrial estates, business parks, universities, shopping and residential cores, reflect different spatial dimensions and degrees of "fit" layered onto the urban framework. This tends to promote an urban design of both fragmented and expanded city quarters.[184]

Coincident with the regeneration of Canton as the third largest city in China and the wealthiest on a per capita basis, investment has also tended to be directed toward the changing status of smaller townships within the Pearl delta agglomerations creating a tiered pattern of urbanization. The absence of a unified land market incentivized the city government to take an increasingly market-driven approach to property development, through disposal of state-owned land that had been repossessed, or a tendering of newly formed land according to zoning criteria, following the established Hong Kong model. A popular expression during the 1990s was *puoqiang, kaidan*: "Knock down walls, open markets." Thomas Campanella has observed that the Chinese character *chai* which means "tear down" or "demolish" that was found on the walls of condemned structures took on the unsettling iconography of sanctioned demolition—a paradoxical extension to the erosion of collective memory carried out under the radical auspices of the Cultural Revolution.[185]

Henry Paulson describes Guangdong Province of the early 1990s, perhaps rather harshly, as "a hothouse of speculation, improvident management, and financial irregularity," depicting the number of corporate failures as indicative of the need for necessary reform of the banking system.[186] There was in fact little in terms of "hands-on" experience to manage the emerging market economy. The first Business School in China was opened only at the turn of the twenty-first century at Tsinghua University, ironically in part from donations extracted from the indemnity paid by China following the Boxer uprising.

Older mansions located in the Thirteen Hongs Area form part of comprehensive regeneration initiatives.

Regenerated Street in the Thirteen Hongs Area.

In Canton, extensive regeneration has created overlapping identities of social space, where economic forces merge and mobilize in new places of associations that act to increase both the complexity and diversity of the city. Spatial organization reflects both responsive physical divisions and changing patterns of use, where the urban environment is cumulatively shaped by a range of forces acting with different degrees of momentum. This is matched by revitalization of older neighborhoods that serve to make them progressively more differentiated and identifiable in terms of their wider urban integration. At the urban margins, situated around the flows and interstices of new transport routes, emerging activities and service centers continue to transform the city fringe, changing the nature of semi-rural and suburban fabric. However, the inner urban fringe has come to represent the coexistence of different parts, where the older quarters still assert an identifiable physical presence, assisted by upgraded secondary streets, pedestrian precincts, and a high level of urban landscape.[187]

The Action of Traction

The tension between control and autonomy—*junxian* and *fengjian*—is not far below the surface in terms of city government, possibly reflecting both the historical persistence of interventionism and the subtle signals occasionally broadcast by the state machinery together with the regular shuffling of senior city officials.[188] Cities are increasingly open to social initiatives and entrepreneurship that have a common purpose, representing a broadly balanced constitutional relationship between state, city, and society. The financial and creative power of Canton has become an economic and social model with a commodified popular culture that forms the ideological basis for new urban lifestyles.

The open door policies have increasingly emphasized private housing production to meet both high space standards and latent demand. Modern urban housing is regarded as an essential component of economic growth, and facilitation of this has become increasingly sophisticated. It has also clearly had an impact on urban form and created the necessity for new urban subway systems at a regional level. Over the reform and open door periods the urban population has risen from 21.1 percent in 1982 to around 60 percent in 2020, significantly exceeding the rural population. The urban density in Canton averages 13,000 people per square mile, roughly comparable to London or Barcelona, with a high per capita land use. The growing maturity of the housing market effectively ensures diversity of investment, but also indicates that the predominant urban spatial structures will inevitably continue to consolidate around clusters of multi-story buildings. At the same time, older and often dilapidated housing stock has continued to be redeveloped for high density uses in response to rising land prices, leading to the re-emergence of a "downtown" commercial district and mixed-use precincts.

Economic and land reform have had a steady impact on growth, with the most significant changes coming through privatization of the old state-subsidized housing market, and a similar replacement of state-owned industry by private industrial and manufacturing investments. In the meantime, land sales have generated a large percentage of annual city income, which has in turn accelerated urban redevelopment and induced relocation of older established communities to the urban fringe.

By the early 1990s the Inner Delta cities such as Dongguan had formed export processing zones, carrying out labor-intensive tasks that could be undertaken by both male and female workers with production expanding at a rate of 40 percent per annum. This spread wealth among the expanding townships in turn generated large-scale construction and urban redevelopment programs. Among the Inner Delta cities and counties, the first tier comprised the centers closest to Hong Kong: Baoan, Dongguan, Doumen, and Panyu, while the second-tier cities of Foshan, Nanhai, Shunde, Xinghui, and Zhongshan grew more slowly but also attracted a greater percentage of entrepreneurs who developed small industries, some of which grew to be large. Second tier cities attracted investment through their ability to offer land and labor at lower costs and were often better integrated within the provincial economy. At the same time, officials were sent to various new growth areas to serve internships and to gain knowledge and experience. Foshan for example benefitted from its consumer industries, developed in the early 1970s. These plants allowed the city to develop a concentration of medium-sized factories that consolidated its traditional ceramic industry producing tiles for the burgeoning construction sector. As the capital of the most prosperous prefecture in Guangdong, its modernizing agenda included both its urban center and surrounding counties as part of a comprehensive development program.

Housing investment from state-owned enterprises increased more than 64 times up to 1992 while annual production of new housing expanded exponentially. The greatest improvements in building and space standards were in the Shenzhen and Zhuhai new economic zones that had higher living standards and better community services. Zhu Rongji, premier between 1998 and 2003, is credited with battling inflation and introducing "corporatization" measures of state-owned enterprises in order to make business more competitive and efficient. The ninth five-year plan from 1996 up to 2000 aimed at an annual growth rate of 11 percent through strengthening the competitiveness of enterprises—greatly benefitting Guangdong Province. This also raised the issue of improving the rate of social and institutional reforms, in particular housing, urban development, and environmental protection. Land reforms during this period helped to alleviate the considerable housing shortage in Canton and improve living conditions.

By the turn of the twenty-first century a majority of households in Guangdong enjoyed higher space standards than public housing tenants in Hong Kong. While the rate of owner-occupation was a major growth sector, public housing rental returns were insufficient to cover even construction and maintenance costs, despite a considerable increase in household income. Housing reform was therefore directed at a more sustainable but still subsidized system that covered all costs as a possible precursor to home ownership, although this was reliant on production capacity, and the best means to utilize housing resources relative to purchasing power and mortgage capacity while reducing incentives for speculation.

The 22 cities in Guangdong Province tend to fall into three categories: the historical cities of Foshan, Huizhou, and Zhaoqing; resource rich cities such as Maoming and Shaoguan that provide oil shale, metallic ores, timber, and coal; and the port cities of Canton, Jiangmen, Shantou, and Zhanjiang. The port of Canton incorporates the former Huangpu Port and is the largest in South

China with an international maritime reach of around 300 ports in over 80 countries. This facilitated a program of divergent growth trajectories during the reform period. The majority of cities have established an industrial base with a high level of diversification and dispersal within the urban and inner suburban fabric, attracting a range of tertiary support industries such as transport, which includes water-borne cargo transport, passenger ferry services, and container vessels. Canton itself has experienced a vigorous construction period from the mid-1980s, for both residential and commercial uses, and as a result has the most extensive built-up area.

Canton's transport links, including new bridges across the Delta region, have consolidated its connection with southern core development areas, in particular Dongguan to the east, Panyu to the south, and the Shenzhen Special Economic Zone, which continues to facilitate growing economic interaction within a network of centers that form part of an intensive growth framework. This establishes the structural backbone of the Greater Bay Area that is intended to promote economic development in Guangdong as a whole, including Hong Kong.

The introduction of the latest technology, modern equipment, and management systems has served the industrializing economy well, and helped it compete successfully with other developing Asian countries. Investment in infrastructure has made it possible for many small producers to reach markets, opening up a large domestic catchment, while its special access to Hong Kong and overseas Chinese communities has provided the means to reach markets around the world. From the beginning of the reform process, leaders also took steps to improve educational standards and impose training programs in order to develop a competent and efficient bureaucracy.

Following agreement on the return of Hong Kong to China, border procedures were simplified and regional commercial and recreational links consolidated in the run-up to 1997. While Hong Kong businesses continued to locate manufacturing plants in Guangdong, government agencies and commercial enterprises from China established offices and operational activities in the new Hong Kong SAR. This has extended to joint agreements on water supply, power installations, transportation systems, and university faculty exchanges—creating new social, professional, and financial interactions. Canton has remained the political center of the Guangdong-Hong Kong region, within a dynamic corridor of industrial output, technology transfer, and commercial turnover, with a rate of industrial growth that exceeds all other provinces in China.

The province itself was administered under a "special" policy, which granted it substantial leeway for new development initiatives. One of the main reasons was its historical links with international trade, reflecting the fact that up to 80 percent of Chinese overseas migration over the preceding century had come from the Province. There were therefore historical and continued financial links between overseas Chinese compatriots and their ancestral home. In addition, it was felt that cooperation with neighboring Hong Kong would attract technological and business management support. To prepare for modernizations in accordance with patterns of increased urbanization in the topographically flat coastal regions, the former prefectures were divided into workable metropolitan regions, creating a more efficient means of urban management.

Road represents the
itional dried food market
of Guangzhou. Arcaded
ets and buildings, which are
heritage landmarks, have
ed the status of the street as a
ed-use trading area.

The Flowery Pagoda, first built in 537 BCE and restored in 1900. It forms part of the Liurong Temple and is known as the Temple of the Six Banyan Trees. The nine stories seen from the outside are divided into seventeen stories internally.

Chapter 9

Remaking the Canton Metropolis

econfiguration of the City

Over the past 150 years, development in South China has been constantly interwoven with marked changes in patterns of urbanization. Much of this reflects a stylistic interface between Chinese and Western influences that have accompanied social, economic, and political change. Urban design has therefore, in certain areas, come to represent an amalgam of both foreign and Chinese characteristics. Extended trading access, social reforms, and continuing urban growth through the beginning of the twenty-first century have led to a "community of interests" with strong planning ramifications.

Modernizing influences in Canton since the mid-1980s have increasingly focused on comprehensive urban design initiatives, including the accelerated accommodation of private investment in determining the priorities of inner-city regeneration, and new Central Business District activities. The Asian financial crisis in 1997 necessarily motivated a far-reaching reform of China's industrial system, inclined toward global trade and binding together both political and economic strategy. Since that time a policy of strengthening regional cooperation and the development of an extensive framework of infrastructure throughout Guangdong Province has brought together many expanding townships and urban clusters known as *Guangfo*, in particular the operational partnership between Canton and Foshan. These form complementary roles with new strategic industries and technology hubs.

Private housing construction has almost totally outpaced public housing programs, and is therefore focused less around government and institutional uses and more on the wider domain. As a result of this the public realm has become more autonomous but also more contrasting in its nature. Collectively this has produced increasingly diversified and complex urban patterns within the regenerated neighborhoods. It has also produced a high level of spatial variety in downtown districts, with pedestrian precincts that attract large numbers of visitors at all times of the day.

There is a large floating population facilitated by the ability to travel more freely in response to market changes, increased industrial opportunities, and shifts in the economics of agricultural production. This is not such a new phenomenon though. David Strand has noted that even in Ming cities the intense mix of commercial uses attracted large numbers of rural migrants or *liumin*.

In Canton this has produced a realm of workers equally at home in both city and countryside generating new forms of social consensus.[189] In recent times the remittance of funds and the injection of business experience to the countryside has in turn helped to transform rural social conceptions and economic networks.

It is estimated that there were, by mid-2008, somewhere between 150 million and 200 million "floating" workers in China's cities—a migration unprecedented in history. It can be justifiably claimed that the urban transfiguration of major cities has, since the late 1980s, been essentially built by a migrant population from the countryside. A dual social and economic structure emerged between those with entitlements for housing, education, and medical care, and those without the necessary essentials. This has impeded social mobility for those members of the "floating" population in the unskilled labor market who want to remain in cities and enter the labor market, but lack an urban *hukou* status and so remain disenfranchised and poorly integrated with city life.[190]

The interactive consequences of state and market procedures have acted to incentivize redevelopment of state-owned industrial land to high intensity commercial uses through a leasehold system, while deriving substantial revenues for the ongoing upgrading of urban infrastructure, urban spaces, and waterfronts. This has also led to the re-shaping of new business districts and the spatial restructuring of older ones, which epitomizes the distinctive mix of global and local capital investment and plays an important but hidden role in the restructuring process.[191]

Regeneration initiatives in Canton have absorbed certain indigenous or heritage elements, together with typologies derived from past patterns of urbanization that act to reduce homogeneity of form and add identifiable signatures to the city. The architectural residue of the treaty port city, with its distinctive patterns of use, has acted to transform some of these into suitably commodified elements within new cultural settings. The reconfigured port city can therefore be seen as a multiplicity of constitutive urban quarters, event areas, and relationships that substantiate crucial urban differences as well as global similarities.

Outlying neighborhoods offer a combination of high-rise estates and low-density suburbs, along with their integrated amenities occurring within the city jurisdictions. In these areas, housing and employment opportunities have been loosely synchronized as industrial investment is attracted to new development zones. Canton is Mainland China's leading commercial and manufacturing region, and the municipality was expanded in 2000 through the amalgamation of the Huadu and Panyu districts, and the acquisition of Nansha and Luogang.

Planning and Lands Mechanisms

The progressive devolution of planning authority from central government has allowed the cities to exert effective control over the negotiation of multinational corporate investment and facilitated the ability to plan for urban expansion through powers to absorb the economic administration of counties or by redesignating these as cities.[192] Thus, powerful shifts in the globalization of capital and spread of technology have been matched by a range of institutional changes that have had a

An afternoon of Cantonese Opera in Liwan Lake Park.

significant impact on the economic, social, and physical reconfiguration of major cities in China, and consequently on their urban design and spatial patterns. These have led to a simultaneous vertical remodeling and horizontal expansion, resulting in reorganization and restructuring of city space through negotiated land pricing and changing land ownership.[193]

This can be divided into three types: *leased land* owned by the state where rights over use can be subject to paid transfer; *administratively allocated urban land* owned by the state but unable to be transferred to other uses; and *rural land* which is collectively owned by farmers but which can be officially acquired by the state.[194] Land leasing, which has become the most significant source of funding to municipal authorities, has fueled massive redevelopment programs and a highly complex urban landscape through clear incentives to capitalize on the difference in value of land under existing use, and that under the best and most intensive use.[195] In addition, pro-growth environments and tax incentives along with simplified regulatory rules have attracted outside business to invest in local economies.[196]

The leased land system was officially introduced in 1987 and although it only covers a relatively small amount of land, it produced a sea of change in terms of urban development as it has allowed city authorities to control its supply and designated use through tender or auction procedures. This provides a substantial source of revenue, not dissimilar to Hong Kong's historical revenue accumulation from lands-related income, which is used for public infrastructure, and which in turn is expected to increase land value.

An additional source of housing land comes from less developed urban fringe locations that generates an incentive for municipal governments to acquire or requisition suburban land in its agricultural status at low prices and convert this to development land for both residential and industrial purposes, rapidly accelerating the urbanization process. Land has therefore acquired a substantial commercial value which has led to an active secondary land market.

In Canton the pace of change is also leading to conversions of older street-based neighborhoods, commensurate with environmental improvements. New housing, arts workshops, and galleries have emerged from the conversion of old industrial buildings, while specialized retail, cafe, and restaurant uses have become an energizing part of mixed-use quarters and special interest areas. This reflects the post-reform commodification of urban development through negotiated land transfer and marketisation of housing and has led to a massive growth in urban consumption. Urbanization has become the driver of economic growth, assisted by institutional instruments that help to enlarge and engineer urban expansion together with the support components of urban infrastructure. The physical manifestation of new tranches of city building is the development of new spatial forms, distinctive urban places, and innovative landscapes within the city.[197]

The Extended Metropolis

During the first tentative phase of reform in the early 1980s, Canton was still held in economic abeyance, as emphasis was instead given to new economic zones. The Guangzhou Nansha Export Processing Zone was founded in 2005 close to Nansha Port, and the National People's Congress approved a development plan for the Pearl River Delta in January 2009. By 2019 the Pearl

River Delta Economic Zone, formed by nine cities, accounted for 12 percent of China's gross domestic product, mainly from tertiary industries. The polycentric regional corridor between Canton and Hong Kong has constantly transformed and reinvented itself over 20 years, reflecting shifts in need just as much as it stimulates change within its constellation of Foshan, Dongguan, Zhongshan, and Shenzhen. This embodies a complex interpenetration of urban and rural identities that cannot be clearly demarcated by traditional boundaries, but has evolved a cooperative sense of collective conurbations, interwoven through urban growth to form interdependent relationships that can adjust rapidly to economic change.[198] In certain cases this effectively breaks down the distinction between city and countryside.

The new agglomeration economy of the Greater Bay Area is in effect a regional economic network, where core cities continue to develop symbiotic relationships with neighboring urban development areas that are able to apply skilled technical, managerial, and other market expertise through joint ventures. This has led to a geographically extended urban region centered on a number of urban cores that continues to break down the urban-rural divide that was a strong characteristic of the pre-1980 city structure. Canton has become the beneficiary of new central policies that facilitates greater autonomy and investment potential, bolstering a broadened economic role that has powered the economy from the turn of the twentieth century. Indirectly this has also facilitated the ability to invest in regional infrastructure and other key facilities within new growth corridors.

Most aspects that were proposed as part of a twelve-year development blueprint, together with stimulus measures for Guangdong issued by the State Council and the CCP Central Committee in 2009, are now complete. These include the construction of new economic zones, industrial zones, and large infrastructure projects including new rail links, highways, power plants, and water control projects and have involved cross-boundary cooperation between the delta cities including Hong Kong and Macau. This is aimed not just at overcoming existing economic problems but at strengthening the Pearl River Delta as the most vigorous area in the Asia-Pacific region, with hi-tech industries, services, finance, automobile manufacturing, steel, petroleum, and chemicals as the basis of the delta's future development, moving away from labor-intensive industry. To attract knowledge workers, Canton has raised spending on education to 18 percent of its total budget, with around 76 percent of its special fiscal account devoted to education programs.

Expanding settlements in rural townships is often referred to as "rural urbanization." This tends to reflect industrialization of rural and urban fringe areas, but also state-sponsored urbanization. Cities within the Province therefore form part of an emerging urban hierarchy. For the Canton metro area, the population is around 14 million people, although official figures tend to reflect only the *hukou* registered population. The 2020 population for Guangdong Province as a whole is 113 million—an increase of 2.58 percent from 2019—making it the most populous province in China within a land area of 69,420 square miles.

Historic building renovation in Canton has assisted the process of rejuvenation and economic upgrading creating a connective system of narrow pedestrian streets and small public spaces linked to the Litchi Bay Canal project.

Heritage and Restoration Districts

A significant feature of inner area urban renewal has been an emphasis on the upgrading and integration of selected heritage areas, and their pedestrian connections with new visitor attractions. The notion of historical memory has propelled a need to reconnect with the past through regeneration initiatives that encompass entire urban quarters, in the form of upgraded or reconstructed streets built around the preservation of traditional uses such as temple compounds, shophouse neighborhoods and areas of historic character. These form new and revitalized configurations within the fabric of contemporary urbanism, with low-rise interventions in the otherwise high density inner city areas, helping to breath both urban contrast and new life into them. Mixed-use quarters tend to successfully articulate cultural heritage with commercial acumen, creating both livable and walkable urban places.

The Yue Xiu and Liwan districts adjoining the former foreign compound on Shamian Island represent the historical core of the city and embody an important part of Canton's urban heritage. In recent years a program of upgrading has been directed at local streets and alleyway connections that characterize parts of the area. One of the problematic aspects, as it is in other developing port cities, has been the fragile urban context that reflects several decades of unplanned growth that continues to pose challenges for coordinated planning. However, substantial improvements to transport infrastructure have relieved the pressure on some of the older urban streets. New development inserts have partially broken up the older shop-house and low-rise—or *tong lau*—tenement pattern, although the pedestrianization of Zhongshan Road continues to exert a catalytic effect on the adjoining street network. Within this framework, land use restructuring measures have focused on re-location of most manufacturing industries into new suburban districts or business parks to release more land for housing and infrastructure, together with some redistribution of the resident population to lessen pressures on downtown neighborhoods.

The application of Lingnan principles represents a "tied-together" urbanism so that urban space has a positive and connecting function with a renewed design emphasis on the street and the urban place. This places a focus on pedestrian-friendly and energy-efficient environments, which allows for constant realms of adaptation and incremental inserts, distinguished and embellished by vertical landmarks as reference points.

Heritage restoration districts and such initiatives as the "Lingnan experience" provide both a re-packaged and nostalgic contrast to redevelopment for higher density uses. Well-researched architectural reproductions of lingnan architectural styles, or restoration of the original forms, successfully act as historical stage sets for entertainment and retail uses, branding the identity of gathering places oriented to new patterns of consumption. These now form the focus of a burgeoning internal tourism industry, that combines heritage conservation with a wide mix of commercial uses, cultural representations, and street markets.

Gentrification of older urban districts is carried out in part by reconstruction and selective clearance, older buildings being restored through implantation of parts from demolished buildings.

Historic building renovation in Canton has assisted the process of rejuvenation and economic upgrading creating a connective system of narrow pedestrian streets and small public spaces linked to the Litchi Bay Canal Project.

e regenerated waterway tem in Liwan District.

The integration of pedestrian precincts offset the buildings and provide a people-oriented framework for circulation. Sun Wen Xi Road was revitalized in the late 1990s through the creation of a commercial streetscape from upgraded and cosmetically reconstructed shophouses, incorporating refurbished shops and restaurants on several levels. The pedestrianized street snakes through several kilometers of the central city, joining together incidental spaces, plazas, and "tributary" streets that come alive at night with signage and floodlights that beckon users into the main pedestrian stream. Canton's jade market, for example, forms a vibrant matrix of narrow streets and pedestrian courts that incorporate outside display areas associated with retail precincts.

The Metropolitan Stimulus

The Canton metropolitan region is one of China's nine "National Central Cities" and one of the three largest in China that represent the main engines of urban growth, where the formation of city clusters forms part of a national strategy. Its area extends into the neighboring developing cities of Nansha, Foshan, Dongguan, Zhongshan, and Shenzhen, contributing to the overall framework of the designated Greater Bay Area. Its eleven divisions are divided into 136 subdistricts, 34 towns, 1,533 residential communities, and 1,642 administrative villages. The urban population in China, taken as an average, is approximately 58.5 percent while in Guangdong Province it is 70 percent—the fourth highest rate in China.

The Pearl River Delta makes up 1.2 percent of China's land area, with 4.5 percent of its population, and accounts for 10 percent of China's foreign direct investment. In common with other Chinese cities experiencing urban growth, Canton's urbanization program has been driven since 1980 by investment in industrial and residential development and a reliance on land conversion.

However, since 2017, the transference of rural land into building land, together with the accompanying revenue for urban land-use and construction taxes, has increasingly become an important means of government revenue generation. The outstanding debt in 2018 was 240 billion RMB but the debt completion rate is around 85 percent, and Canton is allowed to issue a large amount of "special debt" due to its massive land revenues, and a high price of land.[199] There is therefore a key incentive to perpetuate a booming property market, although there is only a limited supply of publicly owned land. The result has been an intensification of density on spatially separate sites, which has resulted in rapid urban development although somewhat compromised growth patterns.

The social reality of Canton in 2021 is shaped by a new metropolitan culture on the back of urban development, closely related to the economic advances of Guangdong Province and the Special Economic Zones. The relationship with the Hong Kong Special Economic Region is ambiguous on a number of levels, in many ways bypassed by vigorous economic and population growth on the northern side of the boundary. While "One Country Two Systems" might well have faltered in meeting its well-intended

motivation, Hong Kong maintains a strong interface role between China and the international community and is an active participant in the ongoing implementation of the Greater Bay Area strategy.

Effective planning requires a strategic allocation of land, labor and capital that is intended to ultimately reduce the rural-urban disparities, provide the means to better shape the urban landscape, and establish more efficient growth models. While land reform acts to reduce migration pressures, Canton still retains the capacity to increase its urban density, with a reduction in energy intensity that can help to induce a carbon neutral future in the coming decades. At the heart of successful urban planning is effective land management that marries consolidated growth with the potential to resolve problems of pollution, and resource depletion. This calls for constant evaluation of the urbanization agenda.

In 2017, Canton was designated as the pilot city for a national comprehensive transport hub that includes 800 kilometers of total travel length including extensions to Nansha and Foshan, with eight million passenger trips per day. In the process it has brought relatively distant suburbs in commuting distance of the central city and its business district in order to maintain a high labor catchment.

Commensurate with the reform of land management is a continuous need for agricultural modernization and an increase in rural income levels. Rural land in China is collectively owned, while urban land belongs to the state through municipal governments that allow land use rights to be leased, creating up to 60 percent of local government budget revenue. Working toward a progressive urbanization model requires ongoing reform of the *hukou* system, which is already taking place, linked to a residency registration system whereby access to affordable housing, education and welfare services are extended to all residents. At the same time the revenue base must be maintained through consumption taxes in order to generate a stable and sustainable source of finance and efficient use of resources. A unified system of land registration, together with precise zoning and planning standards, acts to facilitate more efficient development, and refine urban design standards for the ongoing city-building process under which the wider benefits of urbanization can be realized. Canton has an impressive record in terms of urban greening through a strong landscape, tree planting, and maintenance program that enhances the objective of a livable city and helps to combat environment pressures. This includes the strengthening of environmental standards and resource efficiency at a regional scale.

In 2021, China's urbanization accounted for 800 million people or around 60 percent of its total population. However, a large part of urban population growth has arisen from the *in-situ* transformation of smaller settlements into integral parts of urban economies. The National 14th Five Year Plan that became national policy in 2021 emphasizes growth control as a crucial aspect of national urbanization policy, and its aim is to drive toward a "moderately developed" economy, with a per capita GDP at almost three times the 2020 level. Urbanization is a key driver of productivity through the process of agglomeration, and Canton, in common with other large Chinese cities, has moved from a concentration of industry toward an innovation and service economy through its access to international markets. In 2019, Canton's total GDP reached 363.1 billion USD—a quarter of the provincial total. It operates 217 international container routes with cargo throughput and container

The former ancestral home of Bruce Lee's family in Yongqing Fang. The house was owned by Lee's father Lee Hoi Chuen, a famous Cantonese opera performer, and has been since converted into a museum dedicated to the martial arts legend after many years of abandonment. Its original layout has been restored and retains the carved girders and colored glass screens. Yongqing Fang's arcaded structures are monuments to the lingnan architecture of the period, and the street together with the adjoining Enning Road now represents a regenerative approach to urban physical and economic rejuvenation in restoring the original architecture.

business the fifth highest in the world. The urbanization trend in China is projected to continue through 2035 and beyond, reaching around 65 percent, or a population of around 950 million in cities. In Canton, this continues to create new economic opportunities through technologically advanced industries including high-end manufacturing and services.

The China-Singapore Guangzhou Knowledge City project that commenced in 2010 for an estimated 280,000 people is situated approximately 40 kilometers from the city center and covers 123 square kilometers of the Huangpu District. The project now has the status of a National-Level Bilateral Cooperation Project, with eight "pillar industrial clusters" including some of the world's largest companies. This is part of a long-term technologically inspired growth plan associated with the provincial capital, administered by the Guangzhou Development Zone and the Guangzhou High-tech Zone that will employ an envisaged 600,000 professionals. The new urban district of Nansha in Panyu is also gradually absorbing a cluster of technology and service industries.

Innovation-driven development is at the core of Canton's economic growth, with a number of science and technology agencies promoting and driving its development in competition with Beijing, Shanghai, and the nearby special economic zone of Shenzhen, which has been responsible for many of China's major high-tech start-up companies. Investment is directed at various strategies: research and development; commercialization of innovation; support for basic research; and improvements to current institutional and market environments. Canton was one of the first cities in China to use the "Public Private Partnership" structure on the White Swan Hotel on Shamian Island that opened in 1983. It was also undertaken through a build, own, and transfer model of overseas investment, under a partnership with the Fok Ying Tung Foundation. At the present time there are 17 PPP projects in Guangzhou including transport infrastructure and city center works.

Strict limits are imposed on floor area ratios in central area situations that constrain overall building densities, but this needs also to be equated with proactive planning controls and urban design parameters to ensure a well-planned and lively public realm. The Greater Canton conglomeration, which includes new development areas such as Nansha, has sufficient urban land to accommodate future urbanization and there is considerable scope for greater levels of densification. In addition, older and redundant industrial land is also likely to be converted into necessary commercial and residential land, which meets growing needs and generates greater efficiency. This level of urban intensification is also an indirect driver of consumption, which, as a percentage of GDP, remains relatively low by international standards. In Guangdong Province as a whole, investment in infrastructure projects in the twenty-first century has been colossal, and the existing skeleton of major highway, high speed rail, and bridge connections in the Greater Bay Area will facilitate a continued rate of urbanization.

Canton has a high rate of home ownership for urban *hukou* households at around 80 percent compared to only 10 percent of ownership for migrants. Affordability is subject not just to income but to a constant escalation in urban house prices at least four times since the turn of the twenty-first century. Since 2007, a social housing program has been implemented that includes various

Characteristic curved gable ends were often incorporated in lingnan residential buildings, traditionally representing success in the examination system.

categories including low-cost rental, public rental, and assisted home ownership. Ongoing demand requires a diversification of supply, availability of land for development at increased densities, and specialized non-profit organizations to expand and manage low-income housing supply to complement local government expenditure. All of these can assist the development of a more inclusive society and overcome the dualism of local *hukou* and migrant populations.

Industrial transformation through the pilot special economic zones in Guangdong Province has effectively opened the region to the global economy and in the process has fueled urbanization.

Large-scale investment and capital formation has also enhanced a continued move toward a value-added manufacturing, service, and technology economy, with new specialist services and business districts that benefit from agglomeration. Canton benefits from the city's cultural legacy of older shophouse and treaty port mixed-use and residential areas that create inner districts of urban interest, character, and contrast. The uniqueness and diversity of these areas support strategic opportunities for socio-economic development and promote an informal dialogue between all stakeholders. The existing fine-grained street grid in the older areas fosters people-friendly environments and inculcates a sense of memory and belonging. Attractive locations attract private sector investment but also allow for changes in use and, where viable, land-use intensification.

City Building and Regeneration

The land market system is based on two tiers of land use rights, comprising an administrative allocation to the state and its conveyance from the state to private users under prevailing market rates for fixed periods—dependent on the nature of uses. The planning system follows a hierarchical structure from economic and sectoral planning undertaken by the State Council to urban planning at the municipal level. Various national plans also cover transport, land, and water resources, while regional planning, economic, and social development plans are centralized through the National Development and Reform Commission.

In the modern age of political self-confidence and transformation, the most enduring buildings and urban quarters have taken on a new perspective as China comes to terms with its modernist twentieth-century history through the lens of contemporary urban growth that corresponds with its foremost position in the global economy. But a consensus among designers for a Chinese architectural identity remains elusive. As the essentially functional focus of modernism rejects superfluous detail or decoration, so the historical roots of Chinese architecture only find a means of expression and compatibility in an older cultural context. Far from being seen as a symbol of foreign imperialism, the treaty port architecture of Shamian has survived virtually intact, and is now admired as a finely orchestrated urban quarter, with one of the best clusters of neo-classical buildings and elegant urban landscapes in Asia, symbolic of the nineteenth and early twentieth centuries. Since 1996 the island has been designated as one of China's protected historical sites.

Huijixi Lu between Guangxiao Lu and Liurong Lu.

Planning must ensure that compact and vibrant city neighborhoods are maintained. In China more than 90 percent of urban growth happens at the low-density urban edge through fragmented new town and economic development zones. However, Canton and similar older cities have a wealth of traditional environments that signify their identity. Conservation and regeneration of the public realm must match a policy of planned urban regeneration zones to prevent sprawl, while accepting that the urban area will gradually increase in size. There is a need in new development areas for a more hierarchical and fine-grained system of urban neighborhoods that can create a coherent and deliberately intimate urban fabric. While a high degree of road engineering expedites traffic flow, livable urban design must meet effective standards for high-density urbanism, with regularized street patterns, an attractive cityscape, and the necessary achievement of sustainable and carbon-neutral initiatives.

Perimeter blocks with intersections of between 100m and 150m, and street block systems of five to seven stories provide a higher development density than isolated towers that only occupy a small percentage of a site, with the added advantage of establishing a continuous street frontage and a coherent public realm. This development framework can facilitate a "joined up" urbanism but also a more permeable one, where individual sites within the street blocks can be developed separately or in combination with a high level of densification. This allows the overall framework to operate for the betterment of the urban environment as a whole by reducing the distance between intersections while commensurately increasing the number of interactions within the urban matrix, enabling it to perform a meaningful connective function at a scale appropriate to the local context. In terms of city building and place making, a compact urban environment enhances usability, levels of amenity, social inclusiveness, and economic efficiency. Canton's older urban morphology and its upgraded local street connectivity, along with a mix of commercial and residential uses, provide good examples of pedestrian accessibility, proximity to a range of local services through easy cycle access, and public transit systems.

The regenerative approach can be used with a degree of flexibility to create new grid-based inner district neighborhoods that embody a range of opportunities in tune with existing development initiatives. An intensification of uses establishes an energy-efficient urban form while providing for a highly functional environment that can be developed in self-contained stages, allowing different levels of performance to be measured at each phase to test its effectiveness in meeting set standards.

Some modifications of planning regulations can ensure the effective articulation of the small-block model at an increased building and population density. This requires:

- Flexibility with regard to sub-division of street blocks through leaseholds in order to facilitate a range of lot sizes within each block that can be developed individually or in combination;
- The co-existence of large-, medium-, and small-scale developments to a consistent scale;
- Establishment of a commercial/residential zoning category to encourage flexibility to meet market conditions and encourage a mix of uses, and the regulation of active ground-level uses along designated streets;

The Yuexiu District of Guangzhou overlaps with the historical core, with its street boundaries of Renmin Road, Yuexiu Road, and Yanjiang Road coinciding almost exactly with the Qing dynasty city edges. Various conservation and rehabilitation projects have been initiated, focused on Beijing Road and Zhongshan Road, and around the restoration of the Temple of the City God.

Establishment of the long pedestrian precinct of Zhongshan Road was accompanied by the relocation of old manufacturing quarters. Shophouse buildings have been upgraded and in some cases re-constructed to establish an energized shopping and restaurant environment, linking together new urban spaces and focal points. Its mix of uses is reflected in a range of styles but with an overall consistency of building profiles, unified at ground level by colonnaded shop fronts. This great street unifies the central city, attracting crowds of users throughout the day and long into the night when its vocabulary of radiant lighting and fragmentary signage give way to a complex and colorful visual collage.

Lingnan architecture is eminently suited to street making. Visual appreciation is strongly geared to aesthetic considerations, cognitive understanding, and cultural values that influence how we perceive and interpret our surroundings. This can be seen in the main street of Chungshan.

A formal or ordered situation, articulated by strict repetition of building forms can be aesthetically pleasing according to a sense of harmony and balance. However, both visual identity and user experience in an urban situation can embrace variety through an overall sense of likeness tempered by difference. A cognitive sense of organization tends to synthesize seemingly random elements into unifying sequences through patterns of visual correspondence. This allows for similarity of shape, texture, and form to be applied to a street wall made up of different building elements and functions, but unified by certain features. These might comprise colonnades along the street edge providing an interface between the private and public realms. In Cantonese this known as *qilou*. A consistency of fenestration and rooflines allows for the simultaneous existence of novelty and pattern that is most suitable to the integration of Lingnan architectural elements and provides both urban design emphasis and a sense of Chinese identity. We find precisely this sense of contrast in older urban environments that have experienced constant change and additions over time.

- Introduction of building frontage alignments to ensure continuity of street facades, with some flexibility for individual ground-level setbacks for pocket spaces and seating;
- Incorporation of building corner setbacks at street intersections; and
- An appropriate increase in plot ratio limits in accordance with urban design considerations, and with a commensurate increase in land transactions, which should cover the infrastructure costs associated with the development of fine-grained neighborhood layouts.

A primary benefit of high-density street blocks with floor area ratios of between 3.0–4.0 is in its achievement of a vibrant public realm, where the connective and permeable network of streets and associated spaces promote walkable urban environments attuned to the wider pattern of movement at a district level with multiple access points. Such a system allows for a hierarchical matrix of route alternatives with the potential for sequences of streets to become pedestrianized or traffic-calmed, and at the same time optimize traffic flows. The built fabric associated with a variety of blocks provides for diversity and a greater level of choice, reducing the disparity between income groups. In this way compact and revitalized neighborhoods become self-sustaining, and stimulate both activity and employment.

High-density neighborhoods should ideally be associated with mass-transit station nodes, so that use of private cars can be minimized, while increased connectivity with major hubs via integrated modes of public transport can leverage economic gains to the agglomeration economy. It can also reduce commuting time, which is currently an average of 48 minutes in Canton.

Lingnan Streetscape and Urban Design

Lingnan architecture is eminently suited to street making. Visual appreciation is strongly geared to aesthetic considerations, cognitive understanding, and cultural values, and this influences how the urban population perceive and interpret their surroundings.

A formal or ordered situation, articulated by strict repetition of building forms can be aesthetically pleasing—creating a sense of harmony and balance. However, both visual identity and user experience in an urban situation must embrace variety through an overall sense of likeness tempered by difference. A cognitive sense of organization tends to synthesize seemingly random elements into unifying sequences through patterns of visual correspondence. This allows for similarity of shape, texture, and form to be applied to a street wall made up of different building elements and functions, but unified by certain features. These might comprise colonnades along the street edge providing an interface between the private and public realms. In Cantonese this is known as *qilou*. A consistency of fenestration and rooflines allows for the simultaneous existence of novelty and pattern that is most suitable to the integration of Lingnan architectural elements and provides both urban design emphasis and a sense of Chinese identity. We find this sense of contrast in older urban environments that have experienced constant change and additions through the fourth dimension of time. It establishes a link between the complex patterns found in a typical older street that incorporates a diverse collection of incidental uses and superimpositions, often interwoven with quite simple building fabric. Repetition of similar forms is alleviated by a multitude of textures and individual details that sustain engagement and enrich sensibility. In this respect the ordered and unified grain of the street pattern establishes a responsive framework within which richer qualities associated with a reinterpretation of Lingnan characteristics can progressively unfold.

In Canton's older and street-based neighborhoods, most buildings were designed and developed in the form of small groups and terraces. In these situations, both consistency and variety were expressed through differences in lot width, vertical divisions, the rhythmic patterns of roofscape, fenestration, and material texture. Adherence to the vernacular tradition, with its many proven ingredients, reflects the incidental accretions and adjustments to built form and identity that accrue naturally and make for identifiable urbanism.

In the upgraded and regenerated Beijinglu Street, Zhongshan Wulu Road, and Hui Fulu Road that comprise the revitalized central core of the shopping district, a mix of forms and styles are united through continuity of street colonnades. These configurations reflect older references within a contemporary urbanism of flamboyance, contrast, and complexity. This allows for individuality at the local level, and consistency in a more totalizing sense, drawing on familiar forms as part of a street-based urbanism that triggers economic activity, variety, and functionality. It also establishes a consistency of design interpretation from a palette of features that can be customized and applied to different situations. In this way, urban design achieves an acceptable level of spontaneity and extracts public gain from private development over the course of time, including its primary and residual spaces, and connective links.

Achievement of Green Urbanization in Guangdong Province

China has a comprehensive environmental legislation system, and since 1970 it has enacted many regulatory controls. The essential challenge is in ensuring compliance by both private and state-owned firms. To be more effective, it is necessary to increase resources, encourage community participation, and strengthen incentives for compliance including allocation of additional resources for environmental management. It is also necessary to ensure an improved connection between national governmental goals and local government priorities, and to co-opt the business body in stressing the importance of green growth.

Canton's massive economic progress has come at a certain environmental cost. Tackling the problems associated with rapid urban growth is high on the agenda of China's 14th Five-Year Plan, as environmental degradation compromises economic and social objectives. This includes integrated policies aimed at preventing water pollution, dealing with hazardous waste, resource preservation, ecological protection, and restoration as it seeks to attain a continued growth trajectory based on efficient production. This demands that resources can be recycled and regenerated to accord with imposed environmental management systems.

The CCP amended the party constitution in 2012, which technically put environmental sustainability on an equal footing with economic growth. This was followed by China's pledge at the United Nations in 2020 to achieve carbon neutrality by 2060, along with reduction targets and timelines.

REGENERATION OF CHUNGSAN IN GUANGDONG PROVINCE

The amalgam of styles establishes a link between the complex patterns found in a typical older street, which incorporates a diverse collection of incidental uses and superimpositions, often interwoven with quite simple building fabric. Repetition of similar forms is alleviated by a multitude of textures and individual details that sustain engagement and enrich sensibility. In this respect the ordered and unified grain of the street pattern establishes a responsive framework within which richer qualities associated with a reinterpretation of Lingnan characteristics can progressively unfold.

Mandates have been set for watershed protection, environmental management, and restoration of biodiversity. A "Green Financial System" has been prepared in association with the UN Environment Program to effectively direct capital toward sustainable low-to-zero-carbon projects. As this needs to be policy-led, mandatory targets must be set within an enforceable regulatory framework rather than through market incentives that are more geared to free-market economics. This involves a long timeframe and a great deal of expertise within the financial services industry, which must be largely directed toward mobilizing capital for green investment, but at the same time incorporate returns to the community through managing environmental risks, with the overriding need to limit global warming toward 1.5°C. The 14th Five-Year Plan has established targets to meet this goal and implies a swift transition to the use of renewable energy sources such as hydrogen and bioenergy at a cost of around 2.6 percent of annual GDP over the coming 40 years. It will in turn have a significant impact on urban planning, transport, and construction.

EXPRESSIVE TEXTURE AND ACTIVE STREET MARGINS

Healthy cities experience a constant process of change and revitalization. This represents opportunities for a responsive urban design that emphasizes cultural and historical aspects unique to particular urban places and situations. The application of Lingnan principles to the contemporary urban environment requires a "tied-together" urbanism so that urban space has a positive and connecting function. Regeneration calls for a renewed design emphasis on the street and the urban place, and an equal focus on pedestrian-friendly and energy-efficient environments that allow for constant realms of adaptation and incremental inserts, distinguished and embellished by vertical landmarks as reference points.

Shophouses fronting De Zheng Road in Guangzhou built under the qilou system, whereby buildings fronting streets of less than 24 meters required a permit to construct covered, colonnaded structures over the pavements.

The 14th Five-Year Plan, as the primary policy document of the CCP, draws on carbon pricing and emissions trading that was launched in various cities in 2017, with new regulations announced in late 2020. The plan also announced that the use of non-fossil fuels in primary energy consumption would be increased to 25 percent, solar and wind power capacity would be extended, and forest cover boosted with the help of both technology and investment. This will require a range of policy instruments, including an increase in tariffs for water, energy, and other resources that at the very least meet the costs of providing them, complemented by integrated land use, transport, and energy planning. Sectoral actions might include: a gradual shift from private transport to clean public urban transport and autonomous vehicles; renewable energy sources; promotion of green building technology such as tight energy intensity reduction targets; waste disposal, and reduction programs; and secure safe water systems through prevention of polluting discharges and improvement of resources.

Canton is in a good position to shape energy needs. Its spatial form and overall mix of new and old, at relatively compact physical densities, broadly influences resource efficiency. It is still technically able to raise its urban density to a higher level in the urban core, and has the theoretical capacity to decrease its per capita urban energy use and maintenance costs for urban services. The intensification of new development sites through a compact, small, street-block fabric, coupled with urban regeneration strategies that mix housing with services and employment, can best establish low-carbon development planning. Such an initiative calls for a review of statutory planning regulations in order to deal with current urban design and environmental issues. It is also necessary for the targeted percentage of open space to be applied at a city-wide scale as far as possible through a connective system of urban spaces, traffic free places, and pedestrian channels.

Canton has many essential prerequisites necessary for the acceleration of a greening agenda. This can draw on a sustainable energy and emissions planning process related to the enabling actions dictated by urban planning and secured by municipal stakeholders in accordance with benchmarking tools that set specific targets and prioritize necessary actions. At a more detailed level, mandatory building regulations must enforce energy-efficient and green structures, perhaps through an incentive process including an increase in gross floor area, in common with Hong Kong's Green Building Council and Singapore's Green Mark rating systems that promote ongoing improvement in environmental performance. A further optimization measure is an increase in the use of renewable energy through generation tariffs, cost-effective transmission pricing, and effective extension of wind and solar energy programs. Rooftop photovoltaic systems are used quite extensively in Chinese cities and new business models, with investments financed by service providers, would provide added value to the growing solar energy market. Other important initiatives are the protection of water resources and quality by necessary investment in water supply and treatment infrastructure for wastewater that can be returned to natural water bodies, along with improved efficiency of solid waste management. It is somewhat easier to tackle environmental problems in new development areas than in older cities. It is also equally possible to move toward more balanced economic and environmental conditions with the provision of affordable urban infrastructure, along with a continued adjustment of production toward value-added and high-tech industries.

The urban village of Shipai covering one hundred acres.

Transformation of Urban Villages

Villages on the urban fringe and even the far outskirts of Canton, with long genealogies that date from their foundation as agricultural settlements, have developed new landholding structures in recent years that have become gradually absorbed within the expanding fabric of the city. Over several hundred years their recorded lineages formed the connective element that bond together families and individuals, many of whom had left to form futures elsewhere, with their ancestral roots. After 1949, the government imposed a series of land reforms on the rural countryside, and in 1958 the People's Commune System was applied to all villages, dividing their populations into labor units that reshaped rural society while respecting the family clan system. In the midst of the Cultural Revolution, when village land was collectivized into a commune structure, village boundaries were recalibrated, transforming both the social structure and the agricultural economy. However, following the market reforms of 1978, land was redesignated as either urban—under control of the state—or rural, under the control of collectives. The imposition of a household registration or *hukou* system essentially established residential criteria for indigenous villagers, enabling them to participate in the urban transformation. This reinforced both their territorial affiliation, and later their economic and political autonomy, not dissimilar to the effective control of village land in Hong Kong's New Territories.

The movement of migrants from rural to urban areas over 40 years has resulted in increased urban growth but also a dualism where newcomers have lacked a local *hukou* status. This form of household registration was relaxed in small- and medium-sized cities under the 2019 Urbanization Plan as part of a more open economy and to increase China's rate of urbanization. It is estimated that there are around 300 million migrant workers in China, accounting for approximately 35 percent of the total working population. In Canton, migrant workers have found it difficult over the years to access local public services, including education and healthcare, even though the quality of these, together with market integration in Canton, is quite high. Canton has the highest net migrant inflow among all China's provinces, with urban migrants making up more than half of the city's population, although they remain vulnerable to social and economic instability. However, migrant workers can be granted an urban *hukou* if they fulfill certain criteria including educational qualifications and technical expertise. Canton has adopted a point-based system to vet applicants for *hukou* status in line with the national aim to improve labor mobility within the economy. While *hukou* reform has progressed, it remains under tight control. More than half of the current population of Shenzhen is made up of rural migrants, although approximately half of these are skilled professionals who have transferred their *hukou* registration from their place of origin. Accordingly, the average gross floor area of living space per capita is greater than other major cities in China, including Canton.

The intensification of land and redevelopment of individual house lots through the floating population of migrant workers from the beginning of the reform period, brought about unprecedented physical as well as social change. As the older villages within expanded city boundaries were only subject to nominal planning control, the influx of migrant workers incentivized a process of infill and redevelopment of previously low-rise village house sites to provide an intensified level of accommodation for affordable rental. The demand for new development has effectively doubled the size of the Canton-Foshan urban area to 1,225 square miles in 2020, with a population in excess of 14 million. In the process, urban land acquired a new status and increased in value, while village fabric became transfigured with a greater commercial emphasis. Within 20 years the indigenous village communities had decreased to only 20 percent of the total village population, the remainder being migrant workers who rented accommodation for residential and business uses.

The change in land use status has had a profound influence on the city structure through the expropriation of land, negotiated with indigenous villagers through the Reserved Land Policy.

The Li Wan District covering around 12 square kilometers adjacent to Shamian Island integrates a number of traditional street markets specializing in local products that help retain the cultural identity of the area.

The Yuenzheng jade and ceramics market north of Changzhou street in Guangzhou represents a regenerated complex of buildings, preserving the older fabric and street life while reorganizing the vehicular traffic around the area, allowing new retail activity to be inserted within a series of pedestrian precincts.

Under this, a percentage of expropriated land was reserved to cater for the village collective's future requirements. As the city continued to expand the preserved urban villages became embedded as isolated and contrasting elements within the encompassing regenerated city fabric, where collectively owned land was outside planning controls.

Low-income workers who came to the city in search of a better quality of life and with temporary residence permits found affordable rental accommodation in the urban villages and stimulated a massive process of incremental redevelopment of individual lots at a much increased building density, putting severe strains on the adequacy of service infrastructure. At the same time the open-door policy attracted investment from returning emigres so that the enterprise system expanded rapidly, characterized by an intensification of interaction between urban and rural areas. By 2000, between 60 and 80 percent of the village populations were from migrant groups, and this had begun to radically change the spatial and social structure of the communities. As a result, the urban villages began to assume the economic characteristics of specialized trades and industries, with a large number of small shops, restaurants, and workshops. The building owners themselves, as part of the collective system, became comparatively wealthy,

Historic building renovation in Canton has assisted the process of rejuvenation and economic upgrading creating a connective system of narrow pedestrian streets and small public spaces linked to the Litchi Bay Canal Project.

and indigenous villagers in many cases corporatized their collective assets, so that they became shareholders, earning dividends from their combined holdings.

Three-dimensional redevelopment has tended to erase almost all evidence of an older lifestyle, while traditional village architecture has been largely replaced by an ensemble of modern infill and high-rise incursions, giving rise to extensive remodeling of the older village structures. As village development was unconstrained by building regulations, older lots were simply extruded upward, delineating an assembly of "pencil" towers up to ten stories in height, served by an effective matrix of narrow pedestrian streets and passages, not too different from those within the nineteenth-century walled city. However, in most cases the new high-density conglomerations have incorporated the ancient ancestral temples, with the tight spatial matrix progressively reconfigured to provide for local schools, markets, and other community uses.

The process has led to an erosion of past cultural traditions and historical texture, which could have injected a sense of heritage and memory to expanding conurbations. However, on the positive side, villages within the city or in close proximity provide affordable housing for migrant populations, allowing newly industrialized areas to attract a steady stream of workers. Low-cost accommodation has provided opportunities for entrepreneurs to instigate start-up businesses at affordable rents within compact and high-density enclaves that are highly efficient and convenient to new residents. In this sense they offer a secure and diverse urbanism as an alternative to the privately managed high-rise estates on the urban outskirts. The underlying planning problem is that while urban villages have contributed to the city's dynamic economic development, the process of spatial transformation has compromised the areas between the city and its periphery.

In 1988 the sale of land use rights was introduced along the lines of the Hong Kong land use zoning model, with development capacity dictated under a Buildings Ordinance. This has created a land market using land owned by government as a commodity on which to generate revenue, acting to intensify Canton's hegemony and extending its city boundary to incorporate two existing counties while promoting new infrastructure networks. In 2000, it was announced that 138 urban villages, including some of the most prominent and intensely developed, would be subject to a sweeping redevelopment and environmental upgrading exercise. The city also began to plan for a new central business district in the Tianhe area, along with a new "University City" in Panyu District comprising ten separate campuses.

Shipai Village is Canton's largest urban village, around five miles to the east of the old city center in the Tienhe District. It dates from the Song dynasty and once covered several thousand acres of cultivated land. In 1980 the village was surrounded by farmland and engaged largely with agricultural production. Only ten years later, the farmland had given way to an intensity of infill and consolidation, divided by more than 170 narrow streets, making the achievement of coherent urban form and infrastructure installation difficult. The creation of a new central business district, extending along a new north-south axis in the Tianhe neighborhood also involved the creation of land for a large-scale sports complex, and in the early 1990s additional expropriation was carried out for a technology zone, high density commercial development and the relocation of government offices. The previous village space was therefore incrementally separated into different parts containing entirely new urban functions.

In 1997, the village committee in Shipai was replaced by a joint-stock company that managed the real estate resources, with administrative functions incorporated within the city, and economic functions operated by the collective. The four main clan families in Shiphai were the Pan, Xian, Chi, and Dong, and created a social basis for community concentrations around ancestral temples that reinforced the spiritual identity of the various village quarters. Many ancient temples have been preserved and now serve as points of attraction and activity, creating spatial breaks in the dense fabric. By 2000, the village had an indigenous population of 9,000 people, but a floating population of around 45,000.

Other major urban villages in Canton include Wangshengtang in Yuexiu District, with a population of around 100,000 and employment centered around footwear manufacturing with associated warehousing and wholesale markets that have driven both economic growth and redevelopment of the older environment. Sanyunalin Village, known for its stand against the British in the Opium War, is a center for leather wholesale markets, with a population of 85,000 in an area of only 6.8 hectares. By way of comparison, various urban centers within Guangdong Province have experienced similar growth patterns. The Shenzhen Special Economic Zone has three urban villages within its boundary: Xiasha, Dafen, and Ganxia, housing a total of around 120,000 residents. Leide, an 800-year-old Song dynasty village, stood in the way of a planned cultural and recreation sector including an Opera House, the Guangdong Museum, and the Asian Games stadium. Dachong Village, which housed around 70,000 residents, was effectively razed and the indigenous residents compensated to make way for new office and industrial zones.

Around 20 percent of current urbanized land in Canton comprises village renewal. As urban development has gradually encroached on agricultural land, the economic and social makeup of traditional villages has changed to the point where they have become necessary vehicles of a diffused urbanization process, where urban and rural uses coexist in environmentally challenging proximity. A rise in land values through urban encroachment then stimulates successive stages of redevelopment with more intense forms of spatial signatures that often lack coherent and properly serviced layouts. A constant concern has been insufficient infrastructure, uncontained growth, and a less than positive impact of such settlements on the urban landscape.

Shareholding cooperative companies take a central role in the development process by mediating between government and developers during the complicated process of land requisition. There were few local dissenters to redevelopment as financial compensation inducements to indigenous villagers formed a potent factor against opposition. This effectively exploits the redevelopment value of urban land at increased floor area ratios, rather than a regeneration process that could aim at social investment and retention of established uses within a revitalized and attractive urban framework, where all participants would contribute to a balanced urban form in keeping with a wider district network. Informal redevelopment scenarios in and around Canton impede strategic growth when compared to the new city business centers of the economic zones in the south of the Province. The city blueprint for growth and regeneration entails the "Four Transformations Principle" through a

A range of roofscape elements and mix of two-, three-, and four-story structures along Shang Xia Jiu Road induce a complex compositional geometry geared to the pedestrian scale.

sequence of operational stages, intended to re-orchestrate the existing system toward a more comprehensive redevelopment approach. This involves a transformation of the collective shareholding system into a corporate entity while handing all villagers an urban *hukou* status. Resident committees are then technically able to replace village committees.[200]

In 2007, a compensation package was agreed on the basis of an urban exchange whereby one square foot in a village house, up to its legal limit of four stories, could be exchanged for the same area in a new apartment. Hong Kong developers were invited to participate in this process, and three large parcels of village land were auctioned, with designs produced by the Guangdong Design Institute consisting of 37 towers along with five reconstructed ancestral halls. The master plan for the city calls for the "complete transformations" of eight of the largest urban village concentrations.

The central dilemma is essentially one of equating rising land values in central city locations as part of a transition process that impacts socially mixed environments. Indigenous villagers possess land rights that must be respected within a situation of almost constant urban growth and change, but more informal migrant communities, who have in many cases invested in property, are the most negatively affected stakeholders.

Social housing remains a key factor in China's five-year plan launched in 2021, where local governments have a key role in providing affordable accommodation through controlled enterprises that might involve private developers. Both the economics and management of public rental housing requires careful monitoring and evaluation to meet the pressing needs of low-income households. In large part, the requirements for public housing must relate to eligibility criteria and the considerable rise in private property prices. However, large-scale public housing is not the ultimate social goal, and needs to equate with prescribed limits in order to genuinely contribute to social cohesion and inclusiveness. Shenzhen now follows along the lines of the Singapore housing model, that has a high rate of home ownership with purchase and affordable mortgage payments tied into a Central Provident Fund, which pioneers a new direction in social housing. In Canton this must meet the needs of low-income migrant households as part of a coherent city-building process and must be equated with the capacity to provide affordable rental homes and mixed-use environments within core parts of the city. It is also necessary to ensure affordable spaces for specialized businesses and shop-front streets within properly laid out settlement patterns and upgraded infrastructure that contribute to green neighborhoods. The overall approach calls for incremental upgrading with regeneration objectives, improving street profiles, providing public facilities, and inserting pocket spaces for use by communities.

The risk to orderly city growth is that continued elimination of the older settlement patterns replaces the urban and cultural values associated with the memory of ancestral traditions and fellowship that once created a sense of identity and contrast to older urban environments. The "village in the city" can all too easily give way to self-contained spatial entities in contrast to the patterned and street-based intricacy of older city quarters. It is what might be termed a "Foustian bargain," by appeasing indigenous populations only to stimulate further problems relating to the achievement of livable characteristics further downstream.

Pedestrian precinct along Shang Xia Jiu Road in Canton with upgraded shophouses, linking together new urban spaces and focal points

The Political Paradox

China's transformation from a planned economy to a more market-oriented one has been as breathtaking as it has been meteoric. In 2003, China announced the goal of a "harmonious society," and since that time has sought to protect the interests of society as a whole, even as it was announced in March 2021 that the number of "mega-rich" had swollen dramatically over the previous year. The following month the *Forbes* annual rich list announced that Beijing was home to more dollar billionaires than any other world city, narrowly beating out New York.

By the end of the 1970s there was wide acknowledgment as to the failure and immediate consequences of the Cultural Revolution, but in its aftermath there was also a residual hankering for the persistent values of a state controlled socialism, that ideally seeks to perpetuate the values of community and equality. This contrasts with the perceived excesses of capitalism, even as China pursues something very much like it in the context of a contested global marketplace. It also represents an ambiguous interpretation of orthodox Marxism but one that appears to be well suited to the social mores and unified tradition of Chinese society, just as it is necessarily responsive to world events.

A perplexing alchemy of factors seeks to fashion a political system that has proven remarkably responsive in catering to the needs of Chinese society, and legitimizing its identity. It is supported by the country's economic transformation that retains a robust international outlook, but with a strong sense of nationalism and a nuanced version of Western modernism. Cantonese traditions cannot be detached from those of China, but its trading past and treaty port history helps to define a distinguished independence in relation to its cultural characteristics.

In something of a direct comparison with Mao Zedong, Xi Jinping's speech on "Socialism with Chinese Characteristics" was enshrined at the 19th Party Congress in 2017, notably underscoring a centralization of power. At the same Congress, Xi Jinping stated that "Chinese society faces the contradiction between unbalanced and inadequate development, and the people's ever-growing need for a better life." Of equal interest is that Xi has frequently drawn on Confucian philosophy to reinforce the goals of the political system in developing a virtuous and equal society. Xi retains close Politburo relations with former associates dating back to his time as Party Secretary in Zhejiang, and his virtually unchallenged position provides the means to synthesize the Communist Party agenda and priorities through campaigns directed at the population of China as a whole, including the Hong Kong SAR.

China's partially closed political system is arguably fortified by the country's economic transformation and its increasingly vibrant society. Capturing this reality as it applies to the socio-economic advances within the cities is not so difficult if we take things at face value rather than from a fixed ideological perspective. The legal system in China is not truly independent of the Party, so that a "socialist" rule of law remains almost exactly in line with the tone laid down by the leadership. From a Western perspective freedom to express dissent and to speak freely is a fundamental right, but as China has gained in economic strength it has become politically more assertive. A less than independent media, outside affiliations with the state, must therefore prudently engage in self-censorship if crackdowns are to be avoided. This remains a conundrum in terms of political relations, but arguably raises interrelated questions over prescribed levels of censorship over society in general, in exchange for commitment of protection by the state and the attainment of balanced development. While the West can point to the Chinese government's hold on political power, shaped partly through its monopoly of information, China can equally point to widespread disinformation available all too readily elsewhere, including that which led to the invasion of Congress in Washington on January 6, 2021. To Western accusations that control of the media inevitably leads to distrust of official information sources, China can legitimately claim that its single-minded approach to national reform achieves a minimum of controversy or dispute, and has created a stable society where social responsibility has contributed to a system that has lifted millions out of poverty, and just as many into unprecedented affluence.

A globalized world strengthens competitive instincts, just as it demands a tolerant approach to complex social and economic challenges. From the onset of the Reform and Opening Up period, China's growth model has percolated through a changing economic system to meet continually rising expectations. However, an old Chinese saying is that a rising tide allows all boats to float, but a receding one leaves many craft floundering in the mud. The underlying strength of a market economy and the politics behind it must have a built-in capacity for self-correction that cushions stress, addresses weaknesses, and encourages open exchange with the world. Liberty and the pursuit of happiness can only be realistically sustained through putting well-being of the community on the same plain as that of the self-interested individual, at whatever geographic level. To maintain the country's momentum for development and prosperity there must exist a cooperative external environment, but also an international responsibility to act in the broadest possible public interest. This is something that must increase interdependence and collaboration through shared interests, an example being the landmark agreement on climate change between China and the USA, signed in 2014.

Temples devoted to Taoism and Buddhism date back to the first century CE. A survey in 1840 showed up to 124 in Canton, each dedicated to a particular deity. Buddhism shaped Chinese tradition and culture, and is China's oldest imported religion—combining Taoism and Mahayana Buddhism that spread to China from India via the silk route and across the Indian Ocean. Teachings were passed down over several centuries until the first scriptures were written in the second century BCE and brought to China. It is centered around the "four noble truths," which teaches that there is no intermediary between humankind and the divine. The first Buddhist scriptures in China can be traced back to the Han dynasty when it was merged with Taoism. The modern religion comprises four main schools and there are a multitude of Buddhist religious cities across the country, despite setbacks during the Tang dynasty. Religious rituals revolve around the temples, and a large number integrate a monastic focus as well as catering for lay believers. The Guangxiao Temple in Canton is one of the oldest in China, and played a prominent part in propagating Buddhist education and translation of scriptures.

Religion and Philosophy

The CCP officially frowns on orthodox religion for party members. While Marx famously stated that "religion is the opium of the masses" it is unlikely he was referring to the more philosophical ideologies that are widely practiced in China. However ambiguous, restrictive policies are in place over the free practice of mainstream religions, while unsanctioned religious groups are subject to a cautious policy of toleration.

Chinese religion is centered less around theological concerns than philosophical teachings, which have served it well in its modernization process and have historically allowed it to embrace Western ideologies in a way that has, in general, been culturally positive. The three harmonious belief systems of Chinese culture are Confucianism, Taoism, and Buddhism, all of which establish a moral relationship of the individual in relation to certain hierarchical

externalities—family, neighborhood, city, and nation.[201] This is less to do with a god and more a basis for personal identity in a visionary sense, spelled out by Matteo Ricci, that relates to different cultures in a complementary rather than a contrasting form. Of the three teachings, Confucianism sets out a strict but humane and righteous creed of social etiquette that has much to do with respect and care within society. Taoism is centered on a life of virtue and interdependence, symbolized by *yin* and *yang*, where each side incorporates part of the other. Buddhism on the other hand is based on the teachings of Siddhartha Gautama where positive outcomes arise from following a peaceful and positive path to enlightenment. In general, these teachings have coexisted throughout much of Chinese history and are together manifested in ethical guidance and practice. Political policy can then be viewed as following not dissimilar lines.

At a time when the world seeks a complementary relationship between cultures, responsive to pressing needs, it is necessary to respect the full dimensions and characteristics of Chinese culture through a measure of insight. While Chinese history reflects almost 5,000 years of well-documented knowledge, theories on Western social science arose through much more recent historical experience, based largely on a multitude of religious perspectives. The quintessence of Chinese culture, which has been described as a belief in harmony with diversity, therefore needs to form part of a process of mutual understanding.

Unification of contrasting ideas must overcome the constant hurdle whereby "the virtuous see only virtue and the knowledgeable see only knowledge." This is clearly subject to an elusive realm of ethical belief, less concerned with rationality and more with reason, where a unifying position relates to both knowledge and intelligence. Lai Zi's *Dao De Jing* states that, "the model for man is the earth; the model for earth is heaven; the model for heaven is the Way; and the model for the Way is Nature." Hu Yao-bang, general secretary of the CCP between 1982 and 1987 stated, "that party philosophy should not be pitted against either culture or science, possibly reflecting the Confucian philosopher Cheng Yi who stated that, "knowledge precedes practice, but must be integrated with it—one who knows but cannot practice does not truly know."

Traditional Chinese philosophy with its independent set of concepts and categories cannot be adequately applied to Christian religious concepts as it incorporates a variety of ideas and layers of meaning, some of them quite abstract, whereas Christian religion has a determined relationship between heaven and humanity. It is also the basis of differences between the Chinese philosophy of unity—opposite and complementary—rather than Western philosophy, which is concerned more with making distinctions.

Following the Cultural Revolution, philosophical studies broke free from the bounds of dogmatism, concentrating more on advancing a pragmatic prospect for Confucianism based on both cumulative knowledge and benevolence, and the relationship between humans and society as a basis for humanism. This is applied to the new modernization plans, and an emerging relationship with the West, with an inevitable but often elusive synthesis of a capitalist market economy and socialism, subject to bewildering changes of focus amidst constant references to nationalism and patriotism to explain varying realms of political restrictions.

The founding of the International Confucianism Association in Beijing in 1994, and the importance attached to it by government, is almost certainly a factor in its ideological resurrection, and its culturally conservative relationship with many other Asian countries. Its ethnical core strikes a chord with the goal of achieving a united China, and therefore continues to serve the interests of government. It has arguably become a political basis for Chinese sensitivity and wariness over what might be construed as "Westernization." In a not dissimilar way, it might also reflect the popular interpretation of *The Book of Changes* or *I Ching* as embodying specific aspects of Chinese culture that rely more on intuition than on demonstrable concepts of a Marxist class struggle.

The Underlying Ideology

China's opening up to the world in the twenty-first century is subject to significant restrictions in terms of foreign business registration. Non-government organizations must be formally affiliated with government bodies, and regulatory mechanisms are in place to prevent foreign influences deemed to be potentially malignant, from seeping into society at large. High-principled regulations now govern all parts of the Chinese government, the bureaucracy, and senior military officials, even facilitating the pursuit of those miscreants who have fled the country with ill-gained resources. Whether this necessarily creates a virtuous system of meritocracy is a moot point, but it does indirectly contribute to excessive prudence and inhibition amongst officialdom as to what is said and done.

A number of campaigns from 2013 have emphasized both the need to improve the relationship between CCP members and the public at large, and the need for party officials to offer critiques and self-criticism, while perhaps also underscoring their unequivocal support for the frontal position of the core leadership. In stressing the need for constant rectitude and unification however, this has increasingly positioned China in a somewhat different corner to the ostensibly liberal values associated with civil society in the West, and even those within its own borders who espouse more tolerant ideologies. A campaign to educate the country about Communist Party history, according to its official narrative announced by Xi Jinping in February 2021, is seemingly intended to consolidate support for party loyalty and to renew its legitimacy as part of a national security program overseen by Xi himself.

The equation of China's championship of a free market with the underlying ideology of Marx and Engels in their 1848 *Communist Manifesto*, even under the elusive policy of a socialist market economy with Chinese characteristics, might be stretching a point. This argument, stipulated and justified by Deng Xiaoping, was that the country had to engage in economic growth that combined a dominant state-owned enterprise sector with market capitalism before it could pursue a more egalitarian version of socialism. In economic terms, the country appears to follow most of the hallmarks of a capitalist society, but in political terms it is party-led and state-regulated.

The rule of law in China equates with rule of the country by the Chinese Communist Party, thereby reinforcing the coercive strength of the party state, and establishing a system that can be used to inhibit freedom of expression or indeed any notion of dissent as far as politics are concerned—aspects that are the very essence of Western law. Thus, the role of the Party over the past decade has become increasingly immersed in the regulation of civil society, which inevitably introduces certain contradictions with the outward looking cultural and technological trends that China presents to the world, but with concomitant measures that in practice might well act to inhibit the penetration of external ideas and influences.

It must be stated that China has a long history of controlling information flow. Various forms of censorship have in fact been systematically imposed through a succession of dynastic rulers over 2,000 years, with texts and documents periodically suppressed if they were perceived as threats to social stability or were considered to contain supposedly heretical ideas. The revolutionary philosophy of Mao Zedong deemed it essential to promulgate, first and foremost, social values. Under Mao, the government closed universities and scientific research undertakings for their supposed elitist tendencies, so that both innovation and entrepreneurship were effectively stifled. This was only reinstituted in the early 1980s through the advent of the reform movement and the Four Modernizations.

Inculcating political correctness through ideological control can technically be enforced, for example through targeting universities, but plays into the hands of democratic powers who are not slow to denounce it and threaten reprisals. The clear discouragement of independent points of view, also arguably detracts from a wide appreciation of China's very real economic and social achievements, including the elimination of poverty as a prevailing subtext to China's rise as an economic power. A further and more unpredictable factor is the extent to which rigid ideology induces tensions, while potentially opening a door to extreme measures of enforcement against anything or anyone even remotely deemed to be harmful to national unity. While imposed obedience can catapult a society into divisions and unrest, evidence indicates that the Western world can be only too easily taunted into retaliation at a time when international bodies should be working together to resolve problems of joint concern.

Beijing's reading of political challenges as inciting mutual destruction or *Iaam chau* by what it terms "non-patriots," that is to say those who are considered as being likely to threaten and thwart national interests, extracts any narrative of political counterbalance. Politics then becomes less "the art of the possible," and more of a pro-establishment caucus constructed around an inevitable flattering and sycophantic adherence to favored factions, where too many people have too much to lose by being visionary, open-minded, or simply going against the flow. If the country moves to an ever more dominant hegemony, there will arguably be a need to make government more of a meritocracy that is responsive to different approaches in meeting national interests.

The transparency of the internet in more recent times has unsurprisingly brought a determined but measured reaction from an anxious government with regard to control of information circulation, although social media is used, among other things, to promote favorable profiles of state leaders. The internet is tightly monitored following determined attempts by ambitious netizens to usurp its political potential, and, in particular, anything that can be construed as political content or expression. An army of internet analysts effectively seeks to prevent unfettered website access—a process that continues to make China watchers bristle. At the same time, the internet's usefulness as a vehicle of propaganda to both guide and assess public opinion has also become clear, along with the means to monitor any type of anti-authority mobilization or protest movement.

The Cyberspace Administration of China requires the proffering of official credentials before being able to publish papers, and technically only State media and movers of official propaganda can obtain permission. The cybersecurity law was enacted in 2017, based on a perceived need to protect national security. Data transfer is restricted, and permits are required as a prerequisite to the ability to publish on topics such as political and military affairs, and new rules from 2021 extend this requirement to health, economics, education, and judicial matters.[202] Online creative content is also monitored for compliance with overall internal policy, and State approval is necessary for all material produced by foreign firms, while private technology companies are required to censor their content. This issue represents a paradox, as a loss of credibility through restrictions on the free flow of information can impede innovation and reduce efficiency. It also pits China's considerable promotion of globalization against tightly circumscribed access to the very information that might best achieve it. There are of course anomalies. While the government maintains a computerized database as part of a social-credit program that enables the collection of personal information, large credit-rating companies are at liberty to gather all manner of personal data, willingly handed over by users.

It would, however, be a misinterpretation to view China through that of a Western democratic ideology, particularly at a time when the country is well on its way to becoming the world's largest economy in an era of twenty-first-century globalization. National security might well be an inherent and constant concern of the Communist state, but global leadership brings with it responsibility for creative dialogue, arguably even more so at a time when the well-tested Western institution of democracy is seen by many as an increasingly polarizing rather than a consensus-driven system, and where an insistence on individual rights often appears to override and overwhelm those of the community at large. No single country in the twenty-first century can remain sovereign in an isolated state, and long-term social and economic policies can themselves forge a resilient political cause through a step-by-step approach to increased information access and freedom of expression. At the same time, the West must restrain its threatening tendency to browbeat and ostracize China at the least sign of obduracy.

Arguably an important aspect is China's broad stance on multipolarity—a distribution of power rather than an acquisition and perpetuation of it. Presumably, to be on the safe side China's current annual spending on defense is around USD 250 billion: around one-third that of the United States. There is little or no evidence of China seeking military adventurism, nor does it seek to export its ideology and most certainly not in terms of a doctrinal struggle with the U.S.

Deng Xiaoping's reform initiative has successfully evolved along lines that could scarcely have been contemplated in 1978. The current promotion of a Marxist orthodoxy can be considered purely as a convenient articulation of political theory that is increasingly absorbed within state constitutions, or alternatively as a perceptive recognition that authoritarian rule plays on the essential strengths that underlie Chinese nationalism and helps to regulate it. Taken either way, the present political position is to craft an ideology that justifies its policy making as well as safeguarding party unity. In the process, this establishes clear-cut parameters that demand unswerving patriotism. If the universal truth of Marxism has, in so many cases elsewhere, floundered on the rocks of self-interest and corruption, then it is the "Chinese characteristics" that differentiate its current model by de-emphasizing the class struggle that lies at the heart of both Marxist and Maoist philosophies on modernization. On this basis, economic growth is fashioned on a dominant socialist sector with the private economy supporting the reform policy, and also the goal of a more equal society as the basis of stability. This is generally in line with the four principles of modernization as a key objective of the Party to strengthen agriculture, industry, defense, and technology in China.

Inclusive Urbanization

Local government is largely responsible for financing public services, and a significant amount of revenue is raised from land sales and use conversion, which in turn finances environmental infrastructure in keeping pace with population growth and continued urbanization. The partial result has been a fragmentation of urban development, as growth has extended beyond protected areas, resulting in relatively unsynchronized development patterns at the urban periphery of major cities, including Canton. An emphasis on increasing domestic consumption is bringing about changes in the economic development model toward a policy of regionalization that protects against the negative influences of globalization on China, even as it forms a buoyant role in the international marketplace. However, the primary task of fiscal and monetary policies is to promote economic growth. Boosting domestic consumption is a priority set out in the 14th five-year plan, but the opinion of economists is that this is insufficient as the main driver, although consumer spending made up 54.3 percent of economic growth in 2020. It is likely that investment in infrastructure will continue to increase for the foreseeable future, while stabilizing the leverage ratio of the public sector. Major economic initiatives have been made more challenging in recent times by the COVID-19 pandemic, but perversely this appears to have increased China's competitive ability as well as international influence.

The market finance model relates directly to the regulation of land use through effective urban planning in shaping growth patterns and creating sustainable urban environments that optimize land use for the betterment of the city in accordance with long-term objectives. This process also promotes an effective dialogue between all stakeholders in line with regeneration parameters and agreed land use policy. However, it is necessary that existing planning standards and related building codes are periodically reviewed to ensure they are in keeping with urban modernizations, with particular attention given to context-sensitive urban hierarchies and articulate place making.

Ultimately, property rates or household taxes related to land values must equate with necessary growth in urban expenditure, in line with the need for an efficient use of land, the containment of sprawl, the regulation of agricultural land conversion, and the redevelopment of brownfield sites. A further measure is the imposition of a high tax rate on vacant urban land. In turn, this effectively capitalizes land use rights that incentivizes investment in infrastructure through gradual development intensification in line with demand. Zoning plans must also relate to development regulations associated with explicit spatial strategies.

Canton, together with Guangdong Province as a whole, continues to urbanize, hand-in-hand with economic restructuring, and combines a capital-intensive industrial and technology model with increased domestic consumption. The demographic shift from rural to urban is effectively nearing its maximum, with a new realm of educated migrants arriving in the city along with their entire families, reflecting a requirement for an increasingly skilled workforce in the future. This creates a need to develop integrated social policy reforms in order to realize the full benefits of a residence-based system. Planning must become increasingly aligned to the evolving reach of communication technology that continues to redefine work and social patterns both within and between metropolitan regions.

China's urban land market is effectively divided into primary and secondary sectors. Government is the sole supplier of state land, with land use rights to development granted for a defined period. The secondary market entails a subsequent transaction of state land use rights through leasing these to a third party for the remaining period of the grant, but where land is then often subject to surreptitious changes of use, for example in the renewal of urban villages. This process can be problematic as there is little regulatory oversight of the secondary land market through competitive procedures. There is, however, a tendering process for land use rights to state-owned land, and land concession income has grown continually over the past two decades.

In common with other major cities, Canton must continually fine tune its relationship between local public finance, land development, and value capture to enable more sustainable planning and municipal finance through responsive market-based policies, backed up by legal frameworks and effective institutions. The Shenzhen SEZ in the south of Guangdong Province has proved to be an effective forerunner in land policy innovation, as much of its development has taken place on collectively owned rural land but in coexistence with the formal urban land market under the state jurisdiction. This has acted to exemplify the means of integrating informal collective land rights into the urban development process, thereby consolidating an operative land market for state-owned land within the municipal urban boundary. While this has been clearly assisted by the pace of growth and land value in the special economic zones, it provides an effective model for necessary urban land management, efficiency of urban development, and transferability. This also facilitates the redevelopment of older and inefficient uses, and its success in guiding land market integration is entirely relevant to Canton and other cities, where urban renewal rather than spatial expansion is now a mainstay of urban development. In April 2021 it was announced that Shenzhen planned to add almost 3,000 acres of land to its overall development area, one third of it for residential purposes, as part of government's continuous efforts to control surging property prices, in line with the new centralized land supply policy.

Economic Reform

The state has, for many centuries, effectively managed the Chinese economy, in particular foreign trade, although with a lingering and wary acknowledgment of private enterprise. Following the 1949 revolution, the role of the state was considerably strengthened as a presumed but ultimately misconstrued means of bringing about economic equity. However, the task of reducing inequality and lifting large sections of the population out of poverty in the twenty-first century implies raising income levels, and therefore the need to adopt a policy of market-oriented economic reform, introduced in the post-1978 period. Decentralized economic decision-making was recognized in China's 12th Five-Year Plan 2011–2015, which led directly to its innovative transition from low-end manufacturing to high-end technology and professional services. State-owned enterprises gradually began to be privatized and, in their reformed state, play a significant part in the modern economy, with wide representation. These are also a source of increased government debt and tend to operate at overcapacity, but the CCP leadership role in mega enterprises is deemed to be a political principle, and not a few need to be targeted for reform. However, a central factor in structural reform has been the urbanization model as a means of stimulating consumption levels. China's manufacturing community is estimated at around 150 million and it is credited with an extensive supplier base, innovative technology, fast production, and constant adjustment of products in accordance with changing customer requirements.

A more recent economic initiative is the establishment of priority sectors as a basis for economic growth including information technology, robotics, and aerospace aimed at achieving a dominant global market share in the coming years. Innovation and entrepreneurship are technically something that the CCP leadership supports as being important to the competitive global context, although entrepreneurs must advisedly avoid candid conflict with the machinery of the State, in particular its regulatory mechanisms. This brings into focus the need for transparency of single companies that, by either design or fortune, aim for market dominance in a particular sector—a strategy that is all too evident in such powerful and assertive bodies as the e-commerce behemoths.

Environmental Action

China consumes more natural resources than any other country, which has arguably been necessary to fuel its growth targets. The country has become the largest trading partner for countries rich in these commodities to ensure a ready supply, and this is coupled with massive trade and investment packages, which frequently extend to concessional loans and export credits—often referred to as "soft power engagements."

Environmental pollution in China is a serious issue, in particular the achievement of the World Health Organization air quality standards. This reached something of a crisis point in 2012. China has the world's largest carbon footprint and is responsible for around 28 percent of global CO_2 emissions. Emissions of nitrous oxide have increased significantly over the past 30 years, while the toxic contamination of at least 40 percent of rivers and other water courses through industrial waste is equally problematic. It is estimated that there are 144,000 annual deaths in China linked to pollution from road transport. An apparent shortage of non-potable water is also a challenge in the face of an increasing demand from industrial and agricultural uses. By 2021, China has reduced the use of coal to 50 percent of all energy consumption, but government plans to replace coal-powered plants with nuclear facilities have not necessarily succeeded in achieving public consensus. Economic costs to the national economy from environmental degradation are estimated at somewhere between 3 and 10 percent of GDP.

These are issues that are recognized by the Chinese leadership. In 2017, Premier Li Ke-qiang pledged to "make our skies blue again," with stringent laws put into force with set targets and timetables. Xi Jinping has pledged that economic growth must be matched by ecological protection, and goals have been set to reduce air, water, and soil pollution. In an address to the United Nations in 2020, Xi announced that China would become carbon neutral by 2060 and a range of measures have been put in place to repair decades of environmental mismanagement. This goal is now subsumed within China's current five-year plan to better meet public expectations, and the country is not coming to this from a standing start. It is a leading supplier of clean energy technology, with more than one-third of the world's wind turbine manufacturing companies and around 40 percent of new renewable energy plants. The country also produces 70 percent of all solar panels, although not all of these are successfully employed domestically. One of the priority regions for pollution prevention is the Pearl River Delta, where financial incentives have been set for the reduction of pollution concentrations, and courts have been set up to hear environmental public interest lawsuits.

Ahead of the Earth Day summit in April 2021 Beijing and Washington issued a joint statement pledging to work together to uphold agreements on climate change. A timetable has been set for the attainment of a carbon-neutral environment that includes clean energy, electric vehicles, and a ban on fossil-fuel cars. The country manufactures an average of 24 million cars per year and shows little sign of slowing growth, although it has also invested heavily in electric vehicle manufacturing capacity. Its commitment to increase the adoption of electric vehicles will not only assist a carbon-neutral future, but is estimated to save over 80 billion USD annually on oil imports from 2030—more than sufficient to cover the necessary infrastructure to support electrified transport. In addition battery prices have fallen 20 percent a year from 2010. It is estimated that at the current rate of progress, electric vehicles will account for three out of five cars on China's roads by 2030. At the summit, Xi pledged to strictly control coal-fired power plants, phased over a five-year period. It was announced that China is aiming to reach peak carbon dioxide emissions by 1930, and to reduce emissions per unit of economic output by 18 percent over a five-year period from 2021.

The Political Economy

Deng Xiaoping popularized a strategic aphorism that contained a certain historical wisdom: to conceal one's capabilities, bide one's time, and wait for the right moment. This discreet means of conducting policy has served China well in the modern age, free of its historical vulnerabilities, and even emerging relatively unscathed from the perils of the 2010 financial crisis and COVID-19. The country has been able to assume what its reformist leaders have determined to be its global identity as a rejuvenated power—something ambitiously encapsulated in the 14th Five-Year Plan that commenced in March 2021. This is intent on driving modernization through innovation and technological advancement and promoting high-end green production.

China is now a global power with almost 20 percent of global GDP in 2021. It is also a major source of foreign direct investment, which in recent years has fueled the development of emerging technologies and infrastructure. The current leadership now aspires to shape and influence an international order on several levels, primarily political, institutional, and economic to best suit its long-term interests. The country has, in recent years, played a major part in driving multi-lateral agreements, including the Regional Comprehensive Economic Partnership between Southeast Asian Nations, and the China European Union Comprehensive Agreement on Investment. These promise to open the Chinese market in finance, computing, transportation, and other services, while at the same time absorbing cutting-edge technologies in order to avoid international competition.

Beijing has also shown itself willing to grant market access to foreign manufacturers but largely in return for technology transfer, which has proved to be a point of contention—one that actively discourages competition or excessive collaboration with foreign multinationals. At the same time, the government continues to establish science and technology parks, many of these associated with universities, that accommodate many thousands of high-tech enterprises. In 2020, Chinese universities made up nine of the top international 20 educational institutes, according to the World Intellectual Property Organization. China has been a top source of international patents since 2019 but has been quite slow in converting its research and development into successful product outcomes. China's National Audit Office has stated that government R&D spending converted only 8.4 percent of patents owned by universities into commercial use. The current five-year plan from 2021–25 places self-reliance in critical technological innovation as a central focus, and Beijing has also delegated increased autonomy to Chinese universities in the handling of intellectual property.

China has also developed a massive development fund to assist small business start-ups where innovation is tied to business growth, which includes smart technology and the rapid development of artificial intelligence. This is reflected in a continual narrowing of the technology gap, although China also lags behind many other countries in terms of intellectual property sales. Innovation is helped considerably by financial incentives that have instigated the return of Chinese students from abroad to form part of a large talent pool.

China's leadership is facing a further twenty-first-century issue in tandem with an overhaul of its supporting legal system in order to regulate the country's digital economy which accounts for more than one third of total GDP. The focus is on internet finance, artificial intelligence, big data, and cloud computing that are vital to its national interest, although this is seen as being set within a distinctly Chinese socialist rule of law. Facing up to international challenges, the current five-year plan recognizes the use of international legal tools and the need for compliance in the protection of intellectual property. This accords with what are known as the four-pronged comprehensive political goals: governing the country by law, deepening reform, a disciplined approach to running the Communist Party, and building a "modestly prosperous" society.[203] In effect, this sets out a vision for the coming decades on the assumption that both time and momentum are on the side of China in shaping global and regional institutions that best meet its particular interests.

Xi Jinping has assured various summits of world leaders that China will defend the continuing process of globalization and has promoted lower trading tariffs. He has also used the many Confucius Institutes throughout the world as a forum for this, and globalization on Chinese terms tends to imply the achievement of a rejuvenated nation at a new stage in its history. Such an indistinct strategy presents something of a paradox when balanced against China's enhanced party control that imparts distinct constraints and restrictions as a means of protecting it from the perceived perils of free exchange. This arguably defies the Western viewpoint that a globalized economy requires an interdependence of information, ideas, and capital. China's own strategic vision is to base its immediate future on an enigmatic realization of a capitalist economy with Chinese characteristics. An authoritarian leadership model allows it to assert itself on the world stage and realize its international interests while sacrificing optimal economic growth in the short-term for market dominance and domestic stability in the long-term.

The National People's Congress, the country's Legislative Assembly together with the Chinese People's Consultative Congress, essentially shapes the political agenda. The year 2021 marked both the centenary of the Chinese Communist Party and the commencement of the 14th Five-Year Plan. The latter defines the immediate future of the CCP and how it contends with the international community. It forms a series of social and economic development initiatives that serve to set out strategies for reform, the ratification of growth targets, and detailed economic development guidelines for its regions. In 2021, about 60 percent of China's population, or more than 800 million people, live in cities, and a further 250 million are projected to be urban dwellers by 2050. This necessitates adequate fiscal support. A further factor is prioritizing emphasis on food security and self-reliance, using new technologies to increase the production of foodstuffs through the creation of high-yield arable land to feed its 1.4 billion people.

What has emerged in China is a circumspect accommodation of global capitalism within set boundaries. In other words, there is a need to draw a discreet line between a free market and state regulation aimed at protecting the real economy through anti-trust curbs. Along with the current five-year plan, the leadership has unveiled its "2035 vision"—a blueprint that echoes the opening of the reform period in 1979, but sets a specific target to double the size of the economy by 2035. For this it must continue to boost domestic consumer demand and encourage development of the hi-tech sector. Xi Jinping has signaled that attaining common prosperity to reduce the prevailing income gap is not only an economic issue but a major political one. An immoderate emphasis on China becoming a self-reliant world leader in technology will inevitably heighten international concerns and foster counteracting strategies and even sanctions from Western allies. But there remains a scope for cooperation, as this comes at a time when all countries are seeking financial stability following the economic devastations of the COVID-19 pandemic. Development debt has soared to an all-time high, and China must seek to boost manufacturing and hi-tech industries rather than place a continuing reliance on growth of a property market financed by borrowing.

Canton echoes China as a whole in tightening measures to manage the property bubble, which for the country as a whole is estimated at about USD 60 trillion or 285 trillion yuan—about six times the gross domestic product. This is a reflection of both government's land holding and its need for revenue. Maintaining expectations of property inflation must be equated with measures to tighten liquidity that are necessary to periodically slow down the market and discourage pure speculation, anchored by the Renminbi's soft peg to the US dollar. China is second only to Japan in holding U.S. debt, with around USD 1.1 trillion in treasury holdings. This vital link between the Yuan and the USD contributes to the biggest asset bubble in history, and might be juxtaposed with the U.S. Federal Reserve's balance sheet that represented 6 percent of GDP in 2007 but rose over eight times to USD 7.6 trillion or 36 percent of GDP by March 2021, with the "build back better" stimulus program allocating a further USD 2 trillion up to 2025. Public debt in the U.S. increased to 136 percent of 2021's GDP, and it is projected by the Congressional Budget Office that this will increase to 202 percent of the GDP by the mid-twenty-first century.

The World Economic Forum has described the growing gap between rich and poor as a trend that threatens economic growth and is leading to an evident increase in trade wars and application of tariffs to imports. Thomas Piketty's book *Capital in the Twenty-First Century* focused on soaring income inequality, and the hypothesis of disparities in wealth as opposed to earnings, termed "patrimonial" capitalism. In major world economies increasing inequality has come to reflect an ideology driven by political forces whereby the return on capital grows much faster than national economies. What has been termed "hyper capitalism" increasingly exists outside the social-democratic framework. Piketty points to a central contradiction of capitalism in that through various ways, in particular inheritance, inequality of private wealth is increasing commensurate with the slowing down of economic and demographic growth. The important distinction is between income and wealth. Income relates to the flow of money through salary or social welfare, while wealth relates to assets free of liabilities such as stocks, trusts, and real estate, and this can be exacerbated by the nature of tax policies and by racial disparities. Inequality is measured by the Gini coefficient, which stands at a relatively modest 0.465 in China (where 1.0 stands at complete inequality and 0 represents complete equality). High levels of wealth inequality defy the principles of social justice, long associated with democratic societies, that is contributing to both economic and social polarization, and growing national debt, which effectively acts to reduce state power just as it weakens democracies.

China accounts for around 18 percent of global total wealth while the U.S. share is 29 percent. Divergence of wealth from ownership of capital compared to income from labor is occurring on a global scale including emerging economies, although China is at the lower end of the range. Recent figures suggest that the urban-rural divide and regional disparities play a significant role in wealth distribution. By comparison the unequal distribution of assets among households of the United States in 2020 reached a record level, with the bottom 50 percent of households holding only 1.6 percent of net worth verses 70 percent for the top 10 percent. Many countries have large national debts that are destabilizing democracies, with a drift toward oligarchies, as inequalities between different classes have become entrenched. A further factor contributing to wealth inequality is the growth in technology where both skilled and unskilled workers continue to be replaced by more cost-effective means of production.

China might well be in a stronger position than the West to implement progressive taxation according to income hierarchies, while preserving growth in industry and technology through a dynamic entrepreneurial system, together with the ability to tame the disproportionate power of mega-corporations. In terms of national policy China follows a more egalitarian distribution of wealth which secures a meaningful standard of living and security, and which perhaps in the long term will contribute to increasing political power. However, according to the 2019 Global Wealth Report of the top end of the scale, China has surpassed the United States in having the highest number of residents within the top 10 percent of the world's wealth ownership, with 50 percent of households considered to be middle class. A White Paper, *Poverty Alleviation: China's Experience and Contribution*, was released in April 2020, recording its success in lifting more than 15 million people in the poorest parts of China out of poverty during the previous five years.

China faces certain economic challenges in its shift from labor surplus to scarcity, with a shrinking work force and with a notable emphasis toward innovation as the driver of economic growth. This indicates a continual move of educated migrant workers to the cities, but with a social safety net and training programs in place along with continued investment in research and development. Ambitious environmental goals also suggest a need for innovative technologies to deal with these.

In May 2021, the results of the 10-year census were announced by the National Bureau of Statistics. The population of 1.412 billion, has grown at the slowest pace since the census began in 1953, with a continual falling birth rate which grew at 5.38 percent over the period. The current fertility rate has fallen to 1.3, well below the level of 2.1 that is needed to maintain a stable population level. This confirms previous projections that China's work force will continue to decline, and in response Beijing announced a gradual increase in the mandatory retirement age for both male and female workers. This might also indicate a need to abolish the household registration system which limits the mobility and opportunities of rural workers in order to meet the government's goal of 65 percent of all workers in urban situations. A further initiative might well be the abolition or amendment of policy restrictions on the number of children born to Chinese families and a possible increase in household welfare.

At a more elusive level the new and changing global order requires collaboration with bodies such as the World Trade Organization and the International Monetary Fund in the wake of the COVID-19 pandemic, and in the face of established interests with competing programs. To resolve this conundrum requires international cooperation and continued domestic reforms. China is, to an extent, dealing with this through "dual circulation," which aims to boost the domestic market while attempting to reduce reliance on imports of foreign technology. In order to address containment of the debt-laden property bubble, new financing rules for real estate companies have been set out by China's central bank and the Ministry of Housing and Urban-Rural development to benefit the broader economy.

State control remains as the elephant in the room, albeit an elusive one, although China has the enviable ability to continually nurture creative thinkers and to motivate talented people to engage with the technological challenges of the twenty-first century. A central issue is the extent to which the ramifications of bureaucratic controls, essentially aimed at reinforcing social stability and societal development, can achieve an effective balance with the need to nurture the essential entitlements necessary to carry the new economy forward in an increasingly competitive international order. Klaus Schwab, founder of the World Economic Forum, has stated that in a world where essential public functions and communications are migrating to digital platforms, the government needs to maintain checks and balances. The two conceptual approaches to this are first that everything that is not explicitly forbidden is allowed; the second is that everything not explicitly allowed is forbidden. A blending of these approaches is the challenge facing governments, and for innovation to flourish governments need to effectively engage with citizens.

Insulating the country from foreign interventions and uncertainties is represented by the erection of a "virtual" wall that might be compared to the Great Wall of China itself, from a different age. Both represent strong protective mechanisms, perceived and intended as preventing the possibility of a hostile and threatening opening up, but the former can also be breached just as the latter was, unless it is perpetually reinforced by international relations to match its ascendance on the global stage. Resolving this paradox represents the future challenge.

Acknowledgments

Canton, since 1918 better known as Guangzhou, is a city that I have visited innumerable times since the late 1970s, for both work and leisure. In many ways it encapsulates the modern history of China, from the nineteenth century onwards. Charting the many changes on a frequent basis, stemming from an almost continuous process of regeneration and contemporary insertions within older patterns of urbanization, has in itself been a means of appreciating the prevailing urban character of the city.

As stated in the Introduction, a contemporary view of history, like much of the urbanism we experience in the city today, is a matter of both reference and reconstruction, helping to infuse our perspective on the past with our knowledge of the present. The latter draws on much that is available before our eyes in the modern city that has grown and changed so much over the past forty years. For knowledge of the past, I have drawn on a number of valuable references that I sourced for a previous book, The Urban Design of Concession, on the Chinese treaty ports, published in 2011. A number of distinguished authors and commentators have provided a wealth of historical detail, intelligence, and insight into events during late nineteenth and early twentieth century China.

John Fairbank's Trade and Diplomacy on the China Coast provided exceptional scholarly insight into many of the circumstances surrounding the Western presence in China, the unequal treaties and the early settlement patterns and activities that emerged, covering the period from 1842 to 1854. G. William Skinner's The City in Late Imperial China was a valuable source of detail on the prevailing administrative and economic systems prior to foreign intervention in China. The English in China by J. B. Eames, first published in 1909 and republished in 1974, similarly contains considerable research of historical events in striking and enlightened detail. Grasso, Corrin, and Kort's Modernisation and Revolution in China provided a comprehensive overview from the first treaty settlement through the spiraling sequence of events in the late nineteenth century. Frederick Wakeman's Strangers at the Gate, Chesneaux, Barstid and Bergere's China from the Opium Wars to the 1911 Revolution, and Rhoads Murphey's The Treaty Ports and China's Modernisation also provided scholarly analysis of this same period in terms of tradition and gradual transformation of the port cities. These and many more are set out in the following end notes.

I am also greatly obliged to Jonathan Wattis of Wattis Fine Art in Hong Kong for supplying antique maps and plans of the Pearl River Delta.

I would finally like to record my appreciation to Gordon Goff, publisher of ORO Editions, and to Jake Anderson, managing editor of ORO, for his assistance with the publication and for his valuable editing skills from which the book has greatly benefitted. I would also like to thank Pablo Mandel for the graphic layout and design, overcoming the challenges of reconciling text with illustrative images.

In conclusion a big thank you to my long-time friends and colleagues at URBIS for their constant help and support. I am particularly grateful to my assistant Lily Tam for her invaluable help in typing and coordination of manuscript drafts and her patient and prolonged assistance with the compilation and editing process.

Endnotes

Chapter 1.0 | The Mandate of Heaven

1. Murphey, R. "The Treaty Ports and China's Modernisation: What Went Wrong," Michigan Papers in *Chinese Studies* No.7, 13, 1970

2. Fairbank, J. K. *Trade and Diplomacy on the China Coast: The Opening of the Treaty Ports 1842–1854*. Stanford University Press, 1964.

3. Ferguson, N. *Empire: How Britain made the Modern World*. Allen Lane, 2003.

4. Nylan, M., *The Five Confucian Classics*, New Haven, Yale University Press, 2001.

5. Chesneaux, J., Bastid, M., and Bergere, M., *China from Opium Wars to the 1911 Revolution*, Pantheon Books, NY, 1976.

6. Deng K., "China's Population Expansion and its Causes during the Qing Period 1644–1911," London School of Economics and Political Science Working Paper 215, May 2005.

7. G. William Skinner, *The City in Late Imperial China: Regional Urbanisation in Nineteenth-Century China*, Standard University Press, 1977.

8. Campanella, T. J., *The Concrete Dragon: China's Urban Revolution and what it means for the World*, Princeton Architectural Press, NY, 2008.

9. G. William Skinner, "Cities and the Hierarchy of Local Systems," in *The City in Late Imperial China*, Stanford University Press, 1977.

10. Smith, A. The Wealth of Nations, London, W. Strahan and T. Cardell, 1778.

11. Murphey, R., *"City as a Mirror of Society: China, Tradition and Transformation,"* in Agnew J. A., Mercer, J., and Soshar, D. E., The City in Cultural Context, Boston, Allen and Unwin, 1984.

12. Murphey, R., ibid.

13. Sun Shiwen, "The Institutional and Political Background to Chinese Urbanism," in *AD: New Urban China*, Vol 78 No. 5, 2008.

14. Greenberg, M., British Trade and the Opening of China, Cambridge University Press, 1951.

15. Murphey, R., *"The Treaty Ports in China's Modernisation: What Went Wrong,"* Michigan Papers in Chinese Studies

16. Davis, J. F., *"The Chinese a General Description of China and its Inhabitants,"* 4th edition Vol. II, 1851.

17. Chesneaux, J., Bastid, M., and Berger, M., *China from Opium Wars to the 1911 Revolution*, Pantheon Books, NY, 1976.

18. Johnson, L. C., *Shanghai: From Market Town to Treaty Port 1074–1858*, Stanford University Press, 1995.

19. Chang, S. D., *The Historical Trend of Chinese Urbanisation*, A. M. Geog 53 109–43, 1963.

20. Strand, D. P., "Historical Perspectives," in *Urban Spaces in Contemporary China*, eds. Deborah S. Davis, Richard Kraus, Barry Naughton, and Elizabeth J. Perry, Cambridge University Press, 1995, 396.

21. Wakeman, F., *Strangers at the Gate: Social Disorder in South China 1839–1861*, University of California Press, 1966.

22. Garrett, V. M., *Heaven is High, the Emperor Far Away: Merchants and Mandarins in Old Canton*, Oxford University Press, 2002.

23. Chang, See Chen, "Two Decades of Planning Guangzhou, 1918–1938," unpublished Ph.D. thesis, Feb. 2007.

24. Van Dyke, Paul, *The Canton Trade: Life and Enterprise on the China Coast, 1700–1845*, Hong Kong University Press, 2005.

25. Garret V M op cit P.81

26. Hunter W. C. 'The Fan Kwae at Canton Before treaty Days' 1825-1844. Kelly and Walsh, 1911

27. Fairbank, J. K., op cit.

28. Eames, J. B., *The English in China*, Curzon Press Ltd. 1909; and Harper and Row, NY, 1974, 51.

29. Fairbank, J. K., op cit.

30. Wu Jin, op cit.

Chapter 2.0 | Avenues of Commerce

31. Freedman, M., *Lineage Organisation in Southeastern China*, University of London, 1958.

32. Skinner, G. W., The City in Late Imperial China, Stanford University Press, 1977.

33. Fairbank, J. K., *Trade and Diplomacy on the China Coast:*

The Opening of the Treaty Ports 1842–1854, Stanford University Press, 1964.

34. Garrett, V. M., op cit., 81.

35. Hunter, W. C., *The Fan Kwae at Canton Before Treaty Days 1825–1844*, Kelly and Walsh, 1911.

36. Farris, J. A., "Dwelling on the Edge of Empires: Foreigners and Architecture in Guangzhou," UMI Dissertation Services, 2006.

37. Eames, J. B., *The English in China*, Curzon Press Ltd., 1909; and Harper and Row, NY, 1974.

38. Eames, J. B., ibid.

39. Fairbank, J. K., *Trade and Diplomacy on th e China Coast: The Opening of the Treaty Ports 1842–1854*, Stanford University Press, 1964.

40. Hunter, W. C., "Bits of Old China," *Biblio Life* 2009 (originally published in 1923).

41. Fairbank, op cit.

42. Eames, J. B., op cit., 86.

43. Fitzgerald, J., *Awakening China: Politics, Culture and Class in the Nationalist Revolution*, Stanford University Press, 1996.

44. Hunter, W. C., op cit.

45. Van Dyke, P. A., *The Canton Trade: Life and Enterprise on the China Coast, 17001845*, Hong Kong University Press, 2005.

46. Van Dyke, Paul A., and Schopp, S. E. (eds.), *The Private Side of the Canton Trade 1700–1840*, Hong Kong University Press, 2018.

47. Hellman, L., *This House is not a Home: European Everyday Life in Canton and Macau, 1730–1830*, Leiden, Brill, 2019.

48. Hunter, W. C., op cit.

49. Eames, J. B., op cit., 122.

50. Grasso, J., Corrin, J., and Kort, M., *Modernisation and Revolution in China*, East Gate, 1991.

51. Phatt, L. and Chiang Su-hui, *Six Records of a Floating Life London*, Penguin Books, 1983.

52. Eames, J. B., op cit., 169.

Chapter 3.0 | Adventurism and Hostilities

53. Report from the Select Committee of the House of Common on the Affairs of the East India Company (China Trade), 1830.

54. Van Dyke, P. A., "Floating Brothels and the Canton Flower Boats 1750–1930," researchgate.net/publica-tion 328380053.

55. Virgil Kit-yiu Ho, op cit.

56. Moise, E. E., *Modern China: A History*, Pearson Longman, 2008.

57. Fairbank, J. K., op cit.

58. Eames, J. B., op cit., 201.

59. Eames, J. B., *The English in China*, London, Curzon Press, 1909.

60. Stursberg, P., *Memoirs of Imperialism and its Ending*, The University of Alberta Press, 2002.

61. Eames, J. B., op cit., 232.

62. Fairbank, J. K., op cit.

63. Connor, P., *The Hongs of Canton*, English Art Books, 2009.

64. Fitzgeld, C. D., *China: A World so Changed*, Nelson, 1972.

65. Eames. J. B., op cit.

66. Wakeman, F., *Strangers at the Gate: Social Disorder in South China, 1839–1861*, University of California Press, 1966, 33.

67. Eames, J. B., op cit., 289.

68. Eames, J. B., op cit., 369.

69. Owen, D. E., *British Opium Policy in China and India*, Archon Books, 1968.

70. Fairbank, J. K., op cit.

71. Owen, D.E. op cit

72. Brendon, P., *The Decline and Fall of the British Empire: 1781–1997*, Jonathan Cape, London, 2007.

73. Fairbank, J. K., op cit.

74. Van Dyke, Paul, *The Canton Trade: Life and Enterprise on the China Coast, 1700–1845*, Hong Kong University Press, 2005.

75. P. D. Coates, *The China Consuls: British Consular Offices 1843–1943*, Hong Kong, Oxford University Press, 1988.

Chapter 4.0 | Beachheads of Foreign Influence

76. Wood, F., *Treaty Port Life in China, 1843–1943*, 34.

77. Wood, F., ibid.

78. Richard, Joseph, "Howqua's Garden in Hunan, China," in *The Gardens Trust Gardens of Influence* Vol 43 No., 168–81.

79. Fairbank, J. K., op cit.

80. Fairbank, J. K., op cit.

81. Wood, F., op cit.

82. Chesneaux, J., Bastid, M., and Bergere, M., op cit.

83. Wood, F., *Treaty Port Life in China, 1843–1943*.

84. Yen-P'ing Hao, *The Comprador in Nineteenth Century China: Bridge between East and West*, Harvard University Press, Cambridge, Mass., 1970.

85. Yen-P'ing Hao, op cit., 111.

86. Fairbank, J. K., op cit.

87. Asiasocity.org/chinawealthpower/chapters/weiyuan

88. Farris, J. A., *Enclave to Urbanity*, Hong Kong University Press, 2016.

89. Wakeman, F., *Strangers at the Gate: Social Disorder in*

South China 1839–1861, University of California Press, 1966, 127.

90. Grasso, J., Corrin, J., and Korr, M., *Modernisation and Revolution in China: Breakdown and Invasion,* East Gate, 1991, 65.

91. Grasso, J., Corrin, J., and Korr, M., op cit.

92. Garret, V., op cit., 113.

93. Farris, J. A., op cit.

94. Chesneaux, J., Bastid, M., and Bergere, M., op cit.,179–80.

95. Rawski, E. S., *Agricultural Change and the Peasant Economy of South China,* Harvard University Press, 1972.

96. Cartier, Carolyn Lee, op cit.

97. Spence, J. D., *The Search for Modern China,* Norton, NY, 1999.

98. Chesneaux, J., Bastid, M., and Bergere, M., op cit.

99. Wood, F., op cit.

100. Cartier, Carolyn Lee, *Mercantile Cities on the South China Coast: Ningbo, Fuzhou, and Xiamen, 1840–1930,* Unpublished Ph.D. Thesis, University California at Berkeley, 1991.

101. Cartier, Carolyn Lee, op cit.

102. Ansome, J., *Coolie Ships of the Chinese Diaspora (1846–1874),* Proverse, Hong Kong, 2020.

103. Chesneaux, J., Bastid, M., and Bergere, M., op cit., 281.

104. G. William Skinner, *The City in Late Imperial China,* Stanford University Press, 1977, 220.

105. Chesneaux, J., Bastid, M., and Bergere, M., op cit., 298.

106. Fairbank, J. K. and Goldway, M., *China: A New History,* Belknap Press, Harvard University, 1994, 227.

107. Preston, D., *The Boxer Rebellion,* Berkeley Books, NY, 1999.

108. Preston. D., ibid.

109. Brendon, P., *The Decline and Fall of the British Empire: 1781–1997,* Jonathan Cape, London, 2007.

110. Preston, D., op cit., 337.

Chapter 5.0 | An Emerging Modernism

111. Seagrave, S., *Dragon Lady,* Vintage Press, 1993.

112. Mackerras, C., *China in Transformation 1900–1949,* Longman, 1998.

113. Preston, D. P., op cit., 351.

114. Chang, See Chen, op cit.

115. Cody, J. W., *Exporting American Architecture 1870–2000,* London: Routledge, 2003.

116. Cody, J. W., "American Planning in Republican China, 1911–1937," *Planning Perspectives* 11 (1996), 339–77.

117. Cody, op cit.

118. Chang, See Chen, op cit.

119. Denisen, E. and Guang Yu Ren, *Modernism in China,* Prestel, 2008.

120. Denisen, E. and Guang Yu Ren, op cit.

121. Cody, J. W., "American Planning in Republican China, 1911–1937," *Planning Perspectives* 11 (1996), 339–77.

122. Ho, Virgil K. Y., *Understanding Canton: Rethinking Popular Culture in the Republican Period,* Oxford University Press, 2005.

123. "The New Humanitarian: A Selected History of Opium," in *Encyclopaedia Britannica Opium Trade, British, and Chinese History,* www.thenewhumanitarian.org7.node.

Chapter 6.0 | Forces of Transformation

124. Ho, V., *Understanding Canton: Rethinking Popular Culture in the Republican Period,* Oxford University Press, 2005.

125. Ho, V., ibid.

126. Ho, V., ibid.

127. Fairbank, J. K., *China a New History,* Belknap Press, Harvard University, 1994.

128. Fairbank, J. K., ibid.

129. Chesneaux, J., Bastid, M., and Bergere, M., op cit., 354.

130. Lu Junhua, Rowe, Peter G., and Zang Jie, *Modern Urban Housing in China 1840–2000.*

131. Grasso, J., Corrin, J., and Kort, M., *Modernisation and Revolution in China,* East Gate, 1991, 65.

132. Ferguson, N., *Empire: How Britain made the Modern World,* Allen Lane, 2003, 368.

133. Wright, Mary C. (ed.), *China in Revolution, The First Phase, 1900–1913,* Yale University Press, New Haven, 1918.

134. Grasso, J., Corrin, J., and Kart, M., op cit.

135. Morton, W. S. and Lewis, C. M. N., *China: Its History and Culture,* Mcgraw-Hill, 2004.

136. Chan Lau Kit-Ching, *Anglo-Chinese Diplomacy 1906–1920,* Hong Kong University Press, 1978.

137. Meyer, Kathryn Brennan, *Splitting Apart: The Shanghai Treaty Port in Transition: 1914–1921,* Temple University, University Microfilms International, 1985.

138. Wen-Hsin Yeh, *Provincial Passages: Culture, Space and the Origins of China Communism,* University of California Press, 1996.

139. Grasso, J., Corrin, J., and Kort, M., op cit.

140. Gamer, R. (ed.), *Understanding Contemporary China,* Lynne Rienner Publishers Inc., 1999.

141. Mao Zedong, *The Chinese Revolution and the Chinese Communist Party Selected Works* (English Edition) Vol. 2, Beijing.

142. Fairbank, J. K., *China: A New History*, Belknap Press, Harvard University, 1994, 260.

143. Strand, D., "Historical Perspectives," in *Urban Spaces in Contemporary China*, Cambridge University Press, 1995.

144. Wen-Hsin Yeh, *Provincial Passages: Culture, Space and the Origins of Chinese Communism*, University of California Press, 1996, 207.

145. *"China in Chaos: A Survey of Recent Events,"* published by the North-China Daily News and Herald, Ltd., Shanghai, April 1927.

146. Grasso, J., Corrin, J., and Kort, M., op cit., 87.

147. Grasso, J., Corrin, J., and Kort, M., op cit., 99.

148. Fairbank, J. K., op cit., 321.

Chapter 7.0 | The Socialist Planned Economy 1949–1976

149. Chang, J. and Halliday, J., op cit.

150. Terrill, R., *The New Chinese Empire*, Basic Books, 2003.

151. Spence, Jonathan D., *The Search for Modern China*, W. W. Norton & Co, NY, 1990.

152. Lu Xiao-hong, *Chinese Ambassadors*, University of Washington Press, 2001.

153. Morton, W. S. and Lewis, C. M. N., op cit., 205.

154. Chang, J. and Halliday, J., *Mao: The Unknown Story*, 2005, 398.

155. Chang, J. and Halliday, J., op cit., 379.

156. Chang, J. and Halliday, J., op cit., 432.

157. R. J. R. Kirkby, *Urbanisation in China: Town and Country in a Developing Economy*, 1949–2000, Groom & Helm, 1985.

158. Chang, J. and Halliday, J., op cit., 423.

159. Kam Wing Chan, *Cities with Invisible Walls: Reinterpreting Urbanisation in Post-1949 China*, Hong Kong, Oxford University Press, 1994, 145.

160. Spence, Jonathan D., *The Search for Modern China*, W. W. Norton & Co, NY, 1990.

161. Fairbank, op cit., 359.

162. Zhou Rong, "Leaving Utopian China," in *AD New Urban China*, Whiley, 2008.

163. Gaubatz, P. R., "Urban Transformation in Post-Mao China: Impacts of the Reform Era on China's Urban Form," in *Urban Spaces in Contemporary China*, Cambridge University Press, 1995.

164. Chan, K. W., op cit.

165. Fairbank, J. K., *China: A New History*, 349.

166. Morton, W. S. and Lewis, C. M. N., op cit.

167. Grasso, J., Corrin, J., and Kort, M., op cit, 151.

168. Chang, J. and Halliday, J. P., op cit., 464.

169. Campanella, T. J., *The Concrete Dragon: China's Urban Revolution and what it means for the World*, Princeton Architectural Press, NY, 2008.

170. Lu, Junhua, Rowe, Peter G., and Zhang Jie, op cit.

171. Zhang Jie, and Wang Tau, "Housing Development in the Socialist Planned Economy from 1949 to 1978," in *Modern Urban Housing in China 1840–2000*, Lu Junhua, Rowe, Peter G., and Zhang Jie (eds.).

172. Zhang Jie and Wang Tao, op cit.

173. Wu Jin, "The Historical Development of Chinese Urban Morphology," in *Planning Perspectives* 8:1, 20–52.

174. Zhang Jie and Wang Tao, op cit., 147.

175. Woetzel, J. R., *China's Economic Opening to the Outside World: The Politics of Empowerment*, Praeger, NY, 1976.

176. Arrighi, G., Adam Smith in Beijing: Lineages of the 21st century, Verso, 2007.

Chapter 8.0 | Reforms, Challenges, and Resurgence

177. Clark, P., *The Chinese Cultural Revolution*, Cambridge University Press, 2008.

178. Wakeman, F., *Strangers at the Gate: Social disorder in South China 1839–1861*, University of California Press, 1966.

179. Clark, P., op cit.

180. Lu Junhua, Rowe, Peter G., and Zhang Jie, *Modern Urban Housing in China 1840–2000*, Prestel, 2001; Zhang Jie and Wang Tau, *Housing Development in the Socialist Planned Economy from 1949 to 1978*, 189.

181. Gaubatz, P. R., "Urban Transformation in Post-Mao China: Impacts of the Reform Era on China's Urban Form," in *Urban Spaces in Contemporary China*, Cambridge University Press, 1995, 30.

182. Zhi Wenjun, "Post-Event Cities," in *AD: New Urban China*, Wiley, 2008.

183. Naughton, B., *Cities in the Chinese Economic System: Changing Roles and Conditions for Autonomy in Urban Spaces in Contemporary China*, Cambridge University Press, 1995.

184. Zhang Jie, "Urbanisation in China in the Age of Reform," in *AD: New Urban China*, Wiley, 2008.

185. Campanella, T., op cit.

Chapter 9.0 | Remaking the Canton Metropolis

186. Paulson, H., *Dealing with China*, Headline Publishing Group, 2015.

187. Zhou Rong, "Leaving Utopian China," in *AD: New Urban China*, Wiley, 2008.

188. Strand, D. P., "Historical Perspectives" in *Urban Spaces in Contemporary China*, Cambridge University Press, 1995.

189. Strand, D. P., ibid.

190. Solinger, D. J., "The Floating Population in the Cities: Chances for Assimilation," in *Urban Spaces in Contemporary China*, Cambridge University Press, 1995.
191. Yeh A. and Wu F. L., "The New Land Development Process and Urban Development in Chinese Cities," in *International Journal of Urban and Regional Research*, 1996, 330–53.
192. Cartier, C., *Scale Relations and China's Spatial Administrative Hierarchy*.
193. Ma, L. J. C. and Wu, F., "Diverse Processes and Reconstructed Spaces," in *Restructuring the Chinese City*.
194. Yeh, A. G., "Dual Land Market and Internal Spatial Structure of Chinese Cities," in *Restructuring the Chinese City*.
195. Ran Tao, Fubing Su, Mingxing Liu, and Guangzhong Cao, "Land Leasing Local Pubic Finance in China's Regional Development: Evidence from Prefecture-Level Cities," in *Urban Studies* Vol. 47, No. 10, Sage Publication, September 2020.
196. Si-ming Li and Youqin Huang, "Urban Housing in China: Market Transition, Housing Mobility and Neighbourhood Change," in *Housing Studies* Vol. 21 No. 5, September 2006, 613–23.
197. Wu, F. and Ma, L. J. C., "Towards Theorizing China's Urban Restructuring," in *Restructuring the Chinese City*.

Chapter 10.0 | The Political Paradox

198. Zhi Wenjun, "Post-Event Cities," in *AD: New Urban China*, Wiley, 2008.
199. Niu, M. and Wu, Y., "Financing Urban Growth in China: A Case Study of Guangzhou," in *Aust J Soc Issues* 2019; 55: 141–61, 10.1002/ajs4.87.
200. Crawford, M. and Wu, J., "The Beginning of the End: Planning the Destruction of Guangzhou's Urban Villages," in *Villages in the City*, Al S. (ed.), Hong Kong University Press, 2014.
201. *Confucianism, Buddhism, Taoism, Christianity and Chinese Cultures*. Council for Research in Values and Philosophy, 1991, Tang Yijie.
202. Economy, E. C., *The Third Revolution*, Oxford University Press, 2018.
203. Economy, E. C., op cit.

ORO Editions
Publishers of Architecture, Art, and Design
Gordon Goff: Publisher

www.oroeditions.com
info@oroeditions.com

Published by ORO Editions

Text by Peter Cookson Smith
Drawings by Peter Cookson Smith
Project Manager: Jake Anderson

Book Design by CircularStudio.com
Art Direction, Pablo Mandel
Typesetting, Silvina Synaj

Typeset in Filosofia, and Degular

ISBN: 978-1-954081-64-2

Color Separations and Printing: ORO Group Ltd.
Printed in China.

ORO Editions makes a continuous effort to minimize the overall carbon footprint of its publications. As part of this goal, ORO Editions, in association with Global ReLeaf, arranges to plant trees to replace those used in the manufacturing of the paper produced for its books. Global ReLeaf is an international campaign run by American Forests, one of the world's oldest nonprofit conservation organizations. Global ReLeaf is American Forests' education and action program that helps individuals, organizations, agencies, and corporations improve the local and global environment by planting and caring for trees.